NATIONAL
ACADEMIES

Sciences
Engineering
Medicine

NATIONAL
ACADEMIES
PRESS
Washington, DC

Women's Empowerment, Population Dynamics, and Socioeconomic Development

Anita Raj and Susan C. Scrimshaw,
Editors

Committee on Women's
Empowerment, Population
Dynamics, and Socioeconomic
Development

Committee on Population

Division of Behavioral and Social
Sciences and Education

Consensus Study Report

NATIONAL ACADEMIES PRESS 500 Fifth Street, NW Washington, DC 20001

This activity was supported by a contract between the National Academy of Sciences and the Bill & Melinda Gates Foundation (INV-039679). Additional support was provided by the National Academy of Sciences W. K. Kellogg Foundation Fund. Any opinions, findings, conclusions, or recommendations expressed in this publication do not necessarily reflect the views of any organization or agency that provided support for the project.

International Standard Book Number-13: 978-0-309-72624-5
International Standard Book Number-10: 0-309-72624-7
Digital Object Identifier: https://doi.org/10.17226/27955
Library of Congress Control Number: 2025932139

This publication is available from the National Academies Press, 500 Fifth Street, NW, Keck 360, Washington, DC 20001; (800) 624-6242; http://www.nap.edu.

Suggested citation: National Academies of Sciences, Engineering, and Medicine. 2025. *Women's Empowerment, Population Dynamics, and Socioeconomic Development*. Washington, DC: National Academies Press. https://doi.org/10.17226/27955.

The **National Academy of Sciences** was established in 1863 by an Act of Congress, signed by President Lincoln, as a private, nongovernmental institution to advise the nation on issues related to science and technology. Members are elected by their peers for outstanding contributions to research. Dr. Marcia McNutt is president.

The **National Academy of Engineering** was established in 1964 under the charter of the National Academy of Sciences to bring the practices of engineering to advising the nation. Members are elected by their peers for extraordinary contributions to engineering. Dr. John L. Anderson is president.

The **National Academy of Medicine** (formerly the Institute of Medicine) was established in 1970 under the charter of the National Academy of Sciences to advise the nation on medical and health issues. Members are elected by their peers for distinguished contributions to medicine and health. Dr. Victor J. Dzau is president.

The three Academies work together as the **National Academies of Sciences, Engineering, and Medicine** to provide independent, objective analysis and advice to the nation and conduct other activities to solve complex problems and inform public policy decisions. The National Academies also encourage education and research, recognize outstanding contributions to knowledge, and increase public understanding in matters of science, engineering, and medicine.

Learn more about the National Academies of Sciences, Engineering, and Medicine at **www.nationalacademies.org**.

v

Consultants

KELLI STIDHAM HALL, Associate Professor of Population and Family Health, Columbia University (July 1, 2023–September 29, 2023)
DENNIS HODGSON, Professor Emeritus of Sociology, Fairfield University

National Academy of Medicine Emerging Leaders
in Health and Medicine Fellow

KELLI STIDHAM HALL, Associate Professor of Population and Family Health, Columbia University (December 14, 2022–July 1, 2023)

COMMITTEE ON POPULATION

Reviewers

This Consensus Study Report was reviewed in draft form by individuals chosen for their diverse perspectives and technical expertise. The purpose of this independent review is to provide candid and critical comments that will assist the National Academies of Sciences, Engineering, and Medicine in making each published report as sound as possible and to ensure that it meets the institutional standards for quality, objectivity, evidence, and responsiveness to the study charge. The review comments and draft manuscript remain confidential to protect the integrity of the deliberative process.

We thank the following individuals for their review of this report:

SARAH BAIRD, Department of Global Health, Milken Institute
   School of Public Health, George Washington University
JOHN BONGAARTS, Distinguished Scholar, The Population Council
SEEMA JAYACHANDRAN, Department of Economics and School of
   Public and International Affairs, Princeton University
SUNITA KISHOR, Demographic and Health Surveys, ICF
AGNES QUISUMBING, Poverty, Gender, and Inclusion Unit,
   International Food Policy Research Institute
MARY K. SHENK, Anthropology, Demography, and Asian Studies,
   Pennsylvania State University
AMY O. TSUI, Population, Family and Reproductive Health
   Department, Johns Hopkins Bloomberg School of Public Health
RUTH E. ZAMBRANA, Harriet Tubman Department of Women,
   Gender and Sexuality Studies, and Consortium on Race, Gender
   and Ethnicity, University of Maryland

Although the reviewers listed above provided many constructive comments and suggestions, they were not asked to endorse the conclusions or recommendations of this report, nor did they see the final draft before its release. The review of this report was overseen by **JERE R. BEHRMAN,** University of Pennsylvania, and **CYNTHIA M. BEALL,** Case Western Reserve University. They were responsible for making certain that an independent examination of this report was carried out in accordance with the standards of the National Academies and that all review comments were carefully considered. Responsibility for the final content rests entirely with the authoring committee and the National Academies.

Preface and Acknowledgments

We were charged with leading a committee to examine the evidence on the relationships between population dynamics, socioeconomic development, and women's empowerment in a rapidly changing world. We conducted this work in the contexts of change, persistence, great complexity, and wide variations between countries, regions, and cultural groups.

Throughout human history, cultures have established norms or expectations of women and men (e.g., socially constructed gender norms), in terms of their roles, behaviors, and presentation. These social norms govern key behaviors of population dynamics including women's agency, sexual activity, relationship formation, control over fertility, number and spacing of children, and gender preferences. Gender norms influence socioeconomic development and domestic life including access to education; occupational opportunities; expectations around responsibilities for cooking, childcare, and maintenance of the home; and leadership opportunities. We sought to understand these issues through analysis of women's experiences of restriction but also via exploration of women's empowerment and how women's empowerment across diverse populations can influence socioeconomic development—directly or via increases in women's control over their reproductive and all other domains of their lives.

We had the advantage of a multidisciplinary committee that brought diverse perspectives and evidence to the task at hand. It was obvious that no one disciplinary approach can fully explain the complexities across women's empowerment, population dynamics, and socioeconomic development in our changing world, and that interdisciplinary work is essential to understanding these dynamics. This interdisciplinary approach requires understanding and appreciating the methodologies and theoretical approaches of diverse disciplines and how these can inform the questions at hand. It also requires compromise.

As co-chairs, we wish to express our profound appreciation to the committee members who listened to each other, learned from each other's disciplines, and came together with this report. We would also like to thank the experts who participated in the committee's public meetings and provided valuable input: Daniela Behr, Amanda Clayton, Michele Decker, Arjan De Haan, Nadia Diamond-Smith, Jocelyn Finlay, Margaret Greene, Jody Heymann, Mala Htun, Sandra Pepera, Ndola Prata, Elizabeth Sully, Jakana Thomas, and Aili Mari Tripp. The committee is also grateful for the research assistance provided by Namratha Rao and Edwin Thomas of the Newcomb Institute at Tulane University. Nafeesa Andrabi, Christine Mirzayan Science and Technology Policy Graduate Fellow, also participated with the project.

This report would not have been possible without the strong support of our study director, Krisztina Marton; the steady presence of Malay K. Majmundar, Director of the Committee on Population; and the logistical support of Alex Henderson. We are also grateful to our sponsor, the Bill & Melinda Gates Foundation.

It is our hope that this report will improve understanding of the complex relationships between women's empowerment, population dynamics, and socioeconomic development by generating more multidisciplinary collaboratives, building theory-driven identification of best evidence measures to help advance the field, and creating and evaluating empowerment-focused interventions and policies for their impact. Future work can inform strategies around women's empowerment approaches for women's choice and agency and also for socioeconomic development.

Anita Raj and Susan C. Scrimshaw, *Co-Chairs*
Committee on Women's Empowerment, Population
Dynamics, and Socioeconomic Development

Contents

Boxes, Figures, and Table

TABLE

Summary

While the concepts of women's empowerment, population dynamics, and socioeconomic development have been studied extensively from a variety of disciplinary perspectives, a holistic interdisciplinary review that reconciles the literature on these complex dynamics is absent. The lack of consensus limits the extent to which these concepts can be applied toward accomplishing global health and development goals. The Bill & Melinda Gates Foundation asked the National Academies of Sciences, Engineering, and Medicine to appoint a multidisciplinary consensus study committee focused on advancing the state of knowledge on the impact of women's empowerment and associated population dynamics on socioeconomic development. The committee was tasked with developing a conceptual framework describing these dynamics and setting an agenda for future research and data collection.

To address the charge, the committee reviewed research from a wide variety of social science and health disciplines. While it became clear that existing empowerment frameworks do not fully address the interactions across women's empowerment, population dynamics, and socioeconomic development, these frameworks enabled the committee to identify critical gaps and highlight women's agency as a lynchpin in the empowerment process.

FRAMEWORK OF WOMEN'S EMPOWERMENT, POPULATION DYNAMICS, AND SOCIOECONOMIC DEVELOPMENT

The new conceptual framework proposed by the committee (see Figure S-1) builds on existing frameworks of women's empowerment and highlights the central role of women's agency at the societal, community, interpersonal, and intrapersonal levels. The framework shows how resources can support empowerment and illustrates the role of population dynamics as a potential mechanism through which empowerment can operate to influence socioeconomic development. The framework acknowledges that these relationships are often bidirectional or otherwise interrelated. The framework also recognizes the sociocultural environment, including norms, institutions, and other structural conditions, as a critical moderator of the women's empowerment process and its relations with other constructs in the model. The rightmost box in Figure S-1 shows aspirational development goals, which are the higher-level goals anticipated when basic needs are met, human capabilities are realized, and human rights are guaranteed. We utilized this conceptual framework to guide an in-depth literature examination on the role of women's empowerment in relation to population dynamics and socioeconomic development.

Our review of the research on the *impacts of women's empowerment on population dynamics* found causal evidence related to the roles of family formation and fertility, cash transfers, skills training, employment, and education subsidies in shaping population dynamics. These studies often imply that impacts on family and fertility outcomes flow through women's agency, but findings are largely inconsistent across studies and geographies. Reasons for inconsistencies include differences in the terminology and measurement of women's empowerment, a paucity of research on the agency-related mechanisms through which interventions have their impact, and limited longitudinal data to clarify dynamic relationships between empowerment indicators and outcomes and trajectories of change. Research in this area is typically focused on women's individual and interpersonal empowerment, with limited attention to the understudied higher levels of women's empowerment (e.g., collective resources and agency). Research also lacks attention to the broader gender and policy context, such as the formal institutions and norms that condition the impacts of resources invested in women and women's agency, and in turn, population dynamics. In addition, the interventions studied are often confined to single, small-scale geographies and to relatively homogenous cultural contexts, limiting their external validity and precluding an understanding of their effectiveness at scale.

A substantial body of work focuses on the relationships between women's empowerment and healthcare access, utilization, and outcomes,

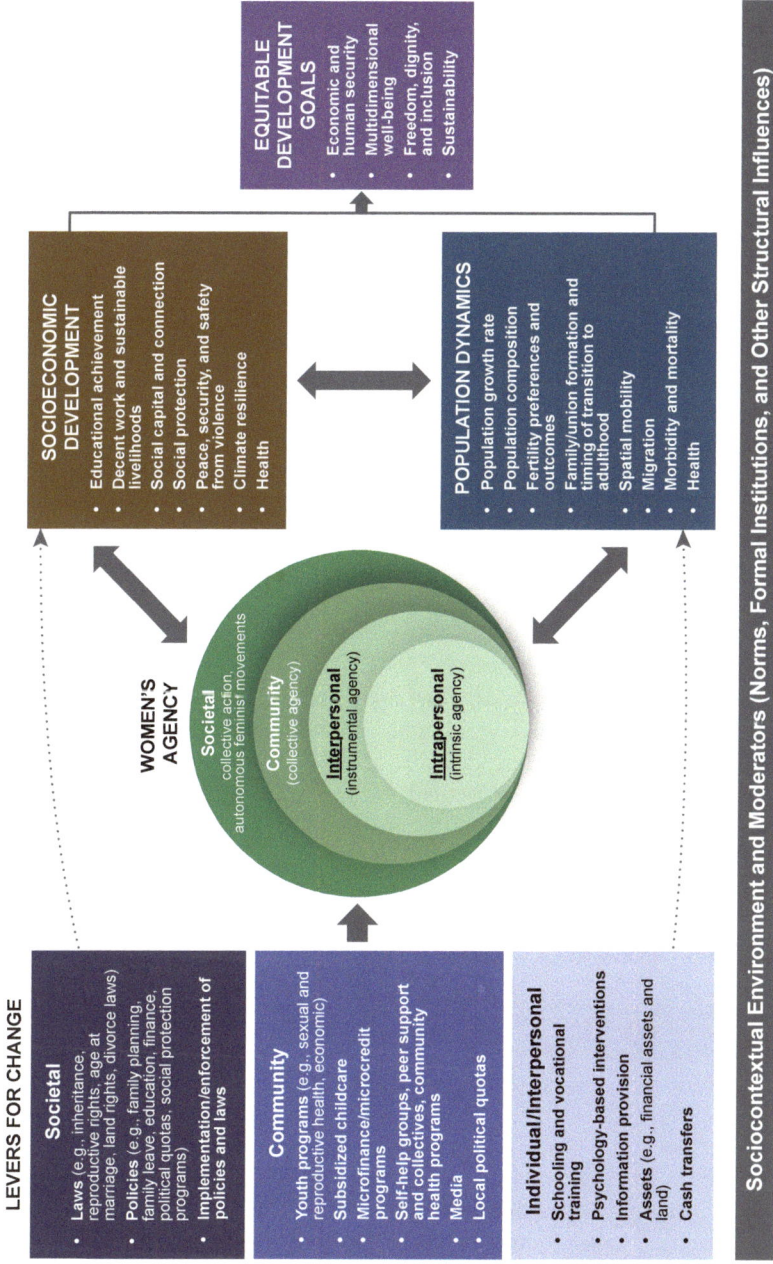

FIGURE S-1 New conceptual framework of women's empowerment, population dynamics, and socioeconomic development. SOURCE: Developed by the committee.

Within the figure:

LEVERS FOR CHANGE

Societal
- Laws (e.g., inheritance, reproductive rights, age at marriage, land rights, divorce laws)
- Policies (e.g., family planning, family leave, education, finance, political quotas, social protection programs)
- Implementation/enforcement of policies and laws

Community
- Youth programs (e.g., sexual and reproductive health, economic)
- Subsidized childcare
- Microfinance/microcredit programs
- Self-help groups, peer support and collectives, community health programs
- Media
- Local political quotas

Individual/Interpersonal
- Schooling and vocational training
- Psychology-based interventions
- Information provision
- Assets (e.g., financial assets and land)
- Cash transfers

WOMEN'S AGENCY
- Societal: collective action, autonomous feminist movements
- Community (collective agency)
- Interpersonal (instrumental agency)
- Intrapersonal (intrinsic agency)

SOCIOECONOMIC DEVELOPMENT
- Educational achievement
- Decent work and sustainable livelihoods
- Social capital and connection
- Social protection
- Peace, security, and safety from violence
- Climate resilience
- Health

POPULATION DYNAMICS
- Population growth rate
- Population composition
- Fertility preferences and outcomes
- Family/union formation and timing of transition to adulthood
- Spatial mobility
- Migration
- Morbidity and mortality
- Health

EQUITABLE DEVELOPMENT GOALS
- Economic and human security
- Multidimensional well-being
- Freedom, dignity, and inclusion
- Sustainability

Sociocontextual Environment and Moderators (Norms, Formal Institutions, and Other Structural Influences)

specifically in the areas of reproductive, maternal, and child health. However, much of this work relies on cross-sectional data and uses unidimensional and/or narrowly defined indicators of empowerment, which limits understanding of the causal relationships between all dimensions of women's empowerment and a broader range of high-priority public health outcomes for women and girls.

In terms of the *impacts of women's agency on socioeconomic development*, many studies document how women's access to resources, including assets and income, positively impacts socioeconomic development outcomes for themselves, their families, and their communities. Laws that reserve political leadership positions for women have been shown to increase girls' career aspirations and educational attainment. They have also been shown to increase women's empowerment by increasing their likelihood of benefiting from employment guarantees and increasing their access to financial services.

However, the evidence base isolating the specific role of women's agency on socioeconomic development outcomes is thinner. Impacts are often presumed to result from changes in women's preferences, yet these preferences are seldom measured directly. In terms of individual agency, self-efficacy is the most directly measured dimension with the greatest empirical evidence. Less empirical evidence exists for direct measures of women's awareness of their rights, locus of control, goal setting, internal motivation, and the actions women may take without others' knowledge, despite their conceptual importance as dimensions of individual agency. In terms of women's interpersonal agency, their decision-making ability is, by far, the most measured construct. However, the specific domain of decision making is not always measured in alignment with theoretical pathways of influence. In terms of community-level agency, causal evidence is lacking on how changes in this parameter (e.g., the expansion of women's networks, changes in collective efficacy, and changes in collective actions) impact socioeconomic development outcomes. Lastly, evidence is particularly limited on how societal-level changes in women's agency affect socioeconomic development outcomes. For example, the influences of policy levers, such as autonomous feminist movements engaged in collective action for social change, have not been adequately explored.

The committee's review of *policies and programs that impact direct measures of women's agency* identified several areas in which interventions have influenced women's aspirations, self-efficacy, and decision making. These areas include (a) financial programs, including cash transfers, microfinance, and job training and placement; (b) women's collectives to support women's economic and health status and build collective efficacy; (c) health interventions, including family planning and sexual and reproductive health programs, community health worker programs for maternal and child health, and peer programs for mental health; (d) youth development interventions, including those focused on early marriage prevention and education promotion, as well as life skills training; and (e) social and legal protections and policies, particularly those related to gender-equal opportunity and safety from gender-based violence. These program and policy approaches align with the areas in which significant changes are seen in population dynamics (e.g., timing of sexual initiation, unions, or marriage; health; and family planning) and socioeconomic development outcomes (e.g., education, women's labor market participation). While studies often show robust impacts of these programs, existing evidence cannot necessarily be generalized beyond often-homogeneous study populations and geographically narrow contexts.

Policies for which evidence appears to be inadequate include those in the areas of marriage, divorce and custody laws, wage equality laws, and family leave policies. Additionally, evidence from low- and middle-income countries regarding the role of agency at levels beyond the individual and interpersonal is generally insufficient. Evidence on collective agency and collective action as outcomes is limited, except in the case of women's self-help groups, potentially because these groups operate with the intention of building solidarity among women. Evidence also is limited on the impact of women's social movements on agency at the individual and interpersonal levels.

We identified three broad areas in which it would be especially productive to concentrate efforts in the near future to better understand the role of women's empowerment in population dynamics and socioeconomic development. These areas, discussed below, include (a) improving the measurement of aspects of women's empowerment, and in particular women's agency; (b) strengthening study designs; and (c) investing in international collaborations and research harmonization.

IMPROVING MEASUREMENT

The committee's review identified inconsistencies, limitations, and gaps in measurement as primary barriers to advancing knowledge of the role of women's empowerment in population dynamics and socioeconomic development and subsequent targeted interventions that increase empowerment. These data limitations often mean that concepts and relationships considered important in theory are poorly defined, poorly operationalized, and not comparable across diverse social contexts, likely resulting in confounding effects. Studies often lack the full range of data elements necessary to measure women's empowerment and to understand the pathways of influence on population dynamics and socioeconomic development. The lack of longitudinal data in particular limits understanding of the trajectories of change. The identified gaps motivated several recommendations.

RECOMMENDATION 1: Data collection on women's empowerment should be expanded to include the range of measures necessary to fully capture elements of women's empowerment, as well as the dynamics and pathways in the committee's new conceptual framework that remain poorly understood. Many of these aspects are multidimensional and should be understood as such. These include

- Sociocultural norms and structures as conditioning factors in the sociocontextual environment.
- Structural dynamics and sexism.
- The role of men, including structural gender inequalities, inequitable gender norms, and masculine dominance.
- Barriers to empowerment.
- Effective methods to reduce gender inequality in productivity, earnings, and profits.
- Effective methods to address norms surrounding women's domestic work.
- Effective methods to eliminate occupational segregation.
- Effective methods to build resilience for women in the face of climate change and other shocks.
- Women's access to health programs (e.g., social protection, insurance, contraception, prenatal and childbirth care, infant and child healthcare, women's healthcare).
- Girls' and women's education and skill building.
- Girls' and women's social networks and supports.
- Couple dynamics.
- Perceptions of rights.
- Time allocation and control over time.

RECOMMENDATION 2: Researchers and government data-collection entities studying women's empowerment should identify opportunities to collect longitudinal data from large-scale studies to better understand change over time, including the determinants of sustained gains in women's empowerment and the long-term effects of women's empowerment on socioeconomic development.

In addition to improving measurement of women's empowerment broadly, this report also highlights work needed to develop better measures of women's agency due to the centrality of agency in the empowerment process, and areas in which it is important to have a better understanding of the role of agency.

RECOMMENDATION 3: Research should prioritize the development of direct multidimensional, construct-specific, and multilevel measures of agency. To the extent that proxy measures are used, researchers should strive for consistency and clarity on how such measures are defined and used, and should be clear that the role of women's agency is assumed and not directly measured. Particular attention should be paid to defining, operationalizing, and assessing the reliability and validity of the following dimensions of women's agency in diverse contexts, leveraging the newest research:

- Individual awareness of rights, aspirations and preferences, goal setting and choice, and internal motivation.
- Control and decision making, including economic and reproductive decision making, at the individual and interpersonal levels.
- Collective agency in formal groups and informal networks at the community and societal levels (e.g., shared goals, collective efficacy, collective action toward shared goals).

Studies of agency would benefit from a life-course perspective—in other words, from recognizing that there are trajectories and turning points as people grow and change across life stages. Agency around life transition points and opportunities, such as reproduction or wage earning, can be particularly important to support women to achieve their life goals.

RECOMMENDATION 4: Research on agency should include studies of women's agency across the entire life course and at key life stages and milestones, with consideration of the socioecological and cultural context and intergenerational influences on key life stages, milestones, and inflection points.

ENHANCING STUDY DESIGNS

While this report prioritizes the discussion of existing research pointing to causal influences on women's empowerment (in particular, agency), and in turn the causal effects of women's empowerment on population dynamics and socioeconomic development, the committee reviewed literature across a range of methods, including qualitative research, mixed-methods studies, and community-participatory and community-engaged research. Considerable gaps exist in some areas in which improved study designs could capture the highly dynamic nature of the interactions, disentangle exposure from outcomes, and establish causality. We also noted that study designs may not be explicit in their terminology related to women's empowerment or about the factors being measured, intervened on, and evaluated, which

represents an additional challenge for the field. Further insight into underlying dynamics could be gained through in-depth qualitative exploration.

RECOMMENDATION 5: Research on women's empowerment and
agency should prioritize study designs that:
- Test causal relationships between dimensions of women's
  empowerment and population dynamics and socioeconomic
  development, and that better elucidate the role of relevant
  concepts as causal factors or outcomes. These designs include
  randomized controlled trials, quasi-experiments, natural experiments, and longitudinal designs to establish causality; to
  examine reciprocal, temporal relationships; and to distinguish
  effects related to the mode of intervention delivery and quality
  of implementation from the content of the intervention.
- Include qualitative data collection to contextualize theories of
  change, to inform intervention and research design, and to aid
  in the interpretation of findings that offer causal evidence.
- Are informed by the perspectives of the women and communities being studied.
- Examine multiple intervention points along the theoretical
  pathways of interest.
- Provide understanding of life-course trajectories and inflection
  points.

RECOMMENDATION 6: Research funders should support studies
designed to examine the effects of programs and policies intended to
enhance women's empowerment and, thereby, socioeconomic development. Study designs should include sufficient follow-up time to examine
sustainability of impacts, as well as measures that permit assessment of
unintended adverse effects of interventions, including outcomes (both
intended and unintended) that may not be immediate.

RECOMMENDATION 7: To establish external validity, more attention should be devoted to understanding the role of interventions and
the specific role of women's agency as a mechanism for social change—
at the institutional and societal levels, as well as across diverse cultural
settings. Also, more attention should be paid to understanding the
feasibility, acceptability, and sustainability of, as well as engagement
with, these interventions.

RECOMMENDATION 8: Studies are needed to better understand the
impacts of integrated approaches to women's empowerment (e.g., cash
transfers to women alongside efforts to address restrictive social and

gender norms) and integrated women's healthcare (e.g., service-delivery models that can address women's sexual and reproductive health as well as psychosocial care needs).

RECOMMENDATION 9: Research funders should support cost analyses and implementation science studies to provide guidance on scaling up efficacious interventions. Such efforts should include systematic tracking of program-implementation data. As evidence from experimental studies continues to grow, comparative effectiveness studies may provide best-practice guidance to government officials and civil society organizations regarding the most cost-effective empowerment approaches in specific country contexts.

COLLABORATION AND HARMONIZATION

Since women's empowerment is deeply embedded into societies' cultural and institutional structures, generalizing research findings beyond limited geographic and cultural contexts is challenging. Comparable data, collected across diverse contexts, are essential for drawing cross-cultural and cross-national comparisons and arriving at conclusions. The interdisciplinary nature of this field further highlights the importance of collaboration to set priorities, coordinate research efforts, and refine measurement approaches that can expedite insights into these questions.

RECOMMENDATION 10: Research funders should establish an international, multidisciplinary group to increase coordination and priority setting for the work in this area. The advisory group could include representatives of funding organizations and other experts and stakeholders, and it would be charged with

- Developing and publishing standards and best practices for development and validation of measures for empowerment, so researchers and implementers can better distinguish among the array of measures in use.
- Coordinating work on psychometric assessment of measures of empowerment and related concepts, and evaluating the possibility of (and recommended processes for) harmonizing measures and global indicators of women's agency and empowerment that would be suitable for comparative use cross-culturally and with various populations.
- Identifying questions and measures that improve measurement of specific empowerment constructs in specific cultures and languages.

- Setting priorities for development of experimental studies to generate causal evidence on relationships that currently are not well understood.

RECOMMENDATION 11: Government, program, and researcher data collections should be better coordinated and aligned. The international group named in Recommendation 10 could facilitate efforts to enhance coordination and alignment across these groups.

1

Introduction

The concepts of women's empowerment, population dynamics, and socioeconomic development have been studied extensively from a variety of disciplines for decades, but attempts to reconcile these perspectives have been rare, particularly in terms of applying a holistic view to the relationships and dynamics. Consequently, consensus on the role of women's empowerment in socioeconomic development remains lacking. This report describes the work of a diverse, multidisciplinary consensus committee charged with synthesizing the current state of knowledge and research strategies for examining the impact of women's empowerment on a range of population dynamics and, in turn, on global socioeconomic development. The synthesis lays the empirical basis for recommendations to improve understanding of these important relationships.

This report builds on a prior study from the National Academies of Sciences, Engineering, and Medicine's (National Academies') Committee on Population (CPOP), entitled *Population Growth and Economic Development: Policy Questions* (National Research Council, 1986). That report examined both the relationship between population growth and economic growth, focusing primarily on macroeconomic issues, and the role of government programs to reduce fertility beyond the provision of family planning services. Since that report, the population growth rate has declined in many parts of the world, and the challenges experienced across population scenarios have changed. Increasingly, researchers from a variety of disciplines have recognized the key role of women's empowerment in socioeconomic development and have argued that women's empowerment warrants attention, regardless of its health and economic impacts (Desai, 2010; Duflo, 2012; Varkey et al., 2010).

Over the past few decades, a range of global women's empowerment indices have been developed to guide research in this area. However, direct measures of women's empowerment, especially specific aspects of empowerment, such as women's agency, are not often included in impact studies. Global data collection at scale is also not routine (Yount et al., 2023). These challenges limit the ability to evaluate the impact of women's empowerment on socioeconomic development and to easily harmonize available findings.

To explore the conceptual, methodological, and policy issues central to the interplay between women's empowerment, family planning, fertility decline, and population and societal impacts, generally and in low-resource settings, CPOP organized a workshop in 2021 that led to the publication of *Family Planning, Women's Empowerment, and Population and Societal Impacts: Proceedings of a Workshop* (National Academies, 2021). In this workshop, experts with a range of backgrounds discussed these issues, with particular emphasis on measurement challenges and limitations in data availability. They noted both an inadequacy of understanding regarding the role of women's empowerment in observed global fertility decline and the need to understand whether and how women's empowerment affects socioeconomic development.

CHARGE TO THE COMMITTEE

The Bill & Melinda Gates Foundation asked the National Academies to appoint a consensus study committee focused on advancing the state of knowledge on the impact of women's empowerment and associated population dynamics on social and economic development. Given changes over the past few decades, including related to women's status in low- and middle-income country (LMIC) settings, timing is opportune for a comprehensive study of these questions. The committee was tasked with developing a conceptual framework describing the complex interactions among women's empowerment, population dynamics, and socioeconomic development. We were also asked to consider policy options, which include identifying evidence-based, multilevel levers for change, to improve women's agency as it relates to development goals. The charge also directs the committee to highlight areas requiring further conceptualization and research. Box 1-1 shows the committee's statement of task.

COMMITTEE APPROACH TO THE STUDY

To address the charge, the committee considered published evidence across a range of relevant topics and disciplines. This review examined

---

BOX 1-1
Statement of Task

An ad hoc committee of the National Academies will undertake a study that will review and assess what is known about the impact of women's empowerment and associated population dynamics on global social and economic development. The study will develop a comprehensive conceptual framework, review the current state of knowledge, critically assess policy options, and set an agenda for future research and data collection; the study may provide recommendations related to these areas.

---

women's empowerment frameworks and their constructs, which highlighted the centrality of agency within the empowerment process. We then focused on women's agency as a critical multidimensional component of women's empowerment and reviewed the empirical literature on the role of women's agency and empowerment in population dynamics and socioeconomic development.

In addition to reviewing existing research, we also held a series of information-gathering sessions to delve into specific topics and to complement the committee's expertise with additional input from a wide pool of experts. The general topics explored in these sessions included

- Emerging challenges and opportunities around women's reproductive agency as an element of women's empowerment;
- The role of social movements, such as feminist movements, in shaping policy; and
- Successes and challenges in the context of implementing policies that affect women's empowerment.

The committee also benefited from additional in-depth research by supporting consultants and a research fellow. A historical overview of population control and family planning access programs was commissioned to provide additional background for our work.

We held a series of closed-session meetings to deliberate on the information gathered and the state of the science. Deliberations drew upon multidisciplinary perspectives and research methodologies and considered the socioecological model as a framework to examine multilevel factors of influence and impact. The socioecological model integrates the individual, family, community, and societal levels of influence in which development occurs. It is important for concepts associated with women's empowerment, such as agency and choice, to be considered at the levels of the individual, couple, family, and community; and for policies, at local, state, and national levels.

The socioecological model also recognizes the life course as embedded in changing contexts, including community and structural factors affecting behavior (Bronfenbrenner, 1975, 1986). We undertake this work from a life-course perspective—in other words, with the understanding that there are trajectories and inflection points as people move through life stages and events, grow, and change over time, and that these points are affected by moment in history, context, and culture (Hutchison, 2010). Applying a life-course perspective allows us to examine contextual exposures and access to resources as factors affecting agency and resultant outcomes during inflection points across life stages (Elder, 1995; Hitlin & Johnson, 2015; Institute of Medicine, 2001; Lee-Rife, 2010; Scrimshaw, 1978).

Given the focus of this study on women's empowerment, population dynamics, and socioeconomic development, we use the life-course perspective to examine the life stages at which women experience major transitions and inflection points related to key areas of population dynamics (e.g., union and family formation) as well as key areas of socioeconomic development (e.g., economic positioning and social participation). While population dynamics and socioeconomic outcomes are relevant at all stages in the life course, this report focuses on outcomes that are especially likely to be affected by changes in women's empowerment and could therefore be of particular interest from the perspective of programs and policies in this area.

When reviewing evidence, we considered research from a variety of social science and health disciplines, corresponding with the multidisciplinary, international expertise of committee members. The research reviewed is based on methods ranging from experimental to observational, including community-participatory and community-engaged research, and extends across national and multinational settings, with a focus on LMICs. The committee's approach was not intended to be an in-depth systematic review of the rich literature on the range of relevant topics. Rather, we relied on our collective expertise and experience to identify the studies that most directly addressed the questions of interest on the basis of strong research designs. Given the report's focus on the impacts of women's empowerment, we prioritized findings from studies that demonstrated causal relationships—in other words, primarily randomized controlled trials but also other statistical approaches designed to produce causal inference from observational data. Where possible, we highlight existing research pointing to the causal effects of women's empowerment on population dynamics and socioeconomic development, as well as causal influences on women's agency as a lynchpin in the empowerment process.

We note that the relationships discussed are often bidirectional or otherwise interrelated, and the literature often discusses them as such. As a result, even though the committee's focus was primarily on the impact of women's empowerment and agency on population dynamics and socioeconomic development, we chose not to limit the discussion to these directional effects. Available findings and data that can shed light on understanding causality versus potential bidirectionality are noted.

In addition to highlighting causal findings, we also discuss qualitative research, which can reveal the nuances and context of social change through the voices and lived experiences of women, girls, and communities. The strength of qualitative research is in the added depth and detail it can provide. For the purposes of this report, we prioritized studies that have been particularly influential or insightful over the years.

One of our goals was to synthesize and comment on the strengths and limitations of existing evidence, as well as methodological challenges and limitations that may preclude an understanding of causal relationships. Prioritizing studies on the basis of the strength of the evidence also enabled us to organize the vast amount of literature into a report that highlights key gaps identified by the committee. We acknowledge that this approach means that studies from some geographic areas are more heavily represented in the discussion than others, and indeed, the need to replicate studies across diverse socioeconomic contexts is an important consideration and finding in the report. This approach also means that the report does not necessarily highlight the most recent research available in a particular area or on a particular topic.

Another goal for this study was to propose a comprehensive framework to guide research and policy. To ensure that a shared understanding of our foci—women's empowerment, population dynamics, and socioeconomic development—informed the evidence review, we developed the working definitions described in Box 1-2, with adherence to standards of the field.

The report focuses on individuals who were assigned female sex at birth and who continue to identify as such, or who are indicated to be women in the studies we reviewed. It is also notable that current research is frequently based on data-collection procedures that rely on a proxy respondent's report, or on interviewers recording male/female based on their interpretation of "gender presentation." Furthermore, the report focuses on heterosexual unions because of the paucity of global evidence from lesbian, gay, bisexual, transgender, queer and/or questioning, intersex, and other (LGBTQI+) persons, particularly from LMICs.

The report focuses on women of reproductive age, including adolescents, unless otherwise noted. Although older and younger individuals may be of reproductive age, available data tend to be limited to individuals between the ages of approximately 15 and 49 years. In addition, as discussed,

---

BOX 1-2
Working Definitions of Women's Empowerment, Population
Dynamics, and Socioeconomic Development for This Report

Empowerment is the expansion and safeguarding of an individual's or group's ability to make strategic life choices and to act on those choices to reach self-determined or collective goals.

Women's empowerment is the application of empowerment (as defined above) to women and girls specifically, recognizing that women's empowerment may occur in the context of restrictive gender norms and gender bias in structures and institutions that disadvantage cis-gender heterosexual women as well as LGBTQI+ individuals, relative to cis-gender heterosexual men. Women's empowerment may be expressed or experienced differently across specific identities—for example, based on race/ethnicity, caste, class, and religion.

Agency is an individual's or collective's ability to act upon personal or shared aspirations toward the realization of self-determined or collectively determined goals. Agency is the component of empowerment that connects enabling re- sources and aspirations to achievements. It operates at multiple levels: individual, interpersonal, community, and societal.

Population dynamics include the growth, composition, and distribution of the population, and the contributing roles of fertility, mortality, and migration, either globally or in given geographic areas. Analyses of population dynamics are typi- cally quantitative and consider factors affecting fertility, mortality, and migration from the individual to the population level.

Socioeconomic development is the process and achievement of social and economic advancement at the individual, household, community, and societal lev- els. This process includes improvements in standards of living, education, health, civil engagement, and state capacity.

SOURCE: Definitions developed by the committee based on existing literature.

---

these are stages of the life course where transition points of particular im- portance for population dynamics and socioeconomic development tend to be concentrated and can be affected by empowerment-promotion efforts. We acknowledge that limitations in the data and research represent major gaps in the evidence base to date and major challenges to fostering more inclusive research paradigms, programs, and policies.

The report also discusses challenges that arise from inconsistent use of terminology across disciplines (e.g., definitions of "empowerment" or "agency"). Unless otherwise noted, summaries of existing research use the terminology employed by the authors of the studies.

ORGANIZATION OF THE REPORT

This report presents the committee's findings and recommendations from the study. The chapters are organized around the main elements of the committee's charge. Chapter 2 provides an overview of existing frameworks of women's empowerment and discusses their limitations and gaps. Chapter 3 presents a new conceptual framework, resulting from this committee's work. The framework describes the interplay between women's empowerment, population dynamics, and socioeconomic development, and highlights the key role of women's agency in women's empowerment. Chapter 4 reviews key indicators of population dynamics most relevant to women's empowerment, including women's agency, and discusses how women's empowerment affects population dynamics at multiple levels. Chapter 5 discusses the literature on women's empowerment and the impacts of empowerment on reproductive, maternal, and child healthcare as well as on women's and children's health outcomes. Chapter 6 reviews how women's empowerment—through an increase in women's agency—impacts socioeconomic development. Chapter 7 sheds further light on the empowerment process by reviewing programs and policy levers (or investments in enabling resources) that have direct measures of women's agency. Chapter 8 summarizes the report's key findings and offers recommendations to further elucidate the dynamic interplay between dimensions of women's empowerment, population dynamics, and socioeconomic development, and to guide national and global priorities on these issues.

Additional background information is included in the report's appendixes. Appendix A contains biographical sketches for the committee members. Appendix B summarizes key attributes of published frameworks of women's empowerment, as a supplement to Chapter 2.

.

2

Review of Women's Empowerment Frameworks and Measures

The term "women's empowerment" has been in use since the early 1970s, building from global feminist and civil rights activist movements that demanded changes in power structures that oppressed women and minority groups (Calvès, 2009). Since that time, women's empowerment has become a global goal of development, as seen in United Nations (UN) Sustainable Development Goal (SDG) 5, one of the SDGs ratified by all 191 UN Member States: *to achieve gender equality and empower all women and girls* (Our World in Data Team, 2023). While national governments have endorsed these goals, global action remains incomplete, in part because of disagreements regarding the meaning of empowerment and how to achieve it (Nanda et al., 2020; Yount et al., 2022). This chapter presents a brief history of the role of women's empowerment in population dynamics and global socioeconomic development and reviews existing frameworks of women's empowerment and associated concepts, such as women's agency, within the empowerment process. We also review measures of empowerment, with a focus on agency, to guide understanding of the state of the field.

A BRIEF HISTORY OF WOMEN'S EMPOWERMENT IN POPULATION DYNAMICS AND SOCIOECONOMIC DEVELOPMENT

A focus on the empowerment of women in global development advanced in the mid-1970s, when the UN General Assembly adopted the *UN Decade for Women* (1975–1985). The goal of that program was to improve policies and address issues such as gender inequities in pay and land ownership, as well as gender-based violence (Calvès, 2009). Key outcomes included the establishment of the *Convention Against All Forms of Discrimination Against Women* (ratified by 170 nations by 1985) and the positioning of women in influential global and regional decision-making forums related to labor and land rights. Other outcomes included the development of the *Commission on the Status of Women*, which organized the first three *World Conferences on Women* (Mexico [1975], Copenhagen [1980], and Nairobi [1985]), and the addition of indicators of women's inclusion and gender inequalities among key development indicators, such as literacy (Zinsser, 1990). However, many feminist researchers and activists criticized the top-down approach in these forums. Instead, they called for a radical transformation of the social, economic, legal, and political power structures that excluded women from planning and decision-making processes and demanded their involvement—with guidance via a gender-analysis framework—on policy formation (McFarland, 1988; Moser, 1989; Rowlands, 1995, 1997; Sen & Grown, 1987). Rowlands (1995, 1997) and Longwe (1995a,b) further spoke of women's empowerment in terms of women's ability to exert power over their lives and to resist and challenge those who have power over their lives, both individually and collectively, recognizing women's capabilities and their entitlement to voice and influence in social and political spaces. Longwe (1995a,b) described the empowerment process as one of liberation, whereby women have to take the power to achieve gender equality.

These approaches and resultant calls for women's mobilization and collective action, demanding their inclusion in vision setting and decision making, were influenced by empowerment principles defined by Freire (1978), a political philosopher and leader in the field of popular education. Freire described empowerment as the process through which oppressed groups cultivate a critical consciousness of their oppression to make demands (e.g., a recognition of self-determined choice as an option) and then move to action. Freire postulated that agency allows marginalized groups to gain freedom from oppression and to achieve self-determination. In 1995, the *Fourth World Conference on Women* was held in Beijing, China. This conference established a progressive and comprehensive blueprint for advancing women's rights that offered the first guidance rooted in Freire's concepts of empowerment, to ensure participatory action of civil society and women's movements for global decision making (UN, 1995). There is some divergence on whether this empowerment is a zero-sum game, as some would say those with power over women have to give that power up for women to have agency over their own lives, where others view empowerment as a process that involves women owning their power over themselves without others having to give up power in the process (Rowlands, 1995).

Concurrently, from the mid-1970s to the mid-1990s, the field of economics began to shift from views of poverty as the lack of basic necessities, such as food, shelter, and clothing, to a capabilities approach, led by Sen (2006) and Nussbaum (2011). This new approach considered the moral values underlying human development and the need for positive freedom. The approach called for a reconceptualization and enactment of development processes to support people's ability to be or do what they need for their self-determined well-being (Gasper, 1997). Kabeer's work on women and development built upon and extended the capabilities approach by documenting how women's grassroots organizing empowered women in ways that could have transformative impacts on their lives (Kabeer, 1999b). This work also clarified the elements of women's empowerment for development as including enabling resources, multidimensional agency, and self-defined achievements (Kabeer, 1999b). This conceptualization differed somewhat from Freire's view, which focused on women and explicitly included enabling resources as part of the empowerment process rather than as an input into empowerment. Nevertheless, Kabeer's approach still aligned with Freire's in its recognition that collective mobilization is a central dimension of agency in the empowerment process, and that several dimensions of agency (e.g., critical awareness and action) are required to achieve self-determined goals.

Following these transformations in theory, all UN Member States created and ratified the UN *Millennium Development Goals* (MDGs) for 2000–2015 and then the SDGs for 2015–2030. MDGs and SDGs provided normative roadmaps for development to achieve healthy and secure societies. Both sets of goals included the goal of achieving gender equality and empowerment of all women and girls, covered first under MDG 3 and more recently under SDG 5 (Jackson, 2007; Our World in Data Team, 2023). SDG 5 targets are as follows:

- 5.1 End all forms of discrimination against all women and girls everywhere.
- 5.2 Eliminate all forms of violence against all women and girls in the public and private spheres, including trafficking and sexual and other types of exploitation.
- 5.3 Eliminate all harmful practices, such as child, early, and forced marriage and female genital mutilations.
- 5.4 Recognize and value unpaid care and domestic work through the provision of public services, infrastructure, and social protection policies and the promotion of shared responsibility within the household and the family as nationally appropriate.

- 5.5 Ensure women's full and effective participation and equal opportunities for leadership at all levels of decision making in political, economic, and public life.
- 5.6 Ensure universal access to sexual and reproductive health and reproductive rights as agreed in accordance with the *Programme of Action of the International Conference on Population and Development* and the *Beijing Platform for Action* and the outcome documents of their review conferences.

Concerns regarding the lack of clear metrics on empowerment were identified first in the MDGs (Kabeer, 2005), with indicators focused on gender inequalities, such as gender gaps in wages or education, or experiences of gender-based violence, rather than empowerment. Many goals related to existing SDG indicators, particularly those related to empowerment, remain undefined, unmeasured, and untracked (Our World in Data Team, 2023). For example, indicators for monitoring sexual and reproductive health and rights focus on contraceptive access and use but tend not to address women's reproductive choice and agency (Our World in Data Team, 2023; Raj et al., 2021). Researchers have argued that the world is not on track to achieve existing targets for these indicators, even as a post-2030 agenda for women's empowerment is being developed. These concerns have given rise to theories and frameworks focused on women's empowerment across disciplines, to help transform lofty goals into concrete indicators for monitoring progress.

REVIEW OF EXISTING FRAMEWORKS
ON WOMEN'S EMPOWERMENT

To understand existing guidance offered by frameworks of women's empowerment for socioeconomic development, the committee reviewed conceptual models and frameworks that were designed explicitly for research or the implementation of programs. The goal of this review was to evaluate how existing frameworks include and define empowerment and its subconstructs.

Our review found a shared recognition of empowerment as a transformative process contributing to self-determination, but there was divergence across frameworks, primarily in terms of purpose and intended audience, level of specificity of constructs, and development outcomes of focus (see Appendix B for a summary of frameworks reviewed). Purposes and anticipated audiences were varied and included global and key national program and policy constituents, organizational and system-change leaders, and researchers working in measurement and evaluation. The frameworks were largely designed to highlight elements of women's empowerment and pathways to increase it. In turn, the frameworks illustrated how women's empowerment may influence women's health and development outcomes in low- and middle-income countries (LMICs), particularly among low-resourced and socially marginalized populations. Our review did not identify frameworks focused specifically on the role of population dynamics in the conceptualization of connections between women's empowerment and global socioeconomic development. The remainder of this section outlines key findings regarding

- The conceptualization of empowerment by purpose of the framework (e.g., for theory synthesis or research application);
- Definitions of the components or elements of empowerment; and
- Specific outcomes or achievements related to women's empowerment.

Conceptualizing Empowerment

Most of the frameworks we reviewed referenced Kabeer's definition of women's empowerment, encompassing enabling resources, agency, and achievements as described above (Kabeer, 1999b). Some frameworks also explicitly referenced Freire's conceptual definitions of critical consciousness, oppression and backlash, and mobilization (Freire, 1978). Across all frameworks, and consistent with the theories of Kabeer and Freire, agency and critical consciousness to achieve self-determination were central to understanding empowerment. All frameworks and their theoretical foundations emphasized the role of women and girls as actors for self-determination, and many recognized the value of participatory action to create change at the levels of the individual and the collective.

Theoretical Frameworks

Frameworks developed for theoretical understanding of women's empowerment have come from economics, political science, psychology, and public health. Women's empowerment in the field of development economics has been led by the work of Kabeer, who defined empowerment as "the process by which those who have been denied the ability to make choices acquire such an ability" (1999a, p. 437), profiling resources, agency, and achievements as the key components of women's empowerment. Conversely, Kabeer defined disempowerment as occurring when choice is denied due to past social, economic, or political inequalities (Kabeer, 1999a). Many of the concepts central to this work were originally built on Kabeer's work in Bangladesh. Choice can be denied due to biased and discriminatory laws or policies, and inequitable social and gender norms (Bill & Melinda Gates Foundation, 2018; Kabeer, 1999a; van Eerdewijk et al., 2017). Hence,

Kabeer recognized the empowerment process as operating at multiple levels (Kabeer, 1999a; Sharaunga et al., 2019). Longwe's (1995a,b) women's empowerment framework also describes empowerment as the process or "route" by which women change the practices and laws that discriminate against them. Longwe developed this framework based on her work in Zambia and other parts of Africa, with an eye toward human rights and liberation processes. The framework describes five levels of empowerment: welfare, access, conscientization, mobilization, and control.

Frameworks for Measurement and Evaluation

Researchers have also produced applied frameworks for survey design and program evaluation, particularly in the fields of women's economic development and poverty alleviation. The framework of Sharaunga et al. (2019), developed to guide research on food security and women's economic agency, describes empowerment in the Kabeer tradition—as a multidimensional process of increasing individuals' and groups' capabilities (e.g., enabling resources and multidimensional agency) to make choices and to transform those choices into desired actions and economic security outcomes. Other women's economic empowerment frameworks, also often guided by Kabeer, include indicators of agency as a combination of women's economic decision-making power, control over income and expenditures, community leadership, control over time allocation, and confidence in handling one's own financial well-being (Kumari, 2020). Empowerment programming frameworks from the field of economics focus on capacity building with women and accountability with institutions, to ensure structural equality of opportunity and support for women, again connecting agency and resources for empowerment, in the economic sector (Mosedale, 2006; Narayan-Parker, 2002).

The Women's and Girls' Empowerment in Sexual and Reproductive Health framework applies Kabeer's framework to reproductive health research (Karp et al., 2020; Wood et al., 2021) but also emphasizes agency in the form of motivational autonomy (e.g., the ability to act on choices; Donald et al., 2020) to support contraceptive choice and use. The framework of Edmeades et al. (2018) focuses on reproductive health and rights. For purposes of measurement and monitoring programs, they define empowerment as power-choice-act: the power to act on choice, freedom of choice, and the ability to voice and act on one's choice as it relates to family planning and fertility practices (Edmeades et al., 2018). Raj et al.'s EMERGE framework (2024), designed for national survey data and measurement in health and development, merges Kabeer's and Freire's theories to elucidate elements of the empowerment process. They view Kabeer's theory of empowerment as centralizing resources as the mechanism for agency and for prioritizing policy and asset-focused interventions at scale; and they view Freire as centralizing *collective action* as the mechanism for agency, predicated on critical consciousness of disempowerment to achieve agency as empowerment, and emphasizing community-based interventions for change. Hence, Raj et al. describe these approaches as both complementary and overlapping, and they apply them in their *EMERGE* framework to describe the empowerment process as ranging from critical consciousness and choice to agency, with agency defined as a "can, resist, and act" dynamic, to achievement of self-determined goals (Raj et al., 2021, 2024).

The Bill & Melinda Gates Foundation commissioned the development of a framework to guide their funding priorities and research and evaluation targets, and to document program and policy impacts for women and development. They define empowerment as an expansion of women's and girls' choice and voice through the transformation of gendered power relations, so women and girls have more control or autonomy over their lives and futures (Bill & Melinda Gates Foundation, 2018; van Eerdewijk et al., 2017). Their framework includes feminist theories from anthropology and sociology, as well as from economics and health, inclusive of Kabeer and Freire. The framework also emphasizes the importance of qualitative research for women's empowerment, given its nonlinear process and context-specific concerns (Bill & Melinda Gates Foundation, 2018; van Eerdewijk et al., 2017).

Frameworks Focused on Structural Empowerment

Some frameworks present empowerment as a process that exists in a context of pre-existing opportunities and constraints, and that thus requires focus on the preconditions in which women have or do not have the capacity to freely decide or act to improve their position or status (Galiè & Farnworth, 2019). Structures can include patterns of relationships and interactions, institutional and family norms and conventions, and policy environments that reinforce and legitimize social hierarchies, including those that devalue women and girls as compared with men and boys (Mosedale, 2005, 2006). The structures can vary by population and context (Richardson, 2018a,b). These frameworks emphasize policy and social change as well as the opportunities that can come from social movements, and they focus on societal-level structures of accountability.

Conceptualizing Agency

Definitions of agency show some variation across frameworks. Kabeer defines agency as the ability to reflect on and to self-determine one's goals and then to engage in actions individually and/or collectively to achieve those goals (Kabeer, 1999b). Donald et al. (2020) built on this definition by synthesizing existing elements of agency, including motivational autonomy (e.g., self-determined choice to achieve one's goals; Deci & Ryan, 1991), perceptions of control, chosen decision-making authority, efficacy to initiate and engage in actions (e.g., bargaining or negotiation) to achieve goals (McElroy & Horney, 1981), and collective action. Karp et al. also use this approach in their framework (Karp et al., 2020; Moreau et al., 2020). Yount et al. (2023) elaborated a comprehensive, multidimensional definition of women's generalized agency that more clearly defines and operationalizes some of its understudied dimensions, including intrinsic agency or "power within" (Miedema et al., 2018; Sinharoy et al., 2023; Yount et al., 2020), instrumental agency or "power to" (Seymour et al., 2024; Sinharoy et al., 2023; Yount et al., 2023), and collective agency or "power with" (Delea et al., 2021; Yount et al., 2020, 2023). Others hold similar definitions, with recognition of agency at the levels of the individual to the collective but using different terminology and emphasizing the role of safety and freedom from backlash (e.g., negative response from those who oppose the actor's agency) as contexts facilitating agency (Bill & Melinda Gates Foundation, 2018; Raj et al., 2021, 2024; van Eerdewijk et al., 2017).

Resources, whether human, social, or material, are described in some frameworks as part of the empowerment process (Edmeades et al., 2018; Leder, 2016; Yount et al., 2020) because they are seen as potentiating agency. In other frameworks, resources are described as inputs into the empowerment process (Bill & Melinda Gates Foundation, 2018; van Eerdewijk et al., 2017). Regardless of these distinctions, the frameworks recognize empowerment as a transformative process, and definitions of agency across frameworks focus on expansion of choice and ability to use resources and internal strengths toward achievement of self-determined goals. The increasing awareness of an expanded landscape of choice (e.g., critical consciousness) as part of the transformational process of empowerment is sometimes defined as a resource (Bill & Melinda Gates Foundation, 2018), sometimes described as a precursor to agency (Raj et al., 2021, 2024), and sometimes considered part of agency itself (Donald et al., 2020; Kabeer, 1999b; Yount et al., 2020). Across these perspectives, critical consciousness is often described in terms of increased awareness of restricted choice or opportunity due to gender inequalities and gender-based oppression.

Conceptualizing Achievements (Outcomes) of Empowerment

Achievements are the outcomes or results of agentic actions. Empowerment frameworks were mostly created to target sector-specific outcomes such as health, water and sanitation outcomes, sexual and reproductive health and rights, agriculture, and nutrition (Caruso et al., 2022; Edmeades et al., 2018; Karp et al., 2020; Sharaunga et al., 2019; Singh et al., 2022a; Sinharoy et al., 2023; Wood et al., 2021). Frameworks that specified achievements or outcomes often prioritized outcomes defined by the researchers and not necessarily outcomes defined by the populations of focus. Kabeer notes that adherence to an empowerment framework requires goals that are determined by those engaged in the process rather than by the sectors providing services or conducting the research; it is important to consider choice and preference of the populations of focus in measurement (Kabeer, 1999b). Outcomes are not characteristics of agentive acts; they are consequences of these acts (Bandura, 2001). It is important for outcomes to be recognized at the individual level, using measures of self-determined goals and self-actualization (Raj et al., 2021, 2024; Yount et al., 2023), and at the collective community, societal, or even global levels, using indicators such as political representation, shared assets, collective efficacy and action, and equitable social and gender norms (Singh et al., 2022a).

Visualization of Empowerment Based on Existing Theories

Based on the critical elements of empowerment that cut across disciplines, the following broad concepts emerge for consideration: *resources* and the enabling environment; *individual and collective agency* as a key element of empowerment; and *achievement of goals* toward self-determination, or in the case of collective agency, toward collective determination and universal human rights. At the national and global scales, equitable human development goals can be considered, in which all people experience security, well-being, dignity, freedom, and social inclusion in a sustainable environment (Figure 2-1).

FIGURE 2-1 Visualization of women's empowerment, building on existing theories.
SOURCE: Developed by the committee.

Measuring Women's Empowerment

Measurement of women's empowerment varies across studies. Research to evaluate the validity and reliability of existing measures is lacking (Donald et al., 2020; Richardson, 2018a,b; Samari, 2019; Yount et al., 2018b) though several new measurement initiatives are expected to yield results in the coming years. Currently, measurement of empowerment often focuses on selected indicators of resources and agency, with much of the published research on LMICs coming from publicly available, multinational surveys such as the Demographic and Health Surveys (DHS; Croft et al., 2023). The DHS includes the following indicators of resources: schooling attainment, having a bank account, and ownership of selected assets (including a house, land, and mobile phone; Croft et al., 2023). The DHS also includes the following indicators of what researchers define as agency: decision making and freedom of movement, as well as attitudinal variables related to the acceptability of partner violence against wives (Basu & Koolwal, 2005; Ewerling et al., 2020; Gram et al., 2019; Jennings et al., 2014; Nahar & Mengo, 2022; Priya et al., 2021; Richardson, 2018b; Upadhyay & Karasek, 2012). These variables generally align with the field's broad definition of agency as the ability to exert control over one's life and to pursue self-defined goals (Alkire, 2008; Beyers et al., 2003; Poteat et al., 2018), aligning with Kabeer's (1999b) prior definition of empowerment.

Views on the measurable aspects of agency can be somewhat divergent by field (Beyers et al., 2003; Steckermeier, 2019; Williams & Merten, 2014). In the fields of psychology and philosophy, agency is often described as having control over one's circumstances, behavior, and behavioral consequences, aligning with the idea of agency as autonomy. Both social and community psychology include collective agency as operating in a similar vein but with the collective seeking control over their shared circumstances, behavior, and consequences. In economics, agency aligns conceptually with the concept of bargaining power, or the relative ability of parties to exert influence over each other for final decision making (Donald et al., 2020; Gammage et al., 2016). This is similar to the concept of autonomy, though social change is usually not emphasized as an outcome in the autonomy literature. Some scholars have conceptualized interpersonal agency as the relative bargaining power of individuals, such as between members of a household (Basu et al., 2006; Rangel & Thomas, 2019) or between employees and employers (Biasi & Sarsons, 2022), while others have focused on collective bargaining between groups (Folbre, 1995). Perspectives across these fields emphasize clarity on perceptions and goals, and offer insight into both individuals and collectives acting for self-determination. In terms of the role of bargaining in the context of agency, feminist researchers discuss subtle, implicit strategies used by women, such as reliance on kin networks (Friedemann-Sánchez, 2006) as well as covert behaviors employed to achieve goals, with the intention of avoiding potential or anticipated backlash, such as covert contraceptive use (Gibbs & Hatcher, 2020; Heck et al., 2018; Raj et al., 2021, 2024; Scrimshaw, 1978; Yount, 2011). Gram et al. (2019) and Raj et al. (2024) highlight certain key features that can be considered to measure and understand empowerment: (a) operation at multiple levels, from individual to household to collective to societal; (b) influenced by internal psychological and emotional barriers as well as external interpersonal, community, and systemic barriers; (c) influenced by past experiences, current circumstances, or fears of the future; and (d) can be enacted independently (self-initiated) or externally (via resources, opportunities, or policies).

Understanding agency also requires an understanding of individual or collective preference to act. For some, the preference to act is described as a process of critical consciousness. This process is characterized by an emerging recognition of options in one's life beyond what has been presented or is expected based on one's social role, value, or positioning, along with the emerging aspiration or goal to select one of these options toward self-determination (Cadenas et al., 2022; Freire, 1978). This process can occur at the individual or the collective level (e.g., self-help groups, community coalitions, informal social networks; Zimmerman, 2000). For women's collectives, this process has been operationalized as shared awareness of gender inequalities (Eger et al., 2018) and the development of shared goals or aspirations that can directly address structural sexism (Gurrieri et al., 2022). The process is affected by changes in sociocultural factors and in the resources available to women, which alter the conditions for preference to act. The process of changing conditions can also be applied at the societal level, via women's autonomous social movements (Htun & Weldon, 2012). For example, #MeToo was a global movement of predominantly women who collectively chose to mobilize against sexual harassment, coercion, and violence aimed at women in the workplace, and to demand retribution from those who perpetrated those crimes (Lee & Murdie, 2021; Vogelstein & Stone, 2021). The consciousness raising and actions in #MeToo predicated change (Lee & Murdie, 2021; Vogelstein & Stone, 2021).

Surveys like the DHS include only a few variables related to preference to act, or choice, as part of understanding agency in empowerment (Basu & Koolwal, 2005; Ewerling et al., 2020; Jennings et al., 2014; Nahar & Mengo, 2022; Upadhyay & Karasek, 2012). Variables in the DHS prioritize preferences regarding fertility goals (e.g., ideal number and sex of children), desire for and timing of pregnancy, and access to and choice of contraceptives. The limited scope of the questions has been used to explain mixed findings regarding associations between "empowerment" indicators (e.g., decision-making agency, freedom of movement) and outcomes (Ewerling et al., 2020; Jennings et al., 2014). For example, a study using DHS data from Sub-Saharan Africa examined associations between women's empowerment and men's involvement in women's antenatal care attendance and found mixed results by country. Authors noted that data on women's desire for male partner attendance could clarify findings (Jennings et al., 2014).

SUMMARY AND CONCLUSIONS

This literature review shows that considerable cross-disciplinary work has been invested in developing frameworks of women's empowerment. Despite some inconsistency in term usage and definitions, our review identified a general agreement across frameworks that empowerment is a transformative process through which individual women and women's collectives come to recognize options beyond those relegated to them, generate new aspirations, set goals, and become agents of social change. Women enact agency using internal and external resources and opportunities, and they achieve goals for self- or collective benefit. Empowerment and agency are lynchpins of goal achievement, and the combination of enabling resources (which may expand options) and awareness of those options may lead to action for achievements, as defined individually or by the collective.

Despite general agreement on key aspects of empowerment, several gaps in these frameworks are notable. First, their application for understanding socioeconomic development and population dynamics tends to be limited. Also, despite conceptual reference to the individual and collective levels, and to a lesser degree structures and organizations, multilevel ecological considerations are generally ill defined or entirely lacking from these frameworks. Moreover, most of the frameworks were designed for specific sectors and thus focus on sector-specific (often researcher-defined) outcomes rather than on socioeconomic development writ large. Furthermore, while the frameworks largely suggest that the expansion of enabling resources could shape and foster the empowerment process (e.g., from expanded choice to agency to achievements), none were explicit in offering guidance on opportunities to create change (e.g., enforcement of existing policies and laws, creation and enforcement of new policies, creation and sustainment of community support groups, the double-edged role of the media). Perhaps most importantly, comprehensive frameworks focused on the relation of women's empowerment with population dynamics—alone and in tandem with socioeconomic development—were lacking, despite the centrality of women's reproductive lives, other population dynamics, other dimensions of health and well-being, and socioeconomic development itself as determinants and outcomes of women's resources and agency.

Similarly, measurement of empowerment is limited and could be strengthened by greater focus on understanding agency and its associated constructs at multiple levels, and the constructs' connection with population dynamics and socioeconomic development. Furthermore, additional work is necessary to assess measurement properties and cross-context, cross-time comparability of existing measures using state-of-the-art approaches to measurement assessment.

The gaps and limitations of the existing frameworks indicate that a new framework is necessary—one that focuses on the process of women's empowerment and that centralizes women's agency to explain their role in population dynamics and socioeconomic development. Such a framework could also advance an understanding of the constructs of agency that can be measured and evaluated to improve the array of outcomes in these two domains.

3

A New Conceptual Framework to Understand Women's Empowerment, Population Dynamics, and Socioeconomic Development

This chapter presents the new conceptual framework proposed by the committee, building on existing frameworks, a review and synthesis of the evidence base, and collective efforts to identify critical gaps and opportunities in the field. In this chapter, we describe the elements of the framework at a high level, while subsequent chapters discuss these elements and supporting literature in further detail. Our new conceptual framework (Figure 3-1) shows enabling resources (indicated here as levers for change) as potential contributors to changes in women's agency at multiple levels of the social ecology. In turn, the process of women's empowerment (i.e., changes in women's enabling resources and multilevel agency toward achievement of self-determined goals) can affect, and can be affected by, changes in socioeconomic development and population dynamics (indicated with bidirectional arrows between these constructs). The dynamic, multilevel relationships between the constructs of women's empowerment, population dynamics, and socioeconomic development are recognized to occur within a broader historical, cultural, and sociopolitical contextual environment. This environment may be enabling or restrictive and may ultimately moderate associations between empowerment and priority outcomes, thus "conditioning" the interrelationships between indicators of women's empowerment, population dynamics, and socioeconomic development. In the case of some of the outcomes, the effects may unfold over generations.

The conceptual framework places women's agency as the focal point. Represented by the circle in Figure 3-1, women's agency contains multiple levels, from societal to intrapersonal. Agency is a key component of

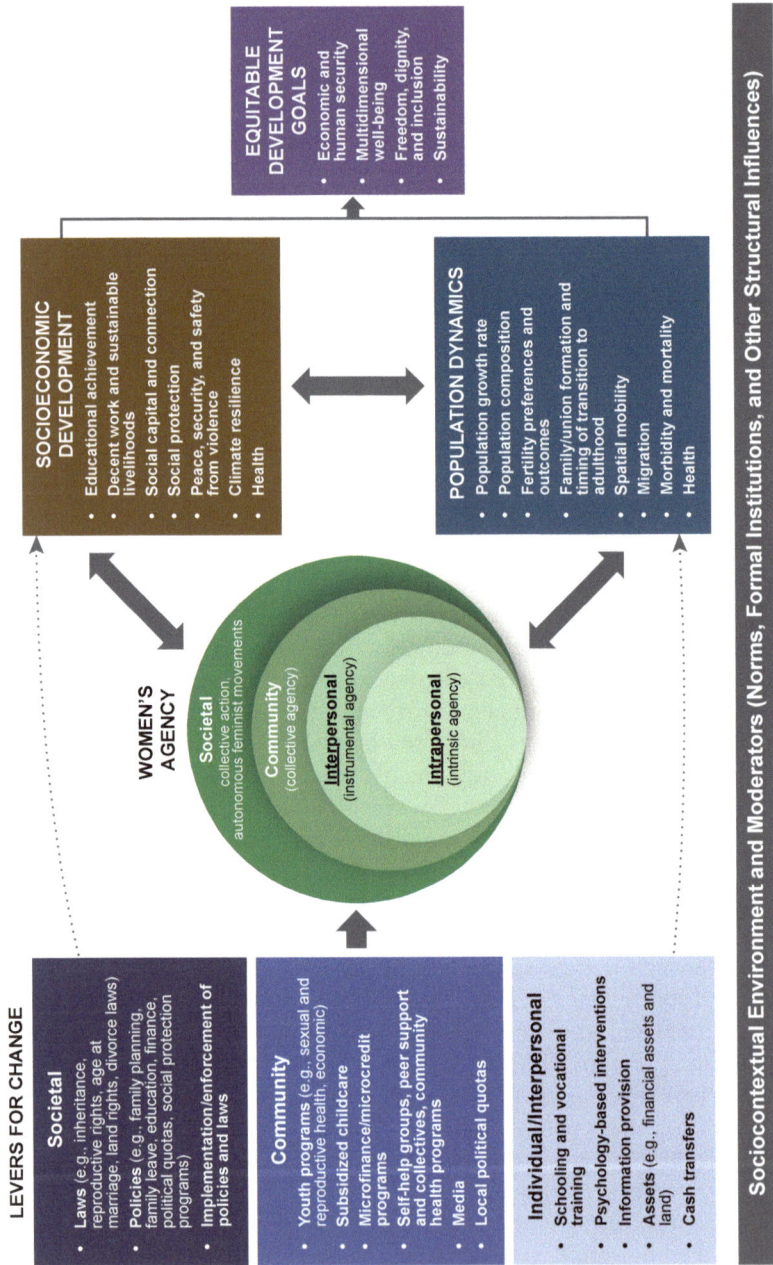

FIGURE 3-1 New conceptual framework of women's empowerment, population dynamics, and socioeconomic development. SOURCE: Developed by the committee.

empowerment. We believe that narrowing the focus to agency allows a clearer view of women's ability to act.

Levers for change, represented in the boxes on the left in Figure 3-1, are the areas we felt could influence agency, and therefore represent potential action items to effect change. These levers range from societal to community to individual/interpersonal. There is a direct arrow between those levers and agency.

The two boxes on the right in Figure 3-1 focus on key indicators of socioeconomic development and population dynamics. The bidirectional arrows between both boxes and women's agency indicate that socioeconomic development and population dynamics are influenced by and influence agency.

The rightmost box in Figure 3-1 represents equitable development goals. These include a set of outcome variables influenced directly by socioeconomic development and population dynamics, and indirectly by agency and levers for change. All these areas fall within the context of the cultural environment and moderators of that environment. Rather than referring to these as social/cultural "determinants," we prefer to use the word "influences," which implies that sociocultural and environmental factors and their moderators are amenable to change.

This new conceptual framework differs from earlier frameworks due to its central focus on agency in the context of population dynamics, socioeconomic factors, and sociocultural factors, and the influence of levers that are possible to change. With the exception of the underlying sociocultural influences, each box or circle in the new conceptual framework is the subject of a chapter in this report. Using a life-course perspective, our discussion focused on the period of adolescence through adulthood, because many elements of population dynamics and socioeconomic development have key inflection points and opportunities at these life stages (Figure 3-2).

MULTILEVEL UNDERSTANDING OF WOMEN'S AGENCY IN EMPOWERMENT

Our new conceptual framework profiles the multiple levels of women's agency in adherence with ecological systems theory (Bronfenbrenner, 1979; Reifsnider et al., 2005), considering levers for change and agency at individual, interpersonal, community, and societal levels. With this understanding, we clarify that empowerment processes operate within and across levels of the social ecology. For example, increases (or decreases) in one woman's empowerment are related to increases (or decreases) in the empowerment of women's collectives at the community and societal levels. Our new conceptual framework emphasizes agency as a core component of empowerment, central to empowerment as a transformative process. In

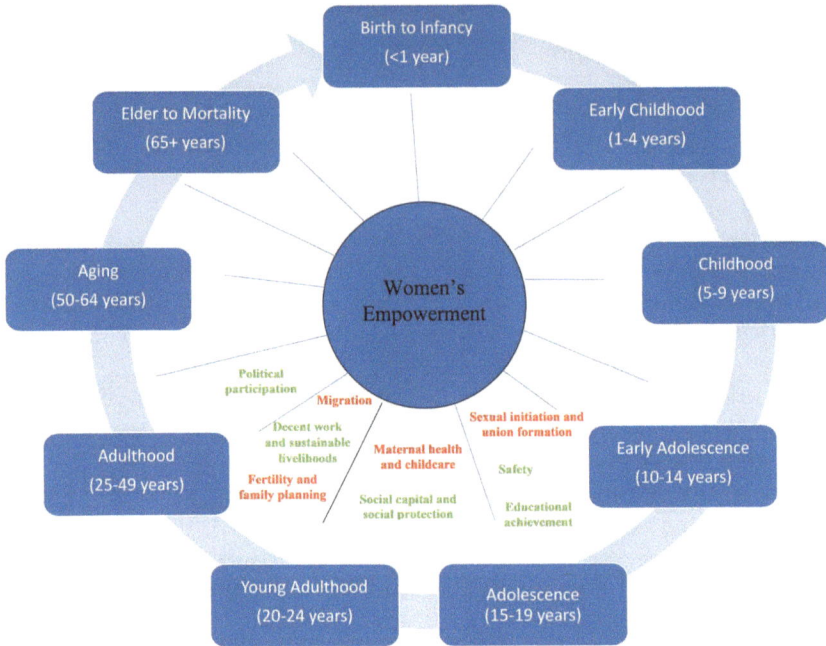

FIGURE 3-2 Women's empowerment and the life course.
NOTES: This figure presents some key inflection points in the life course at which changes in women's empowerment are most likely to affect population dynamics (red) and socioeconomic outcomes (green). The figure is illustrative and does not cover all potential outcomes or all the ways that these metrics may manifest across all life stages. We highlight some of these outcomes to illustrate why much of the work we present focuses on women's years of menarche to childbearing and of secondary education to employment. These are also the years on which much of the literature is focused, for similar reasons.
SOURCE: Developed by the committee.

this new framework, agency is considered at the individual, interpersonal, community, and societal levels.

Individual-level agency involves expansion in one's intrinsic ability to alter their circumstances in context but not directly in relation to others. Individual agency includes the efficacy or felt capacity to enact change and the motivation to enact change or the actions of change. Examples include voting, seeking an abortion, or escaping an abusive marriage. In these cases, a woman may act covertly, without the engagement or even knowledge of others in her household or family, or even in the absence of laws protecting or permitting these rights. Some have argued that this level of agency is decontextualized, as if occurring in a vacuum (Khader, 2016). Our new conceptual framework of women's empowerment explicitly shows how women's individual agency relates with other levels of agency and is conditioned on the broader social and cultural context (Figure 3-1). As such, our framework recognizes that one woman's actions may have differing consequences that depend upon the family, community, and societal contexts in which she is embedded, with important implications for investments in broader social, structural, and policy change.

Interpersonal agency entails the power to exercise one's capabilities vis-à-vis someone else, particularly one with greater authority in the relationship, and to do so even in the face of resistance from others. Some use the term instrumental agency to describe women's actions in relation to others (Jones et al., 2020a). We emphasize the term interpersonal agency to align with its socioecological framework and to differentiate agentic acts that women enact alone (individual agency) from those that women enact in relation to others (interpersonal agency). For women, interpersonal agency is often thought of as occurring within the context of households or families, relative to a spouse or in-laws (Malhotra, 2002). However, interpersonal agency can also occur in communities (e.g., with neighbors) or in work environments (e.g., with co-workers). Women's interpersonal agency may be enacted through increasing voice or the ability to articulate practical needs, personal views, and strategic interests that may oppose the dominant norm in the context of power relations (Gammage et al., 2016; Klugman et al., 2014) and through increasing influence in decisions in which preferred outcomes differ across actors in these various contexts (Abbink et al., 2020; Ashraf, 2009; Doss, 2013; McElroy & Horney, 1981). These acts can be transformational in women's social positioning and gender relations in households, families, communities, and work environments.

Community-level agency involves engagement in or leadership of community-based formal groups or informal networks characterized by shared awareness of gender inequalities (Eger et al., 2018), shared goals or aspirations for change, shared confidence in the ability to act on these goals or aspirations (Bandura, 2001), the coordinated articulation of these goals and aspirations (Gammage et al., 2016), or influential joint actions in the pursuit of shared goals or aspirations (Kabeer, 2011). Community-level agency may be enacted in women's collectives, which engage in community mobilization and participatory action, and have been used effectively to improve the conditions of women's lives with respect to their health, political participation, and economic position (Biskupski-Mujanovic & Najjar, 2020; Brody et al., 2015; Prost et al., 2013). Community-level agency may also be enacted through women's mobilization to increase the presence of women in public spaces, often including freedom from harassment and abuse (Boyer, 2023; Gardner et al., 2017; Yount et al., 2017).

Societal agency involves changing and improving life circumstances, not just for oneself or those within a collective but for the wider benefit of others. To that end, such agency often takes the form of social movements affecting large geographic areas, from cities to nations to transnational environments, and includes efforts to change structures and policies that maintain sexism and heterosexism in society (Beckwith, 2000; Hurwitz & Taylor, 2012; Ray & Korteweg, 1999). Much work in this area comes from the field of political science, in which different terms (e.g., "women's movements," "feminist movements," "women in social movements," "autonomous feminist social movements") yield somewhat different definitions (Beckwith, 2000; Htun & Weldon, 2012; Hurwitz & Taylor, 2012; Ray & Korteweg, 1999). Nonetheless, this work broadly recognizes that these movements often align with or are in response to sociopolitical conditions that the movement deems objectionable, and that movements may take on transformative or even revolutionary tones, with collectively determined goals that drive social and political change. Fukuda-Parr (2003) argued that these types of movements "have been the essential motor behind progress in achieving major policy shifts necessary for human development, such as the recognition of gender equality, the need to protect the environment, or the promotion and protection of a comprehensive set of human rights" (p. 309).

Empowerment Constructs and Terminology

While there is overlap in conceptualization of empowerment and its operation across levels, some inconsistency exists in definitions and terms across studies, and these disciplinary differences in terminology can contribute to confusion. For example, for some in the fields of education, psychology, and public health, choice in critical consciousness is distinct from agency or embeds agency, particularly as collective action, within it (Allen, 2008; Diemer et al., 2017; Freire, 1978; Orsini et al., 2022; Seider et al., 2020). However, other researchers in the fields of economics, sociology, and global development view critical consciousness as a form of agency, specifically defining it as one dimension of intrinsic agency (Bernheim & Whinston, 1985; Jones et al., 2020a; Martimort & Stole, 2009; Navarro-Mantas et al., 2022; Poudel et al., 2022; Yount et al., 2020). Similarly, as discussed in Chapter 2, we noted some disciplinary differences in the use of agency. With consideration of these disciplinary perspectives, Box 3-1 presents key concepts indicative of various dimensions of agency.

Women's goals and aspirations are central to an understanding of women's agency in the empowerment process. In research and practice, this perspective requires attention to women's voices, to know their desires and preferences rather than assuming these based on a priori-determined global health or development goals (Rappaport, 1995; Zimmerman, 2000). Other

---

BOX 3-1
Key Constructs of Agency

- Critical awareness of rights and historical denial of rights
- Locus of control
- Sense of agency (subjective awareness of control)
- Aspirations and goal setting (expanded personal or shared choice)
- Self-efficacy (self-confidence, self-awareness of one's capabilities)
- Motivational autonomy (internal versus external motivation)
- Decision making
- Bargaining/influence in decisions involving others
- Acting on goals
- Freedom of movement (including in previously male-dominated spaces)
- Voice (expressing views that may oppose dominant norms)
- Collective aspirations and goal setting (expanded shared choice)
- Collective efficacy (shared awareness of collective capabilities)

SOURCE: Committee generated.

---

factors important to attend to include the sense of control as well as the cognitive space that individuals and groups need to set well-defined goals (Donald et al., 2020), as well as their internal motivation to pursue self-determined goals (Ryan & Deci, 2000) or their shared motivation to pursue collectively determined goals. Crucially, understanding and measuring agency requires some knowledge of an individual's or a collective's goals.

Observed behaviors that are presumed to be agentic, such as the use of a contraceptive method or employment, may be due to external pressures (e.g., coercive programs or poverty) or social expectations rather than to personal preferences or internal motivations; hence, observed behaviors may not be indicators of agency (Donald et al., 2020; Malhotra & Mather, 1997; Raj et al., 2021; Yount et al., 2020). Conversely, preferences do not always result in observed behavioral agency, as inaction may be the choice taken due to resigned adaptation (Sen, 1987), fear of backlash (Kandiyoti, 1988; Komter, 1989), or the anticipated costs of action (Agarwal, 1997). Hence, it is important for preferences and agency to be understood in tandem with elucidating an individual or group's transformative goal setting and actions toward goal achievement (Allen, 2008; Diemer et al., 2017; Freire, 1978; Orsini et al., 2022; Seider et al., 2020). Furthermore, these choices rely both on women's critical awareness of options and on conditions or resources in the environment that expand the opportunities available to women to consider an extended set of choices. Throughout our new conceptual framework, these resources are contained in socioeconomic development, population dynamics, and the sociocultural environment. The reciprocal nature of these relationships illustrates empowerment as a transformative process at multiple interrelated levels over time.

Population Dynamics

Population dynamics involve the growth, composition, and distribution of the population, with studies analyzing patterns of fertility, mortality, and migration globally or in given geographic areas, as well as the effects of a changing ecology on these dynamics (National Research Council, 1994). Given our charge to understand whether and how women's empowerment affects socioeconomic development directly or indirectly via population dynamics, we focus foremost on the following:

- *Fertility preferences and outcomes*: family size, birth spacing, and child sex composition (i.e., desired versus achieved number and sex distribution of surviving children); population growth; desired versus achieved timing, number, and spacing of pregnancies; contraceptive preferences, access, and use.
- *Sexual initiation and union formation*: first sexual encounter, first sexual union, cohabitation, and first formal marriage (i.e., marriage celebrated and recorded according to local law and custom).
- *Migration*: internal (within country) rural-to-urban migration as well as international migration, voluntary and involuntary/forced migration, migration intentions and outcomes for women, women left behind.
- *Morbidity and mortality*: gender differences in life expectancy, mortality, and morbidity, with emphasis on maternal and child mortality, including age at death and sex differences in child death and in maternal morbidity and mortality.
- *Health*: the state of complete physical, mental, and social well-being and not merely the absence of disease or infirmity (World Health Organization [WHO] 1948) is included in our new conceptual framework as part of both population dynamics and socioeconomic development, because of its fundamental relevance in both areas. Given that our framework also includes outcomes such as social connectedness, resilience, and overall well-being, in subsequent chapters health primarily refers to physical and mental health.

Socioeconomic Development

Socioeconomic development is the sustained improvement in the social and economic well-being of the population, encompassing standard of living (e.g., income per capita, poverty rates, and food security), human development (e.g., education and health), civil engagement, social cohesion, and state capacity (Ruck et al., 2020). Socioeconomic development definitionally requires equitable achievement of these goals across groups in society, including by gender (Chowa, 2019). Reducing the breadth and depth of inequality in the achievement of socioeconomic goals is thus a core component of development. As shown in our new conceptual framework (Figure 3-1), indicators of socioeconomic development are proximal outcomes that may contribute to broader aspirations for society, including human rights and dignity.

The indicators of socioeconomic development we have chosen are tied to global development goals and include the following:

- *Educational achievements*: These indicators relate to Sustainable Development Goal (SDG) 4 and refer not only to the number of years of education obtained by individuals in the population but also to the quality of that education and the skills (technical and socioemotional) imparted. While this indicator primarily concerns children and adolescents, it also includes achievement of "lifelong learning opportunities for all" (United Nations [UN], 2023).
- *Decent work and sustainable livelihoods*: These indicators relate to SDGs 1 and 8 and entail the ability to find a high-quality job and to earn an income. The International Labour Organization (ILO) defines decent work as productive work for women and men in conditions of freedom, equity, security, and human dignity (ILO, 1999). This definition implies that everyone who wants to work should be able to do so, whether in self-employment, unpaid family work, or wage employment in informal or formal sectors.
- *Social capital and connection*: Social capital has been defined as "an instantiated informal norm that promotes co-operation between two or more individuals" (Fukuyama, 2001, p. 7) or as the "features of social organization such as networks, norms, and social trust that facilitate coordination and cooperation for mutual benefit" (Putnam, 1995, p. 67). Social capital contributes to social connectedness, or the degree to which people have relationships that create a sense of belonging, care, value, and support (Centers for Disease Control and Prevention, 2024).
- *Social protection*: This relates to SDGs 1 and 2, and is achieved when the poor are protected from both transitory poverty (e.g., due to economic shocks) and chronic poverty (e.g., persistent food insecurity) through policies and programs designed to provide support to individuals and households facing social and economic risks (Devereux, 2001; Hulme & Shepherd, 2003).

- *Political participation and good governance*: Political participation involves people developing and expressing their opinions on the world and how it is governed, and their participation and efforts to shape the political environment and policy decisions that affect their lives. Political participation is a core principle of human rights and a condition for effective democracies (United Nations for Human Rights Office of the High Commissioner [UNHCR], 2021). More broadly, good governance requires transparent and accountable processes and institutions, an efficient and effective public sector that is responsive to citizens' preferences, and respect for the rule of law (UNHCR, n.d.).
- *Peace, security, and safety from violence*: This construct relates to SDG 16 and includes safety from all forms of violence, including those related to war or violent conflict, criminal violence, gender-based violence, violence against children, and workplace violence. As such, it is also related to SDG 5. "Safety" from violence entails not only that individuals are protected from violence occurring but also that, if violence is perpetrated, the victims are offered adequate resources to heal physically and mentally, and that steps are put in place to prevent reoccurrence.
- *Climate resilience*: This construct relates to SDG 13 and entails the individual and collective ability to mitigate, adapt to, and recover from climate-related shocks and stressors (e.g., extreme weather such as heat waves, heavy rain and floods, and droughts). Effective resilience planning also considers chronic challenges, such as the deterioration of air quality and shifts in population migration related to climate.
- *Health*: (see above).

Equitable Development Goals

Socioeconomic development has a role in supporting equitable human development goals, which are the higher-level goals anticipated when basic needs are met, human capabilities are realized, and human rights are guaranteed. Foundational documents from the UN, including the *UN Declaration of Human Rights 1948* (UN, 1948), the *1987 Brundtland Report* from the UN World Commission on Environment and Development (Brundtland, 1987), and the first *UN Development Programme Human Development Report* from 1990 (UNDP, 1990), describe equitable development goals as security, well-being, freedom, dignity, inclusion, and sustainability. These goals also align with the 2015 UN SDGs with expectations of 2030 achievements (UN, 2015), as well as the planning occurring for the post-2030 agenda (Lutz & Pachauri, 2023; see Box 3-2 for detailed definitions of these goals).

BOX 3-2
Equitable Development Goals

Security
Security includes both economic and human security. Economic security is the ability of individuals, households, and communities to meet their basic economic needs, including food, shelter, and clothing. The right to work and earn gainful livelihoods and fair wages can help ensure economic security, but state-supported health, education, welfare, and environmental programs also are important (International Committee of the Red Cross, 2015). Human security is the ability of individuals, households, and communities to ensure that their physical safety and health needs are met, and their lives are free of fear (e.g., conflict, crime, natural disasters, and disease) and free from want (e.g., poverty, lack of nutrition) (King & Murray, 2001).

Well-Being
Well-being is broadly defined as encompassing happiness, life satisfaction, and fulfillment (Becchetti & Pelloni, 2013; Dahl, 2012; DeNeve & Sachs, 2020; WHO, n.d.); positive social connection, integration, and coherence (Keyes & Shapiro, 2004; Larson, 1993; VanderWeele et al., 2019); and the ability to meaningfully and purposefully contribute to the world (VanderWeele et al., 2019; WHO, n.d.).

Freedom
Freedom is the right to lead one's life as one wishes, as long as one does not infringe on the rights and freedom of others. Negative freedom involves noninterference by others, while positive freedom involves the removal of constraints that impede one's ability to achieve their full potential as they wish (Sen, 1999). Importantly, however, if others, such as the state, impose positive freedom, this can undermine an individual's negative freedom, as the individual may not agree with the state (other) on how to achieve one's goals or potential. Families, communities, or the state can impose coercive constraints on individuals and groups, and social inequalities and discriminatory norms influence the individuals and groups who may be targeted (Vasquez et al., 2021).

Dignity
Dignity is the condition in which one is recognized and treated as having inherent value—that is, value beyond what they can offer in terms of their utility or abilities—and receives respect and ethical treatment from their family, peers, communities, and government. Dignity requires that no human or state treat another human with contempt, abuse, alienation, exploitation, or discrimination, and that all people are worthy of having their basic needs met and being treated equivalently under law (Gewirth, 1992).

Inclusion
Inclusion refers to the ability of individuals, regardless of their backgrounds or identities, to participate actively in economic, social, and political processes. An inclusive approach to development requires challenging both formal institutions and informal institutions (norms) that marginalize individuals or groups based on gender, race, ethnicity, religion, class, caste, sexual orientation, or other identities (Pouw & Gupta, 2017; Yang et al., 2016).

continued

BOX 3-2 Continued

Sustainability
Sustainability is the achievement of well-being and security in a balanced man-
ner that does not compromise the ability of future generations to meet their own
needs. For economic development to be sustainable, it requires the careful management of natural resources and consideration of environmental goals—such as
the conservation of biodiversity, promotion of healthy ecosystems, and tackling
climate change—alongside social and economic goals (Purvis et al., 2019).

SOURCE: Committee generated, based on definitions used in the literature (see citations).

Sociocultural Context

The empowerment process and its connection with population dynamics, health, and socioeconomic development occur within a broader social
and cultural context that can facilitate or impede women's empowerment
and its impacts. Numerous models of the sociocultural context exist for
understanding influences on population dynamics, health, and development
(Anderson et al., 2003; Scrimshaw et al., 2022; Solar & Irwin, 2010). This
report focuses on the sociocultural context for women's empowerment. This
context includes informal rules or social norms; formal laws; and formal
structures including religion, government, education, economic stability,
healthcare systems, and political climates, including those that reinforce
structural oppressions and discrimination (e.g., Bergenfeld et al., 2021).

In this report, we define culture as the socially learned and shared sets
of values and meanings that can govern behavior (Institute of Medicine,
2002). Culture underlies the informal and formal rules in the sociocultural
context and can be modified by lived experience (Garro, 2000), creating
a dynamic sociocultural context that can change in ways that improve or
restrict women's empowerment. Furthermore, the context often includes
social hierarchies and structural oppressions based on gender as well as religion, race, ethnicity, caste, geographic residence, and economic status. These
intersectional hierarchies and oppressions condition trajectories of empowerment for different groups of women and girls. As Sen and Ostlin note in
an analysis for WHO, "Gender norms and relations are a persistent basis
[for] social hierarchies and stratification[...], intersecting with social class,
ethnicity, education, occupation, and income; influencing socioeconomic
position and the distribution of other SDH [social determinants of health];
and being influenced by the wider socioeconomic and political context,

culture, and societal norms and values" (2011, p. 74). More recent efforts to diagnose repressive social and gender norms within institutional contexts offer important examples of how formal and informal institutions (norms) operate to sustain these social hierarchies (e.g., Bergenfeld et al., 2021).

The sociocultural context affecting women may often be most influential at the level of the family or extended family and in the community, particularly in contexts in which women's movement is restricted or options beyond family responsibilities are limited. Here, social norms in terms of what a person thinks others do (i.e., descriptive norms) and what a person perceives others expect them to do (i.e., injunctive norms) can influence women's and girls' opportunities (Raj et al., 2024; Weber et al., 2019). Studies from across low- and middle-income country contexts show that restrictive gender norms affect preferences and behaviors related to freedom of movement, social interactions, sexuality and fertility practices, family responsibilities and roles, and employment participation and opportunities (Marcus, 2021; Weber et al., 2019). These norms can be particularly restrictive in rural settings, where cultural change via lived experience is slower and there is less cultural diversity. However, even in the most restrictive contexts, women overtly and covertly challenge familial norms, societal norms, and formal laws (Scrimshaw, 1978, 1985). Also, cultural norms and women's responses to them change throughout the lifecycle. Social and cultural contexts are considered in Chapter 6, which explores research on the relationships between women's empowerment and socioeconomic development.

SUMMARY AND CONCLUSIONS

Women's empowerment has long been hypothesized as an important means to achieve development goals while also being a goal in itself; however, little work has clarified the role of population dynamics in this relationship at scale. The committee's multidisciplinary review of existing frameworks and theories of women's empowerment led to a novel, comprehensive conceptual framework linking women's empowerment, population dynamics, and socioeconomic development, which addresses key gaps and opportunities in the evidence base. This new conceptual framework can

- Guide a multilevel understanding of agency across the social ecology;
- Consider population dynamics as a potential mechanism through which empowerment can operate to support socioeconomic development; and
- Elucidate necessary resources and how they can support empowerment.

The new conceptual framework is used in this report to guide an examination of the literature on the role of women's empowerment on socioeconomic development, both directly and indirectly via population dynamics. Subsequent chapters examine empirical evidence to assess hypothesized relationships in the framework, as well as programs and policies that may serve as levers for change at various multilevel intervention points along the model, potentially increasing women's empowerment and ultimately socioeconomic development. Research needs are identified in cases when this evidence is weak or lacking.

4

Women's Empowerment and Population Dynamics

This chapter provides a critical summary of scholarship on the relationship between women's empowerment and population dynamics, with a focus on the multilevel elements of agency that may influence population dynamics. The committee acknowledges the bidirectionality of the relationships examined and the largely associational nature of the evidence, and emphasizes plausible causal studies in which women's empowerment (e.g., an expansion in women's resources, agency, or choice) affects population dynamics. Also, while we recognize the relevance of population dynamics at the community and societal levels for economic growth and socioeconomic development—and, as such, we incorporate these levels in our new conceptual framework—this chapter largely focuses on population dynamics at individual and interpersonal levels. Hence, the chapter is structured around sections discussing population outcomes—family formation and fertility, migration, and mortality. Furthermore, as women's and children's health are components of both population dynamics and socioeconomic development, these concepts are briefly discussed in both this chapter and Chapter 6 (socioeconomic development), and we also dedicate Chapter 5 to a primary focus on health, as a bridge between the two domains. Figure 4-1 highlights elements of the framework discussed in this chapter (e.g., fertility, mortality, and migration) as well as topics in women's and children's health that are discussed in Chapter 5.

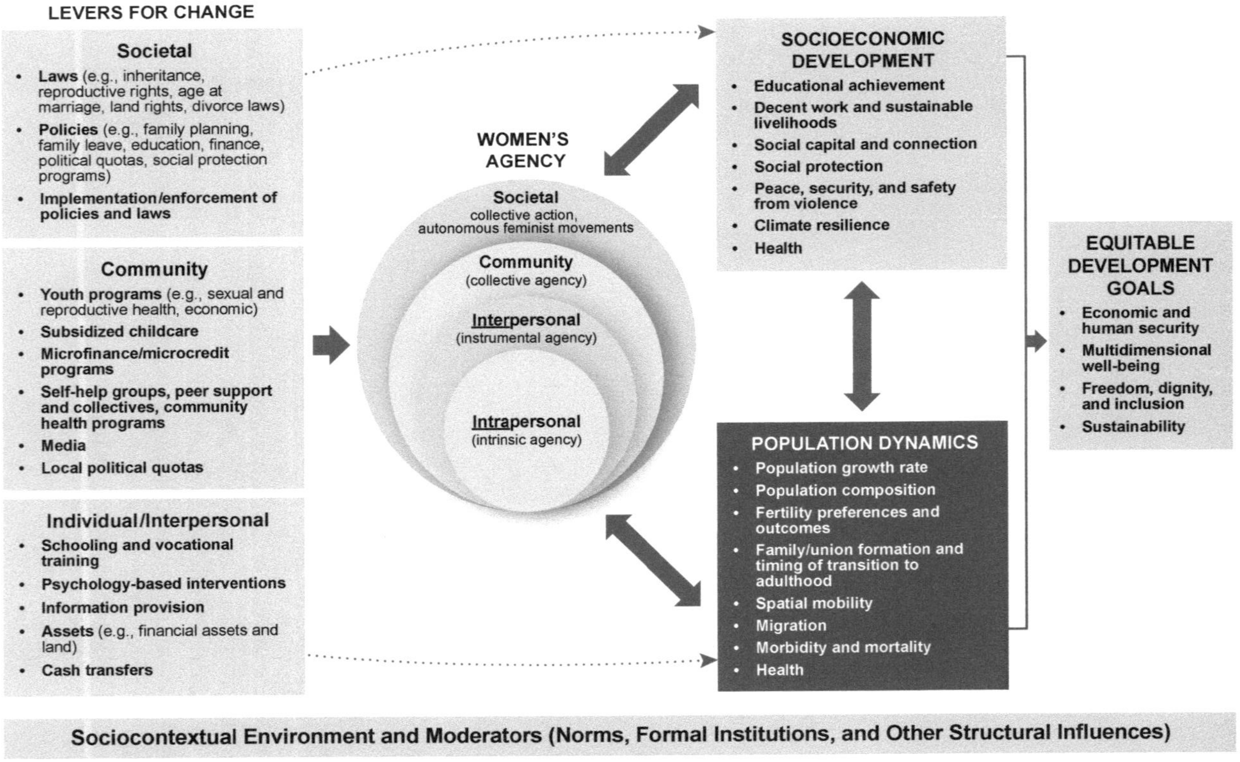
LEVERS FOR CHANGE
Societal
• Laws (e.g., inheritance, reproductive rights, age at marriage, land rights, divorce laws)
• Policies (e.g., family planning, family leave, education, finance, political quotas, social protection programs)
• Implementation/enforcement of policies and laws
Community
• Youth programs (e.g., sexual and reproductive health, economic)
• Subsidized childcare
• Microfinance/microcredit programs
• Self-help groups, peer support and collectives, community health programs
• Media
• Local political quotas
Individual/Interpersonal
• Schooling and vocational training
• Psychology-based interventions
• Information provision
• Assets (e.g., financial assets and land)
• Cash transfers
WOMEN'S AGENCY
Societal
collective action, autonomous feminist movements
Community
(collective agency)
Interpersonal
(instrumental agency)
Intrapersonal
(intrinsic agency)
SOCIOECONOMIC DEVELOPMENT
• Educational achievement
• Decent work and sustainable livelihoods
• Social capital and connection
• Social protection
• Peace, security, and safety from violence
• Climate resilience
• Health
POPULATION DYNAMICS
• Population growth rate
• Population composition
• Fertility preferences and outcomes
• Family/union formation and timing of transition to adulthood
• Spatial mobility
• Migration
• Morbidity and mortality
• Health
EQUITABLE DEVELOPMENT GOALS
• Economic and human security
• Multidimensional well-being
• Freedom, dignity, and inclusion
• Sustainability
Sociocontextual Environment and Moderators (Norms, Formal Institutions, and Other Structural Influences)

FIGURE 4-1 New conceptual framework of women's empowerment, population dynamics, and socioeconomic development, highlighting this chapter's area of emphasis.
SOURCE: Developed by the committee.

WOMEN'S EMPOWERMENT AND UNION FORMATION, FAMILY FORMATION, AND FERTILITY

Association of Women's Empowerment with Marital Dynamics and Fertility Outcomes

A starting point to understand the relationship between women's empowerment (including agency) and family and fertility outcomes lies in recognizing that women's value and status in families and societies are often connected with sex, marriage, and childbearing. Hence, these aspects of population dynamics are particularly salient for considerations of women's empowerment. Age of sexual initiation; age at sexual union formation; age at first marriage; age at first birth; desired family size, composition, and birth spacing; and the desire to become pregnant are considered key determinants of partnership dynamics and fertility.

Jones et al. (2020b), McDougal et al. (2018), and Rao (2015) acknowledged the complex relationship between timing of first marriage and women's empowerment, stressing that child marriage—the most extreme manifestation of early union formation—is a multistage process, and that women's agency can and does play a role, albeit a different role, at every stage. Furthermore, research also shows that social norms and social influences at the level of individuals, families, and communities shape the extent to which agency may matter for marriage decisions. McDougal et al. (2018) reported that girls in Ethiopia and India were infrequently involved in the initiation of early marriage proposals, though their decision-making autonomy was greater in groom-initiated proposals than in marriages arranged by their parents. Girls with greater social vulnerability, such as those without a male caretaker, had more compromised voice, choice, and agency with regard to early marriage. Using extensive longitudinal data from Egypt and methodologies to identify the "correct" chain of causality, Yount et al. (2018a) found that marriage before 18 years restricted women's economic empowerment, while marriage after 18 was positively related to long-term economic empowerment, measured through women's engagement in market work and family economic agency.

Baraka et al. (2022) provided a different perspective on the role of women's agency in shaping early marriage in Tanzanian communities in which early marriage is normative. Their findings challenged the common assumption that early marriages are simply driven by the interests and coercive actions of parents or men, with limited agency of brides themselves (Al Akash & Chalmiers, 2021; Lokot et al., 2022; Miedema et al., 2020). Overall, these findings suggest that, although far from ideal, early marriages may represent a tolerable scenario compared with other alternatives when wider norms restrict women's opportunities for success outside of marriage.

For instance, early marriage may be considered a "better" option when the alternative of remaining unmarried or delaying marriage fails to protect adolescents from risks to well-being such as early pregnancy, increased likelihood of raising children outside of marriage, and amplified exposure to sexually transmitted infections (Schaffnit et al., 2021).

In the context of constrained choices, women's agency may contribute to outcomes that contradict what outsiders would define as beneficial in the realm of marital stability (Baraka et al., 2022; Reniers, 2003). For example, in northern Burkina Faso, Guirkinger et al. (2021) found that as women were increasingly involved in the selection of their spouses, a higher number of divorces were initiated by women, many women had a positive perception of polygamy, and remarriage was on the rise and showed no negative associations with women's well-being. Therefore, they concluded that women showed self-efficacy and internal locus of control in accepting an early marriage, in that they anticipated the ability to divorce and later remarry if they deemed their first union unsatisfactory or unsuccessful. Lastly, focusing on marital satisfaction (rather than stability), and attempting to move scholarship in a more causal direction, Li (2023) used an instrumental-variable approach based on genealogical data and found that higher intrahousehold bargaining power was associated with lower marital satisfaction for women, particularly among older women constrained by external norms.

A related line of inquiry explores the indirect role of agency in marital outcomes by studying outcomes across varying couple configurations, such as couples in which both partners hold the same versus different levels of education or couples in which women's relative earnings are higher than men's. One well-established finding, at least in low- and middle-income societies, is that couples that did not share "status consistency" (heterogamous couples) tended to exhibit higher rates of conflict and marital instability, including more common instances of intimate partner violence (IPV; Behrman, 2019; Pesando, 2022; Weitzman, 2014; Yount, 2005; Yount & Carrera, 2006). In contexts in which new and atypical roles may threaten male dominance (Cools & Kotsadam, 2017; Hornung et al., 1981), when women had higher education, better occupations, or more resources than men, increased conflict between partners could result, including less gender-equal decision making, less female autonomy, and more violence (Ackerson et al., 2008; Flake, 2005; Rocca et al., 2009). Research across 28 countries on women's asset ownership and experiences of IPV suggested that the relationship of women's sole (status inconsistent) and joint ownership of a house and/or land with IPV was highly context-specific (Peterman et al., 2017). Much of this literature, however, adopted proxies for agency that may be seen as developmental outcomes per se, namely female educational attainment, earnings, and occupation. Research using actual measures of agency, including interpersonal agency at the couple level, is lacking.

In contrast to observations on forms of status inconsistency related to resources such as education or occupation, age inconsistency was shown to favor men—age gaps between spouses (e.g., older husbands) were associated with earlier onset of sexual intercourse, less agreement on sexual practices, and less overall use of contraception (Barbieri & Hertrich, 2005; Kaestle et al., 2002). So, increases in income/education for women were shown to create higher vulnerability, while increases in women's age (e.g., reducing the age gap favoring men) were associated with lower coercion. Research also documented that in Indian communities in which social norms dictate greater separation of men and women and in which women have low decision-making power, girls tended to marry at an earlier age (Desai & Andrist, 2010).

Moving to fertility, several analyses of Demographic and Health Surveys (DHS) data from low- and middle-income countries (LMICs) examined the association between women's empowerment and fertility preferences. Haque et al. (2021) analyzed large national surveys for women older than 35 years from 53 LMICs, focusing on the association between women's empowerment (measured by participation in household decision making and attitude toward wife-beating) and fertility preferences (measured by women's perceived ideal number of children and their ability to achieve that preference). The study found that empowered women had a relatively low ideal number of children, irrespective of the measures used to assess women's empowerment (Haque et al., 2021). Atake and Ali (2019) also used DHS data from four countries in West Africa and found that women who were more empowered desired significantly fewer children compared with their less-empowered counterparts, although results varied by country.

On the relationship between women's empowerment and the number of children born, in a systematic literature review, Upadhyay et al. (2014) documented that most studies found an inverse relationship between number of children and at least one empowerment measure. The review reported that most studies including at least some aspects of women's empowerment were linked to increased spousal communication and the capacity to decide whether to have children (Upadhyay et al., 2014). Moreover, the analysis included two studies using DHS data from the Philippines and Bangladesh, which documented a significant association between empowerment measures and unwanted pregnancy. Women's final say in household decisions and sexual matters with husbands was found to be associated with lower odds of unwanted pregnancy (Abada & Tenkorang, 2012; Rahman, 2012). Albeit associational, these findings suggest higher sexual and reproductive autonomy among women with higher levels of agency. Schierl et al.'s (2023) pooled analysis of DHS data from 31 Sub-Saharan African countries corroborated this conclusion: women's empowerment was found to be strongly associated with the ability to make decisions about sexual behavior, including highly empowered women refusing sex or asking their partners to use condoms, which increased women's control over the risk of acquiring HIV (Schierl et al., 2023).

A recent study from Mozambique on the influences of women's empowerment on fertility-related outcomes also showed that women's ability to make independent decisions increased the odds of not wanting more children. Furthermore, beliefs about violence against women and control over resources were positively associated with having fewer children (Lopes et al., 2022). While almost all the evidence reviewed came from cross-sectional studies, one longitudinal study from Egypt showed that women with greater agency were more likely to have had a birth and to have had a greater total number of births than women with less agency. Due to social norms in Egypt favoring a higher number of births, women with higher agency could be fulfilling these social expectations and choosing to have more children (Samari, 2017).

Part of the challenge in evaluating the role of women's interpersonal agency in shaping fertility arises from the fact that, in many instances, spouses have similar fertility preferences (Mason & Taj, 1987). However, when spousal preferences do not coincide, the relative weight of partners' preferences defies generalization, even within the same setting (Blanc, 2001). In contrast to studies focusing on individual-level measures of discordance between spouses, Mason and Smith (2000), looking across LMICs with differing levels of gender inequality in intrahousehold power and across diverse gender contexts within the same country, compared outcomes when spouses disagree about desire for more children. They found that in countries where women have greater autonomy, the decision to use contraception was more likely to be affected by the wife's preferences than it was in countries where gender inequality was greater. This finding was observed for India, Pakistan, Thailand, and Malaysia but not for the Philippines.

A similar importance of social context was observed when interventions were implemented. Many interventions aim at influencing family formation and fertility outcomes by boosting various aspects of women's empowerment. Substantial differences exist, however, across contexts in terms of these issues (J-PAL Policy Bulletin, 2018, Figure 1). The timing of first union formation or marriage is heavily influenced by social norms. In some regions, the practice of dowry payments by the bride's family to the groom's family fuels early marriages, as dowry tends to increase with the bride's age (Chiplunkar & Weaver, 2023; Corno & Voena, 2023). This practice can lead brides' parents to favor early marriages, to reduce dowry costs. Even in the absence of dowry practices, women from disadvantaged households may marry early due to reduced opportunities, such as limited access to education or employment (Batyra & Pesando, 2023; Corno et al., 2020; Kohno et al., 2020). Household income not only affects marriage decisions but also influences decisions related to sexual activity. In contexts in which sex outside of marriage is not against the norm, adolescents in low-income households may engage in relationships with older partners who can support them financially (Luke, 2003). Additionally, income plays a role in adolescents' ability to develop human capital, including education and skills, which can empower them to make informed decisions about sexual activity, marriage, and childbearing and to pursue economic opportunities.

Because family formation and fertility outcomes often co-move (e.g., early marriage is closely tied to decreased sexual and reproductive health and earlier fertility), reviewing the causal evidence by outcome is challenging and risks redundancy. Instead, the text below is organized by type of program investment, distinguishing between economic programs (e.g., financial incentives and/or schooling interventions), social norms interventions (often called "empowerment" programs), life skills training programs, political initiatives, or combinations of these investments. Chapter 5 includes a review focused on sexual and reproductive health, and thus that topic is not a focus here.

Impacts of Women's Empowerment Interventions on Union Formation and Fertility Outcomes

Cash and Asset Transfers

Much of the literature on cash transfers and their potential to influence union and fertility outcomes has targeted adolescent girls, to support their retention in school and delayed marriage and childbearing. Baird et al. (2011) assessed the effectiveness of randomized conditional cash transfer programs (CCTs) and unconditional cash transfer programs (UCTs) on adolescent girls' life trajectories in Malawi. When focusing on adolescent marriage and pregnancy rates, results were particularly strong in the UCT arm. The likelihood of ever being pregnant or married were 27% and 44% lower, respectively, in the UCT arm than in the control group at the end of the two-year intervention. These substantial delays in marriage and fertility in the UCT arm were seen entirely among adolescent girls who dropped out of school after the start of the two-year intervention; rates of marriage and fertility among girls still enrolled in school at follow-up were negligible, regardless of the treatment arm. Additional positive effects of the cash transfers included lower risk for stunting and HIV, as well as delayed marriage and age at first birth (Baird et al., 2011, 2016, 2019). Importantly, effects were lost after the cash transfers ended, and there is some indication that delayed marriage may have affected the quality of available partners for marriage in adulthood. Hence, while the findings from this work, as well as reviews of cash transfer studies (Baird et al., 2013; Kalamar et al., 2016), document the value of conditional and unconditional cash transfers, unanticipated negative consequences of nonadherence to norms related to age at marriage can result from such interventions. These findings highlight the importance of providing broader community- and society-level interventions focused on norms when engaging in economic empowerment interventions targeting women and girls.

In contexts without dowries and in which women had agency over their own marriages, money transfers conditional on staying in school were associated with delayed marriage or childbearing (Alam et al., 2021; Austrian et al., 2022). The primarily nonexperimental evidence from contexts with dowry and arranged marriage is mixed. Alam et al. (2021), in Pakistan, and Hahn et al. (2018), in Bangladesh, found that transfers conditional on education and marriage were associated with reduced child marriage. However, Heath and Mobarak (2015) documented no impact of the same Bangladeshi program using a different comparison group. The only policy effort to condition financial incentives on marriage age alone was the *Apni Beti Apna Dhan* (ABAD) program in Haryana, India. Despite the ABAD CCT's intent to enhance the value of girls in Haryana, the evaluation showed that ABAD did not significantly delay marriages or encourage secondary and higher levels of education, suggesting that financial incentives alone may not change deeply entrenched and gendered social norms (Nanda et al., 2016).

Targeting child marriage, specifically by lessening families' economic pressure to marry girls early through a combination of economic and social norm interventions, Buchmann et al. (2021) evaluated a randomized program in Bangladesh providing financial incentive to families to delay marriage, alongside a girls' empowerment program. They found that girls eligible for two years of incentive were 19% less likely to marry below the age of 18 (the age of consent), while the empowerment program failed to reduce adolescent marriage. As such, the findings suggest that empowerment programs may be ineffective at reducing underage marriage when adolescent brides have limited influence on marriage timing, underscoring the key role of young girls' agency and the influence of an enabling normative environment. This same finding was also reflected in several additional studies (Ashraf et al., 2020; Bandiera et al., 2020; Buehren et al., 2017; Edmonds et al., 2023).

In Bihar, India, the state-run *Mukhhyamantri Balika Cycle Yojana* (Chief Minister's Scheme on Cycle for Girls), designed to close the education gap among girls in the state, provided girls with funds to buy bicycles. This is an example of a "successful" asset-transfer program. A randomized impact evaluation found that the bicycle program improved school enrollment by 32% and reduced the corresponding gender gap by 40%

(Muralidharan & Prakash, 2017). Furthermore, the authors found a 22% decline in sexual harassment on the way to school and documented that the program led girls to express an increased desire to delay marriage and pregnancy. Now piloted in Zambia, a similar randomized evaluation of a bicycle program found that the program had significant effects on enrollment, graduation, absenteeism, punctuality, and empowerment (Fiala et al., 2022).

Education Subsidies

Similarly, several types of educational subsidies have been found to support school retention, delayed marriage, and delayed first births for adolescent girls, though relatively less research on this type of intervention exists compared to research on cash transfers. Duflo et al. (2015) randomized the provision of free school uniforms to students in their last three years of elementary school in Kenya and observed a reduction in adolescent pregnancy among women beneficiaries. In Zimbabwe, using a randomized controlled trial (RCT) design, Hallfors et al. (2011) found that a comprehensive support program for orphan girls, including uniforms and a school-based helper/tutor to solve problems, combined with food programs, increased the likelihood of participants reporting over time that the consequences of sex were an important factor in their desire not to have sexual intercourse. However, the authors did not find self-reported sexual intercourse to be a reliable measure among girls who reported ever having had sexual intercourse at any one of the survey time points. Duflo et al. (2024) randomized secondary school scholarships in Ghana and found large impacts on childbearing onset, age at first cohabitation, partner characteristics, and incidence of unwanted pregnancy. Using a quasi-experimental approach in five Sub-Saharan African countries, Bhuwania et al. (2023) found that tuition-free secondary education reduced the probability of marriage and childbearing before 15 and 18 years of age, respectively, by providing girls with more autonomy and independence in decision making.

Quasi-experimental research in this area includes a study conducted in the context of changes that eliminated primary school fees in Uganda (Keats, 2018). The study found that women with more education tended to delay fertility and had lower fertility overall. A higher level of maternal education was also correlated with improved child health indicators. A similar study examined the role of education on fertility, in the context of the introduction of universal primary education in Nigeria (Osili & Long, 2008). The study found that each additional year of education reduced fertility before the age of 25 by 0.26 births. Ozier (2018) linked eighth grade standardized test score data to responses from a survey of young adults in Kenya and found a reduction in teen pregnancy among women with higher test scores, believed to be associated with admission to government secondary school. A recent study that leveraged the expansion of access to girls' or mixed schools in Jordan, to investigate the effects of access to school on women's education and fertility, found that an additional year of schooling reduced total fertility by 0.3–0.4 births (Zhang & Assaad, 2024).

Knowledge and Skills Training

When social norms allow girls to have some control over their sexual relationships, access to health information may change their beliefs about sexual behaviors and marriage, and building skills to support options beyond marriage and childbearing may, in turn, influence marriage and childbearing outcomes (Chang et al., 2020). Among women regardless of age, contraceptive knowledge and access was shown to contribute to improved birth spacing, which can reduce maternal and infant morbidity and mortality; birth spacing is thus viewed as a proxy indicator of reproductive agency for women (Molitoris et al., 2019; Wolfers & Scrimshaw, 1975). A review by Upadhyay et al. (2014) identified six studies that examined associations between women's empowerment indicators, including decision-making control, reproductive coercion, and birth spacing, and five of these six studies found significant associations, despite differing measures of birth spacing. One recent study from Kenya that used attitudes toward IPV as an indicator of empowerment found that shorter birth intervals were associated with more permissive attitudes toward IPV (Kudeva et al., 2020).

Intervention evaluation studies also show the potential utility of knowledge and skill building on early marriage and fertility outcomes. Using an RCT design, Dupas (2011) showed that equipping young women with information about the health risks associated with sexual relationships with older partners (e.g., "sugar daddies") reduced (typically unwanted) adolescent pregnancies, especially pregnancies with older partners. Blending knowledge and skills training, Amin et al. (2016) used an RCT design to evaluate the effectiveness of a program named *BALIKA*, aimed at delaying child marriage through community-based skills development for girls in Bangladesh. All girls participating in the *BALIKA* program met weekly with mentors and peers in safe, girl-only locations called *BALIKA* centers, which helped girls develop friendships, receive training on new technologies, borrow books, and acquire the skills needed to navigate the transition from girlhood to adulthood. Girls used these skills within their communities, which helped build confidence, demonstrate their achievements, and elevate their profiles within their communities. Girls living in *BALIKA* communities were one-third less likely to be married as children than were girls living in communities not reached by the *BALIKA* program. Girls who were single at the beginning of the study were one-fourth less likely to be married by the end of the study. Relevant for the purposes of this commit-tee, in communities where girls received life skills training on gender rights and negotiation, critical thinking, and decision making, girls were 31% less likely to be married as children at endline than were girls in the control communities. Similar programs leading to declines in child marriage are documented by Stark et al. (2018) in Ethiopia. In contrast, recent studies in Nepal and Bangladesh evaluated the impact of sexual and reproductive health education and training girls for leadership and advocacy, in the con-text of efforts to change community norms among parents and leaders, but found no impact on delayed first marriage (Naved et al., 2024; Yount et al., 2023). Reduced child marriage showed an association with level of engage-ment in the program in Bangladesh (Naved et al., 2024). A positive effect of vocational skills training is also evident from some studies. Bandiera et al. (2020) evaluated a policy intervention aimed at jump-starting adolescent girls' empowerment in Uganda by providing adolescents with vocational training and information on sex, reproduction, and marriage. After four years, the program led to sharp declines in teen pregnancy, delayed entry into marriage or cohabitation, and declines in the share of girls reporting sex against their will. Weaker impacts were observed on outcomes such as views and aspirations tied to the ideal age at marriage. One concern is that scale up of the program was limited. Furthermore, similar programs in Tanzania, Bangladesh, and Zambia found small or no impacts on education, marriage, or childbearing (Austrian et al., 2020; Buchmann et al., 2021; Buehren et al., 2017; Waidler et al., 2022).

Adoho et al. (2014) evaluated the impact of the *Economic Empower-ment of Adolescent Girls and Young Women* (EPAG) project in Liberia, a randomized intervention aimed at providing livelihood and life skills train-ing for 2,500 young Liberian women. The EPAG program increased wom-en's employment by 47% and earnings by 80% through positive effects on a variety of empowerment measures, including increased access to money, improved self-confidence, and decreased anxiety about circumstances and the future. Despite evidence of shifts in gender norms and more gender-equitable allocation of household tasks, the evaluation found no net impact on fertility, sexual behavior, or opinion about the suitable age at marriage for women. Also, in the context of Liberia, Özler et al. (2020) evaluated the effectiveness of *Girl Empower*, a mentoring program combined with a cluster-randomized cash-transfer intervention, which sought to equip adolescent girls with skills to make healthy, strategic life decisions that would keep them safe from sexual abuse. The program led to noticeable positive changes in gender attitudes, life skills, and sexual and reproductive health but did not affect girls' reports of sexual violence, level of school-ing attained, or psychosocial well-being. Nonetheless, adding a monetary incentive to the empowerment program reduced the likelihood of marriage and the number of sexual partners in the previous 12 months by over 50%.

Makino et al. (2021) documented positive impacts of two RCTs in Bangladesh and Zambia. The former, providing academic skills training, had a significant impact on discouraging child marriage in villages where girls' participation in paid work was particularly high. The second study, providing empowerment intervention and safe spaces, had a significant impact on delaying pregnancy, especially for illiterate girls in communities where premarital sex was relatively common.

Employment and Other Economic Opportunities

Studying the effects of the explosive growth in the Bangladeshi garment industry through a natural experiment exploiting the timing of access to garment sector jobs, Heath and Mobarak (2015) found that access to factory jobs lowered the risk of early marriage and childbirth due to two factors: older girls postponing marriage because of a higher likelihood of being employed, and younger girls remaining in school.

Jensen (2012) performed one of the few studies seeking to empirically establish the causal effect of increased opportunity for paid work on marriage and fertility decisions, in contexts in which those decisions are taken by parents. The author worked with business process outsourcing centers to organize recruiting sessions in randomly selected villages in Northern India, providing an exogenous increase in women's labor force opportunities for women in these villages. The study found that women in treated villages were less likely to marry and have children and more likely to pursue additional schooling and training. The study also reported that women in treated areas wanted fewer children and desired to work steadily throughout their lifetimes.

Heath and Jayachandran (2016) reviewed evidence on the effects of increases in female education and labor supply on socioeconomic development. They concluded that

> both education and labor force participation have been shown to delay fertility and lead to healthier children once a woman does have children. However, effects over the life course (such as completed fertility) or that depend on general equilibrium adjustments (such as the timing of marriage or partner choice) are less clearly established and probably context-dependent. A valuable area for future research would be to characterize the factors that determine the heterogeneity in these relationships. Less is also known about potential negative consequences of labor supply on women, such as decreased leisure or increased domestic violence (p. 16).

National Political Quotas and Legal Change

A series of policy levers may affect marriage dynamics by boosting women's agency. For instance, Castilla (2018) conducted a natural experiment in India, exploiting random variation in the cross-district timing of the first election to include reserved seats for women Pradhans, to explore the impact of women in leadership positions on age at first marriage, likelihood of child marriage, and age at gauna (e.g., the ceremony that indicates the start of marital life and the consummation of marriage). She found that the likelihood of child marriage decreased by 20 percentage points, and age at marriage increased by 2.3 years, after reserved seats for Pradhans were implemented, consistent with both a "role-model" effect and increased voice and representation of women. Castilla proposed that changes in gender norms could be a mechanism for the change (Beaman et al., 2009, 2012; Castilla, 2018).

Also in India, Deininger et al. (2013) evaluated the impact of changes in the Hindu Succession Act, which granted equal inheritance shares to daughters and sons, and found that this amendment increased women's likelihood to inherit land, their educational attainment, and age at marriage (by 0.54 years) for women who married after the Hindu Succession Act.

Changes in marriage-related laws—such as changes in the legal age at marriage or laws pertaining to divorce—may affect partnership outcomes through women's agency. A study using a difference-in-difference design showed that the Revised Family Code 2000 in Ethiopia, which increased the minimum legal age of marriage from 15 to 18 years, was associated with an increased age of marriage among young women, which could be a direct effect of the law or an indirect effect of women's changed expectations regarding marriage and their increased economic opportunities (Hallward-Driemeier & Gajigo, 2015). Similarly, evidence from the Egyptian Khul reform, which introduced unilateral no-fault divorce for women in Egypt, showed reduced IPV, increased educational attainment, delayed entry into the labor market, and mechanisms consistent with an increase in women's bargaining power within the couple (Corradini & Buccione, 2023). Other research, mostly in high-income societies, has demonstrated that changes in divorce laws have important consequences on the balance of decision-making power between partners in intrahousehold decision making (Brassiolo, 2016; Chiappori et al., 2002; Stevenson & Wolfers, 2006; Voena, 2015), which in turn may affect marital stability (González & Viitanen, 2009; Matouschek & Rasul, 2008; Wolfers, 2006). For example, Kneip et al. (2014) found that introduction of unilateral divorce laws across 11 European countries was associated with increases in age at first marriage and incidence of divorce, particularly among couples with children.

Pension systems can also affect women's fertility decisions. A quasi-experimental study in Namibia found that women reduced their fertility in response to the expansion of a pension program in the country (Rossi & Godard, 2022). Donald et al. (2024) analyzed data from six RCTs of business-training and land-titling programs in Sub-Saharan Africa that increased women's earnings and household wealth, and found increases in women's fertility—with results driven by those women most in need of sons for support in old age or widowhood. Future research investigating the relevance of these findings for other contexts is important, as is research to causally assess the impact of women's access to social protection and insurance programs on their fertility.

Fertility Decline and Gender Equality

Evidence on the impact of the fertility decline on changes in gender equality is limited. One study of fertility decline and women's empowerment in China (Wu et al., 2012) showed that women with lower fertility do less housework and tend to be more satisfied with their family status than women with higher fertility. Other studies indicated that fertility decline does not predict other aspects of women's welfare, including household gender equality and gender-based violence (Stoebenau et al., 2013). In many contexts around the world, women's employment and earnings decline precipitously after the birth of the first child, whereas men's do not (Kleven et al., 2023). Gendered norms and roles have not shifted alongside or following fertility decline. This resistance to change is mostly attributed to deeply entrenched inequitable gender norms and systems (Yount et al., 2016).

Fertility declines can have detrimental impacts on gender equality through two primary mechanisms. First, when the son preference is strong, a decline in fertility can increase the skewness of the sex ratio. A vast body of demographic research has documented that declining fertility, coupled with continued preference for sons, is associated with declining proportion of girls to boys (Das Gupta & Bhat, 1997; Larsen et al., 1998). Jayachandran (2017) provided evidence that, in India, this association is likely causal: using an innovative survey in Haryana, she showed that respondents reported preferring a more skewed sex composition when asked about a hypothetically low versus hypothetically high total fertility level. The study estimated that the fertility decline could explain up to 50% of India's recent increase in sex ratio skewness in the past 50 years.

Second, increased sex ratio skew can exacerbate the practice of bride importing. To the extent that bride importing is associated with low agency of exported/imported women, this may be detrimental for gender equality (Kawaguchi & Lee, 2017; Mukherjee, 2013). Proportions of marriages with international brides grew rapidly in the late 1990s in Taiwan and early 2000s in Korea (Lee, 2010). This change occurred as the effects of an increasingly adverse sex ratio became noticeable. Bride importing in Taiwan, Korea, and China increased as adverse sex ratios began to create a marriage squeeze (Cho, 2018). In South Korea, for example, male-to-female sex ratios for individuals ages 25–34 began to diverge from 2003 onward. In the same period, the number of foreign brides increased from about 25,000 to about 140,000. Interestingly, despite many economic similarities, Japan saw neither a substantial rise in adverse sex ratio over the period of fertility decline nor a vast increase in foreign marriages, providing a useful counterfactual (Lee, 2010). While international bride import receives considerable attention, substantial import of brides within countries with demographic diversity also exists, generally from distant regions to areas with marriage squeeze. Research in China and India documented a substantial increase in marriage arrangements in which brides were imported into areas with adverse sex ratios (Kaur, 2016). Finally, a study of Indian states showed that states with adverse female-to-male sex ratios had greater reports of child trafficking with a 10-year lag (Prakash & Vadlamannati, 2019). However, child trafficking was also reported more frequently in states with greater women's empowerment, raising questions about whether these states experience more trafficking or greater reporting of trafficking.

WOMEN'S EMPOWERMENT AND MIGRATION

Voluntary Migration

Ample evidence suggests that work migration can lead to large income gains for migrants and the families they leave behind (Clemens, 2011). While the proportion of women among labor migrants rose steadily between 1960 and the early 2000s (Donato et al., 2011; United Nations Population Fund & International Organization for Migration, 2006), work migration remains disproportionately male, raising the question of whether women's empowerment programs can increase women's ability to take advantage of migration opportunities. The answer depends on the context. Social barriers to women's work-related migration are documented by a study in Bangladesh that examined women's migration before and after construction of a bridge that increased communication and reduced mobility costs. Comparing areas benefiting from bridge construction with those that did not benefit, and comparing younger cohorts that came of age once the bridge opened with older cohorts using a difference-in-difference analysis, the study found that increased access improved the likelihood of women's migration for marriage but not for work (Amirapu et al., 2022). The authors suggested that social barriers reduce women's likelihood of taking advantage of reduced migration costs.

In contexts in which women are the primary migrants, such as for domestic labor,[1] the returns from migration (e.g., earnings and well-being while away) may be muted if women migrants lack resources and agency both prior to and during their migration period. Blaydes (2023) provided descriptive evidence from a survey of Filipino and Indonesian women who returned from employment stints as migrant domestic workers in the Arab Gulf states. The study documented high rates of mistreatment, such as excessive working hours and delayed salary payment, as well as nontrivial rates of emotional and physical abuse. Using a different survey instrument, Bazzi et al. (2021) provided similar evidence for temporary migrant women from Indonesia. Women who chose to migrate disproportionately came from poor households and had low education levels, so it is possible that programs that boost female education or local employment opportunities could reduce risky migration behaviors. Using an RCT with Indonesian women, Bazzi et al. (2021) showed how empowering potential international migrants with information on which placement agencies provided higher-quality placements reduced international migration and improved outcomes for women who chose to migrate.

India is an interesting context in which to explore the relationship between women's empowerment and migration. In India, about 208 million Indian women marry away from the villages and towns of their birth, arguably the largest permanent migration in the world. Two aspects of women's agency (and lack thereof) have been shown to be associated with the desirability of marrying women into villages outside their natal villages, particularly at a distance. One aspect relates to kinship norms, particularly in the north-central area, whereby women cannot marry men tied to them in kinship. Hence, women have to marry outside their villages, resulting in migration at marriage (Dyson & Moore, 1983; Ghurye, 1955; Uberoi, 1993). However, women migrate for marriage even in areas where kinship norms do not prohibit within-village marriage (Chatterjee & Desai, 2019). In both situations, lack of women's agency in their marriage choices is a key factor making village exogamy feasible. Even in the 21st century, 95% of Indian women noted the involvement of their parents and other family members in the selection of their marriage partners (Desai & Andrist, 2010).

At a macro level, a policy brief from the Organisation for Economic Co-operation and Development (OECD) suggests that higher levels of discrimination against women in origin countries parallel higher levels of female migration but only up to a certain threshold—very high discrimination

---

[1] In particular, women pioneered and dominated migration from Jamaica and the Philippines to the United States, due to employer preference for female service workers (Foner, 2009; Tyner, 1999).

appears to curtail women's abilities to migrate (Ferrant et al., 2014). While discriminatory social practices may lead to increased migration, migration to countries with lower levels of discrimination may also lead to changes in norms in the origin countries, through what has come to be defined as social remittance (Levitt, 1998). To deal with this reciprocal relationship, OECD data were extended to assess the two-way relationship between discriminatory social institutions and migration, using instrumental variables with the date of ratification of the Convention on the Elimination of All Forms of Discrimination Against Women and religiosity as instruments for the level of discriminatory social institutions (Ferrant & Tuccio, 2015). Results showed that the unequal status of women and their low decision-making power within the family constrained their ability to choose their own development pathways, resulting in a lower probability of engaging in international migration. In addition, an undervalued status of women within the family was shown to reduce the size of the female migration flow. Therefore, high discrimination at the family level seems to affect women's migration opportunities. A similar effect is not observed for men (Ferrant & Tuccio, 2015).

Forced Migration

Literature on forced migration (Klugman, 2022) has documented its impact on the increasing vulnerabilities of women. However, the way that women's empowerment or lack thereof influences the likelihood of forced migration has received much less attention. One study reported results from a five-year-long intervention in Nepal, Bangladesh, and India aiming to prevent trafficking of women workers and their exploitation (Zimmerman et al., 2021). The study did not show that interventions empowering women through knowledge and attitude change resulted in reduced forced servitude. The authors argued that systemic changes and increased support systems for women workers in their destination countries, rather than simply changes in their own knowledge and attitudes, may be important to reduce women's vulnerabilities.

WOMEN'S EMPOWERMENT AND MORTALITY

Estimating the Magnitude of Missing Women

Sen (1990, 1992) was among the first to estimate the millions of "missing" women among the population of the Global South, particularly East and South Asia. Observing that China and India had much higher ratios of men to women than other parts of the world, Sen (1990) concluded that over 100 million women are "missing" due to the neglect and maltreatment of women and girls. These imbalances reflect gender inequalities in several outcomes, including mortality—Sen's original focus—as well as in morbidity and the risk of induced abortion, which is also discussed by Lane et al. (1998) in the context of Egypt. The specifics of Sen's "100 million" calculation remain a matter of controversy. Initial debates focused on whether researchers should use sex ratios from West or Sub-Saharan Africa to estimate the sex ratio that would likely be observed in Asian populations in the absence of gender discrimination (Coale, 1991; Sen, 1992). Subsequent research clarified three core issues that affected the calculation of the missing women: the age structure, the natural sex ratio at birth, and the overall level of mortality in the population. Accounting for these three factors, Bongaarts and Guilmoto (2015) estimated that 126 million women, or 4% of women globally, were missing due to discrimination in 2010. Their results were driven by excess female mortality from birth through late middle age, principally in China and India. Within those countries, they estimated that 10% and 7% of women were missing, respectively.

It could be argued that the absence of these women—along with the implied excesses in morbidity and mortality—result from limits in women's agency, since premature mortality necessarily implies a loss of control over one's life. Greater agency could possibly enable women to avoid premature mortality and unnecessary morbidity as adults, while also empowering them to shield their children, especially daughters, from the same outcomes. These influences could operate at multiple levels—by empowering women at the individual level and also by transforming communities, governments, and societies to protect women and girls.

Among adults, most excess female deaths occur in middle age rather than old age (Anderson & Ray, 2010; Bongaarts & Guilmoto, 2015). Causes of excess female deaths vary by region, but one consistent source in early adulthood and middle age is maternal mortality, defined as death during or soon after pregnancy from causes related to pregnancy or birth. Maternal mortality has declined substantially in all regions but remains very high in some regions (Alkema et al., 2016). Globally, the maternal mortality ratio nearly halved between 1990 and 2015, from 385 to 216 maternal deaths per 100,000 live births. However, maternal mortality remains more than an order of magnitude higher in Sub-Saharan Africa, where deaths stood at 546 per 100,000 live births in 2015, than in developed regions, where it stood at 12. In Sub-Saharan Africa, a woman experiencing 2015 mortality and fertility rates throughout her lifetime would have a 3% lifetime risk of dying from maternal causes (Alkema et al., 2016). Another cause of death is IPV and femicide, which has gained currency in global research and political discourse (Graham et al., 2021).

Mortality

To what extent does women's agency protect against excess mortality among adult women? Data are scarce at the individual level, but at the polity level, event-study evidence indicates that rising women's agency is associated with reduced maternal mortality. Comparing countries that instituted parliamentary gender quotas at different times, Bhalotra et al. (2023) estimated that increases in women's political representation caused maternal mortality to fall. Between 1990 and 2015, 22 developing countries instituted parliamentary gender quotas, which reserve parliamentary seats for women. The timing of these reforms lined up with a 6–7 percentage point increase in the proportion of women in parliament and a 7–13% reduction in the maternal mortality ratio. Antenatal care and skilled birth attendance became more prevalent, fertility declined, and young women's educational attainment rose, all of which may have played a role in the maternal mortality impact.

Additional evidence comes from India, where amendments to the Hindu Succession Act in the late 20th century increased women's inheritance rights in several states. One can think of these legal reforms as simultaneously improving women's rights at the societal and individual levels. Cross-cohort increases in women's inheritance rights at the state level coincided with cross-cohort increases in women's say in household decisions and in their autonomy to travel away from home by themselves (Heath & Tan, 2020). Calvi (2020) demonstrated that these changes also coincided with reductions in underweight status, anemia, self-reported illness, and mortality. These reductions were especially pronounced in older women, highlighting how disempowerment and neglect extend the "missing women" phenomenon to older ages in India, despite its concentration from birth to middle age globally.

Fertility decline reduces maternal morbidity and mortality risks associated with pregnancy and childbirth through a mechanical effect, in that fewer pregnancies/childbirths mean fewer opportunities for pregnancy/childbirth complications. Fertility decline may also reduce maternal morbidity and mortality by decreasing high-risk births—namely, first births among adolescents, high-parity births, closely spaced pregnancies, and births to older women. Women with fewer births may also have the strength and health to withstand complications of pregnancy that women with many births may not have. Using decomposition techniques, Jain (2011) estimated that 38–50% of maternal lives saved in 2008 in India, Pakistan, and Bangladesh could be attributed to fertility decline in these countries between 1990 and 2008.

Evidence on the causal mechanisms underlying these individual associations is scarce, but cultural determinants of women's agency within the household and extended family offer insights. In India, when multiple adult brothers live in the same household, wives of younger brothers are assigned lower status. Pre-marriage characteristics are comparable between wives of younger and older brothers, so that comparisons of post-marriage outcomes shed light on the health effects on women's intrahousehold positioning. Compared to other wives in the same household, wives of younger brothers were found to have less say in household decisions and were more likely to be underweight (Coffey et al., 2022). The weight finding is thought to be related to the practice of eating in order of social rank, such that household heads eat first, followed by their sons, then their grandchildren, and then their daughters-in-law. The youngest daughter-in-law cooks the food and eats it last (Palriwala, 1993). Consistent with this interpretation, other Indian datasets have indicated that women with less say in household decisions were more likely to eat last (Hathi et al., 2021), and women who ate last were more likely to be underweight (Coffey et al., 2018).

The birth of a girl was also shown to reduce a woman's standing in an Indian household (Das Gupta et al., 2003). Using data from India, Milazzo (2018) documented evidence of "missing" mothers of first-born daughters relative to first-born sons, suggesting increased mortality, and found that among survivors, mothers of first-born daughters were more likely to suffer from anemia than mothers of first-born sons. Notably, Indian mothers with first-born daughters reported having more say in household decisions than those with first-born sons (Heath & Tan, 2018), implying that if women's agency explains the health and survival differences, its mechanism of action goes deeper than everyday household decisions. The mechanism is likely related to the tendency of mothers with first-born daughters to endure more pregnancies, more abortions, and more closely spaced births, all of which carry health risks. One can interpret the increased reproductive burden as a restriction on agency, but it is different from control over everyday household decisions.

India displays well-known fissures in women's agency at a societal level, with implications for child survival. Dyson and Moore (1983) famously noted that South India exhibited lower infant and child mortality than North India, which they attributed to the greater agency of women in the South. Along with lower overall infant and child mortality, Dyson and Moore (1983) documented that South India also had lower female-to-male ratios in infant and child mortality, which they again argued was due to greater female agency in the South. Carranza (2014) linked South India's greater equality in survival between boys and girls to the economic value of women, which was seen to be greater where clayey soils prevented deep tillage, as in the South. She documented that women comprised a larger share of workers in districts with clayey soils, and child sex ratios were correspondingly less biased.

Women's education, a well-known driver of empowerment, may also reduce child mortality. Using data from Nigeria, Caldwell (1979) first documented that maternal education predicted lower child mortality. The association is ubiquitous in LMICs (Balaj et al., 2021), although some have questioned its robustness to controlling for the family's socioeconomic status and geographic area of residence (Desai & Alva, 1998). Recent evidence from policy-induced education expansions in Africa suggested an effect, however. In Zimbabwe, an education reform sharply expanded access to secondary schools in 1980. Children of mothers from affected cohorts were substantially less likely to die than their counterparts born to mothers from earlier cohorts (Grépin & Bharadwaj, 2015). In Malawi and Uganda, education reforms sharply expanded access to primary schools in the 1990s. Subnational regions that were more affected by the reforms saw larger declines in child mortality (Andriano & Monden, 2019). Notably, in neither case did the schooling expansion affect women's reported decision-making power in the household.

Son Preference and Girls

Girls experience direct effects of women's disempowerment at a societal level, but the specific effects of maternal agency are unclear. In India, the patterns of girls' excess mortality overall and by birth order suggest gender bias in the allocation of nutrition and healthcare. In classic research on Punjab, Das Gupta (1987) documented that girls' (but not boys') mortality risk rose dramatically with birth order, a result she interpreted as discrimination by son-preferring parents against later-born girls. Furthermore, because parents are more likely to continue having children after a girl than after a boy, girls were also found to have more siblings on average, depleting per capita resources (Clark, 2000). Nevertheless, advantages for boys including increased childcare time, breastfeeding duration, and vitamin supplementation emerged even in infancy, as suggested by a study restricting the sample to families with young children whose mothers had not yet had the opportunity to have other children (Barcellos et al., 2014). Nonetheless, some discrimination against infant girls may be intended to make a subsequent conception more likely (Jayachandran & Kuziemko, 2011). Boy-girl discrimination in India also worsened during droughts and recessions, which disproportionately harmed girls' survival (Bhalotra, 2010; Rose, 1999). In China, infanticide historically played a larger role in skewing sex ratios, at least until ultrasounds enabled a shift toward sex-selective abortion (Coale & Banister, 1994). The practice has a centuries-long history (Johansson, 1984; King, 2014; Scrimshaw, 1984). A large body of evidence suggests that son preference and the preferential treatment of sons over daughters are not restricted to India and China but are observed more widely across Asia, North Africa, and the Middle East (Yount, 2001, 2004).

Prenatal ultrasounds became accessible by East and South Asian parents in the 1980s, leading to a proliferation in sex-selective abortion. In recent data, the sex ratio at birth was significantly male biased in Albania, Armenia, Azerbaijan, China, Georgia, Hong Kong, India, South Korea, Montenegro, Taiwan, Tunisia, and Vietnam (Chao et al., 2019). Due to their large populations, India and China accounted for at least 90% of the 23–30 million missing female births that accumulated worldwide since the late 1970s (Bongaarts & Guilmoto, 2015; Chao et al., 2019). Again, imbalances were concentrated in later-born children (Yi et al., 1993), consistent with sex-selective abortion.

Focusing specifically on sex-selective abortion, Nandi (2015) assessed the impact of a ban on sex-selective abortion on infant mortality in India. In 1996, the Prenatal Diagnostics Techniques Act aimed at stopping prenatal sex determination and sex-selective abortion. Through a quasi-experiment leveraging variation in the timing of the law across Indian states, the study found that the law significantly increased likelihood of female births, thus improving female-to-male sex ratios at birth, while no change was observed in female infant mortality.

The disparate treatment of male and female children and fetuses pointed to persistent norms of son preference and the broad disempowerment of women in many cultures, but not in all (Engle et al., 1984). In countries where there was son preference, efforts to empower women had mixed effects. In India, for example, increases in women's inheritance rights due to amendments to the Hindu Succession Act exacerbated son preference because the amendments made daughters costlier in addition to improving women's rights (Bhalotra et al., 2020). However, in a well-known example from South Africa, pension receipt by grandmothers improved height-for-age and weight-for-height among granddaughters but not grandsons (Duflo, 2003).

SUMMARY AND CONCLUSIONS

This chapter critically reviewed the evidence on the relationships between women's empowerment and a range of population dynamics, with particular attention to family formation and fertility, migration, and mortality. We included associational evidence, which more often operationalizes measures of relative resources (e.g., relative schooling, work, age, and assets) as well as direct measures of individual and interpersonal agency (as defined in this report) and related these measures to interpersonal population dynamics. We then emphasized causal evidence, mainly taken from RCTs, which allowed us to isolate the impacts of investments via cash transfers, educational subsidies, skills training, and political and legal changes.

We documented a rich range of causal studies that explored impacts on marital and fertility outcomes. Importantly, the majority of these studies implied that impacts on marriage and fertility outcomes flow through women's agency; however, they do not assess mediation explicitly. Causal studies related to leading causes of mortality are more limited and more often take the form of natural experiments rather than RCTs. Lastly, experimental and quasi-experimental studies in the migration domain are virtually nonexistent.

While a vast literature attempts to link indicators of women's empowerment to population dynamics, results are often inconsistent across studies and geographies. These discrepancies may in part result from the diversity in indicators and lack of attention to mechanisms through which these relationships are expected to operate. In many cases, presumed indicators of empowerment, such as women's education, cannot be disentangled from secular trends in societal development; and women's education (both a resource and possibly an achievement) does not directly measure or guarantee her choice and agency. As discussed, studies showed that educational expansion resulting in decline in child mortality in Sub-Saharan Africa was not accompanied by increases in women's decision-making agency (Andriano & Monden, 2019). Second, some of the analyses of the effects of women's empowerment broadly, as well as women's agency specifically, on population outcomes ideally require longitudinal data over an extended period to understand immediate and sustained social change. Unfortunately, these kinds of data are rarely available. Third, most of the research focused on women's individual and interpersonal empowerment (e.g., resources and agency), yet the gender context seems to be an important moderator of individual-level relationships (Blanc, 2001; Desai & Johnson, 2005; Mason & Smith, 2000; Nanda et al., 2016; Peterman et al., 2017). Mason (2002) found that 40–80% of the variation in women's reported empowerment in the domestic sphere could be explained by aggregation of responses to normative questions about women's and men's roles. Unfortunately, interventions are often limited to small geographic areas within single countries, and thus to relatively homogenous cultural contexts, which hinders inferences to wider contexts as represented in the committee's new conceptual framework and certainly limits inferences to other national settings. Fourth, data limitations often affected the committee's ability to derive comparable results across diverse social contexts and to eliminate confounding effects.

Comparing the available empirical evidence to theoretical pathways along the dimensions of individual, interpersonal, community, and societal levels of agency, a few patterns emerge. First, existing evidence adequately maps theoretical pathways at the individual and interpersonal levels only, particularly in the areas of fertility and family formation. At the individual level, agency is most often measured as self-efficacy or through indirect measures of skills and knowledge, while intrinsic motivation and aspirations are rarely measured explicitly. Conversely, at the interpersonal level, agency is most often proxied, relying on measures of status inconsistency between partners, such as differences in age, education levels, decision-making power, and occupation. Empirical evidence measuring agency with clear constructs at the community and societal levels is missing, primarily due to the complexity, vagueness, and, at times, sensitivity of measuring social and gender norms.

5

Women's Empowerment and Women's and Children's Health

This chapter reviews research on the relationship between women's empowerment and various dimensions of women's and children's health and well-being, focusing largely on the strongest evidence base related to sexual and reproductive, maternal, and newborn/early child health. The committee has adapted the World Health Organization's (WHO's) definition of health as a state of complete physical, mental, and social well-being and not merely the absence of disease or infirmity (WHO, 1948). Health—and importantly the highest standard of health—is considered a universal, fundamental human right, regardless of economic or social position, political beliefs, religion, or race and ethnicity (WHO, n.d.). Yet stark differences in outcomes and opportunities for health and well-being exist between men and boys compared to women and girls worldwide. Gender is an important social influencer of absolute health outcomes, and of disparities in health outcomes, for women and girls. The health of women and girls is heavily shaped by structural environments, cultural and gender norms, societal roles and relationships, and inequities in access to the social and environmental conditions for good health (WHO, n.d.). Beyond biological differences in risk and susceptibility between females and males (as assigned at birth) that may contribute to higher rates of some of the leading diseases and lower rates of survival among women, underlying structural and social factors drive gender-based health inequities for women and girls (Langer et al., 2015). As such, empowerment of women and girls has significant implications for health—as empowerment relates both to population dynamics and to socioeconomic development, and more broadly to societal well-being and Sustainable Development Goals.

Given the significant overlaps between key dimensions of health and both population dynamics and socioeconomic development, as well as related empowerment, the committee conceptualizes health as operating within both of those domains. As in the prior chapters and indicated in the framework presented in Figure 5-1, we acknowledge the bidirectional nature of the relationships between empowerment and health. But in this chapter, where possible, we place greater emphasis on how women's empowerment—at various levels of the social ecology—impacts health-related outcomes. We operationalize health outcomes as done in several key areas with the largest evidence base: access to family planning (including contraception, abortion, sexual activity); access to women's healthcare and health service utilization; women's physical, mental, and maternal health outcomes; and child health (including nutrition). Due to overlaps in the literature, some topics that can be considered health related are primarily discussed in other chapters (e.g., mortality is discussed in Chapter 4). As mentioned, for practical reasons, in this report the committee chose to focus on women of childbearing age, but we acknowledge the critical importance of understanding the link between women's empowerment and health at older ages as well.

WOMEN'S EMPOWERMENT AND
ACCESS TO FAMILY PLANNING

When it comes to reproductive choice, women's empowerment and agency are important for the right to decide about the number, timing, and spacing of their children; to decide about their reproductive activities; and to realize fertility goals and preferences. The interpersonal and sociocultural context includes the roles of women's male sexual partners, family, peers, community, and environments. Women's choices are influenced by the likelihood and actuality of the survival of their children to adulthood, as well as by broader multilevel influences discussed later in this chapter. Among the means defined above, contraceptive acceptability and effective, desired use result from the complex interplay between women's agency and partner dynamics and are conditioned by the same fundamental drivers inherent to assurance of reproductive rights—equitable access to services and methods, freedom from discrimination, economic and environmental resources, and supportive cultural norms and policies. Contraceptive use results from interactions between the availability of safe, acceptable, and affordable contraceptives; women's agency; sexual partner communication and power dynamics; family pressures; and cultural norms.

Evidence on family planning programs designed to improve women's agency and sexual and reproductive healthcare utilization, contraceptive use, and birth spacing is robust. Empirically, increased options in

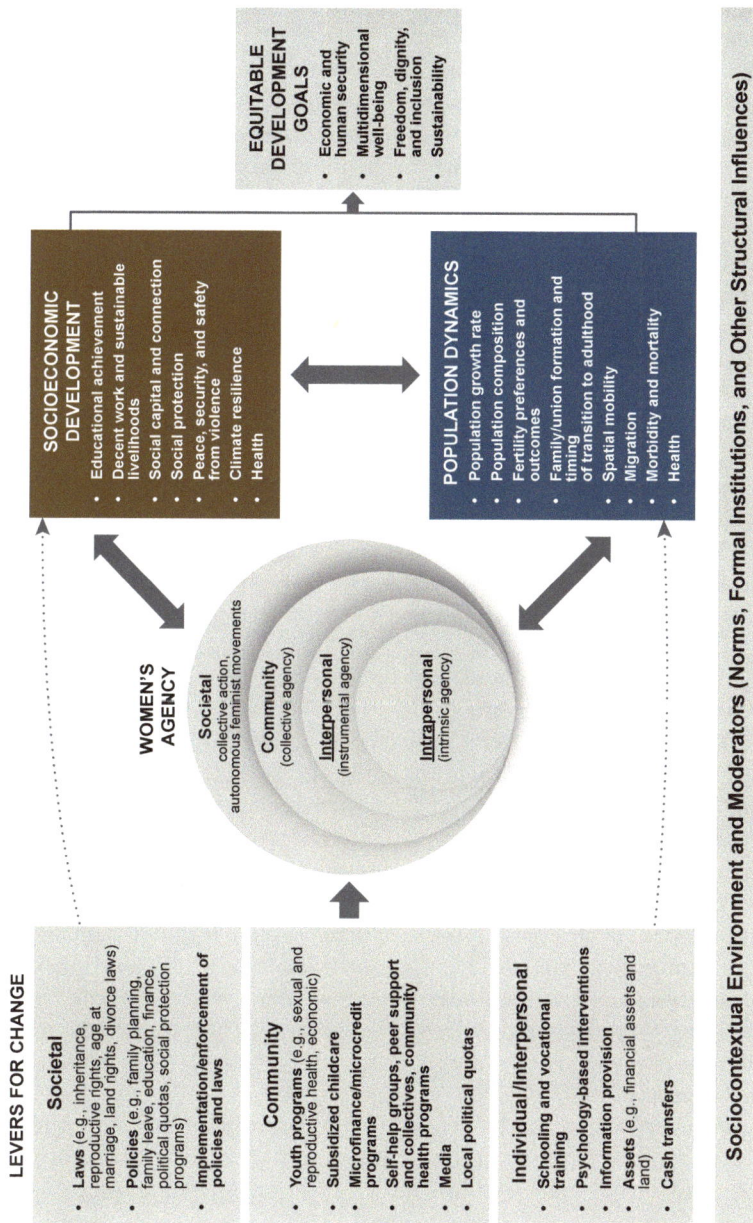

FIGURE 5-1 New conceptual framework of women's empowerment, population dynamics, and socioeconomic development, highlighting this chapter's areas of emphasis.
SOURCE: Developed by the committee.

LEVERS FOR CHANGE

Societal

- **Laws** (e.g., inheritance, reproductive rights, age at marriage, land rights, divorce laws)
- **Policies** (e.g., family planning, family leave, education, finance, political quotas, social protection programs)
- **Implementation/enforcement of policies and laws**

Community

- **Youth programs** (e.g., sexual and reproductive health, economic)
- **Subsidized childcare**
- **Microfinance/microcredit programs**
- **Self-help groups, peer support and collectives, community health programs**
- **Media**
- **Local political quotas**

Individual/Interpersonal

- **Schooling and vocational training**
- **Psychology-based interventions**
- **Information provision**
- **Assets** (e.g., financial assets and land)
- **Cash transfers**

WOMEN'S AGENCY

- **Societal** collective action, autonomous feminist movements
- **Community** (collective agency)
- **Interpersonal** (instrumental agency)
- **Intrapersonal** (intrinsic agency)

SOCIOECONOMIC DEVELOPMENT

- Educational achievement
- Decent work and sustainable livelihoods
- Social capital and connection
- Social protection
- Peace, security, and safety from violence
- Climate resilience
- Health

POPULATION DYNAMICS

- Population growth rate
- Population composition
- Fertility preferences and outcomes
- Family/union formation and timing of transition to adulthood
- Spatial mobility
- Migration
- Morbidity and mortality
- Health

EQUITABLE DEVELOPMENT GOALS

- Economic and human security
- Multidimensional well-being
- Freedom, dignity, and inclusion
- Sustainability

Sociocontextual Environment and Moderators (Norms, Formal Institutions, and Other Structural Influences)

contraceptive products and contraceptive access provided privately, as well as life skills training, can increase contraceptive use, which can in turn translate into informed choices about sexual activity and, at times, later onset of sexual intercourse (Ashraf et al., 2014; Bandiera et al., 2020). A randomized controlled trial (RCT) in Mozambique found that introducing female condoms to women led to a substantial increase in the proportion of women who used female condoms, especially among women with lower bargaining power, who were previously having unprotected sex (rather than using male condoms; Cassidy et al., 2021).

RCTs evaluating family planning counseling and education interventions have shown significant impact on contraceptive use among women across multiple national settings and world regions (Mwaikambo et al., 2011; Nanvubya et al., 2022; Zakiyah et al., 2016). They have also proven cost effective (Zakiyah et al., 2016). More recent evidence indicated that gender-transformative family planning interventions (e.g., those that counter traditional gender norms by including male partners and centralizing women's voice and choice) also showed significant positive effects on contraceptive use but primarily in the form of condom use (Ghanotakis et al., 2017; Raj et al., 2016, 2022). Bapolisi et al. (2020) provided a clear example of these gender-transformative sexual and reproductive health interventions engaging men, in the context of the Democratic Republic of the Congo. Using a longitudinal parallel mixed-methods approach combined with matching techniques, the study assessed the impact of the *Mawe tatu* program, an intervention linking village savings and loan associations for women with men-to-men sensitization, to transform gender-inequitable norms and behaviors. These two project arms were combined with an educational component about family planning and sexual and reproductive health. The authors found evidence of a positive effect of this combined intervention on the household economy, on child nutritional status, on the use of reproductive health services including family planning, and on reducing sexual and gender-based violence. Studies on gender-transformative family planning with married couples in India yielded similar findings regarding increased contraceptive use, male engagement in family planning, men's reports of relationship quality, and women's reports of satisfaction with family planning, as well as reductions in partner violence and traditional masculinity norms (Averbach et al., 2023; Chatterji et al., 2023; Fleming et al., 2018; Raj et al., 2016, 2022).

A quasi-experimental trial design by Ahmed et al. (2015) in rural Bangladesh examined the effect of integrating family planning with a community-based maternal and newborn health program on improving postpartum contraceptive use and reducing short birth intervals (< 24 months). The study found contraceptive prevalence rates in the intervention arm to be 15% higher than in the control arm at 12 months, and birth intervals of less than 24 months to be significantly lower in the intervention arm. Similarly, Karra et al. (2022) conducted an RCT in Lilongwe, Malawi, to assess the causal impact of improved access to family planning on contraceptive use and pregnancy spacing. The intervention arm received four services over a two-year period: (a) up to six family planning counseling sessions, (b) free transportation to a clinic, (c) free family planning services at the clinic or financial reimbursement for services obtained elsewhere, and (d) treatment for contraceptive-related side effects. The authors found that contraceptive use after two years of intervention exposure increased by 5.9 percentage points, mainly through an increased use of contraceptive implants. Furthermore, the treatment group's hazard of pregnancy was 43.5% lower 24 months after the index birth, suggesting longer birth spacing. Moreover, a recent study showed that providing personalized digital counseling to women regarding modern contraceptive methods may be as effective in increasing contraceptive use as providing subsidies (Athey et al., 2023).

Additional evidence comes from Naz and Acharya (2021), who evaluated the impact of the *Family Advancement for Life and Health (FALAH)* project, a family planning program implemented in 31 districts in Pakistan, using a quasi-experimental approach comparing outcomes of multiple children from the same mothers before and after the project. The study found that *FALAH* increased interbirth intervals by 2.4 months on average and reduced the proportion of short birth intervals by approximately 7.1 percentage points.

One relatively understudied aspect of access to family planning is access to infertility treatment. A recent systematic review and meta-analysis by WHO indicated that, globally, approximately one in six people have experienced infertility at some stage in their lives, equivalent to a lifetime prevalence of 17.5% and a period prevalence of 12.6% in 2022 (WHO, 2023). Availability and access to infertility treatment remain limited in low- and middle-income countries (LMICs), especially in Sub-Saharan Africa. We are not aware of any causal study examining the relationship between women's empowerment or agency and uptake of infertility treatment. Conversely, correlational studies have shown that infertility is associated with various physical and mental health issues. Infertility can lead to social ostracization or divorce; intimate partner violence; and poor economic, mental, or other health indicators (Kiani et al., 2020, 2021; Polis et al., 2017).

WOMEN'S EMPOWERMENT AND ACCESS TO ABORTION

Comprehensive abortion care, which includes information provision, abortion management, and post-abortion care, is an integral component of women's sexual and reproductive health. In 2020, WHO included comprehensive abortion care in its published list of essential healthcare services.

The WHO Abortion Care guideline released in March 2022 strives to facilitate evidence-based decision making for quality abortion care that is effective, efficient, accessible, acceptable, person-centered, equitable, and safe (WHO, 2022).

Clarke and Mühlrad (2021) examined the impact of progressive and regressive legislation targeting access to abortion services on women's health in Mexico using a two-way fixed-effects approach. While the Federal District of Mexico decriminalized and subsidized early-term elective abortion (progressive), other states increased sanctions on "illegal" abortions (regressive). On the progressive end, the authors documented sharp declines in maternal morbidity, especially due to hemorrhage in early pregnancy, suggesting considerable improvements in health outcomes flowing from legal access to abortion. On the regressive end, small or null impacts on women's health were observed in the states that increased sanctions. It is important to note that when women are denied legal access to abortion, some will seek other means to terminate a pregnancy (e.g., Scrimshaw, 1985).

In the context of India, Rastogi and Sharma (2022) explored whether legal restrictions on prenatal discrimination against females led to shifts by parents toward postnatal discrimination. Leveraging the same cross-temporal and cross-spatial variation described in Nandi (2015), they also documented an increase in female births, yet this was accompanied by less human capital investment in those children, providing evidence of postnatal discrimination. Specifically, females born in states affected by the ban were 2.3, 3.5, and 3.2 percentage points less likely, respectively, to complete grade 10, complete grade 12, and enter university. The study found these effects to be primarily concentrated among the poorest households that had no resources to evade the ban.

WOMEN'S EMPOWERMENT AND WOMEN'S ACCESS TO HEALTHCARE AND SERVICE UTILIZATION

Beyond family planning, associations between women's empowerment and health-related knowledge, behaviors, care access, and service utilization in LMIC contexts are well documented, particularly in relation to sexual and reproductive health (e.g., HIV), maternal health (antenatal/postnatal), and newborn/early child health services. A multitude of studies have conducted secondary analyses of Demographic and Health Surveys (DHS) data across various countries and settings globally. For example, Htun et al. (2021) analyzed Myanmar DHS data to identify barriers to accessing healthcare among 7,779 married women aged 15–49 years. This study focused on women's decision-making power and disagreement with justification of wife-beating, which are described in the study as indicators of women's empowerment but could also be considered indicators of women's agency. Barriers to healthcare access include not getting permission to go to the doctor, not being able to get the money needed for advice or treatment, long distances to a health facility, and not wanting to go alone. Using logistic regression, the authors found that women with high empowerment scores experienced fewer barriers when accessing healthcare services generally when compared to married women with low or middle empowerment scores. Barriers to healthcare access were also reduced among women residing in urban areas and those with a higher level of education, fewer children, and richer households. Reviews of the literature involving LMICs show similar predictors of women's control over decision making to seek healthcare for themselves, including women's education and employment; husbands' education and employment; and household wealth (Idris et al., 2023; Osamor & Grady, 2016).

In an analysis of Nepal DHS data, Khatiwada et al. (2020) identified significant associations between various dimensions of women's empowerment, which they defined as including education, occupation, owning a bank account, media exposure, internet use, and access to skilled birth attendants during delivery. These findings were consistent with those of a prior analysis of DHS data from 31 countries where data on women's empowerment were available, 21 of which were African countries (Ahmed et al., 2010). That study found that women experiencing empowerment inequities were less likely to utilize health services. Empowerment was measured based on five questions, with a possible score of 0–5, asking women about their involvement in decisions related to their own healthcare, large household purchases, daily household needs purchases, visits to their family or relatives, and daily meal preparation. Women with the highest empowerment scores were found to be significantly more likely to have attended four or more antenatal care visits and to have had a skilled birth attendant than were women with the lowest empowerment scores.

There is also growing research specific to the role of expanding information and communication technologies such as mobile phones, be they simple-feature phones or smartphones enabling full internet connectivity. With technology maturation and expansion of mobile data networks, mobile phone capabilities have expanded from enabling communication to provision of information and delivery of services (Aker & Mbiti, 2010). The increased affordability of mobile phones has also translated into enhanced financial independence and better labor market prospects, especially for women (Suri & Jack, 2016); food security and dietary quality (Bhandari, 2017; Sekabira & Qaim, 2017); better educational outcomes (Aker et al., 2012); and more decision-making power for women in domestic and public domains such as care work (Wekwete, 2014) and politics (Abubakar & Dasuki, 2018; Varriale et al., 2022). One influential study leveraging a natural experiment suggested that access to the Kenyan mobile money system M-PESA increased per capita consumption levels and lifted 2% of Kenyan households out of poverty. This study also documented more pronounced impacts for female-headed households, which seemed to be driven by changes in financial behavior (e.g., higher saving) and labor market outcomes such as occupational choice, especially for women who moved out of agriculture and into business (Suri & Jack, 2016).

A large-scale study covering over 200 countries found that the expansion of mobile phones was associated with lower gender inequalities, higher contraceptive use, and lower maternal and child mortality, with particularly strong associations among the poorest countries and communities (Rotondi et al., 2020). By complementing macro-level information with micro-level data and quasi-experimental techniques, the study also showed that ownership of mobile phones narrowed the information gap about reproductive and sexual health and increased women's independent decision making (Rotondi et al., 2020). Some of this evidence is consistent with a correlational study from India suggesting that women's mobile phone use is positively associated with women's physical mobility, nonsurgical contraceptive use, and higher community connectivity among women (Rajkhowa & Qaim, 2022). Associational evidence even suggests that benefits may transmit intergenerationally. For instance, using DHS data from 29 countries, Pesando and Qiyomiddin (2023) found that infants born to women owning mobile phones fare consistently better in terms of birth weight. Identified mechanisms are consistent with the idea of broader knowledge and access to healthcare services, and associations were found to be stronger in countries where infant health is poorer, yet mobile phone diffusion is higher, highlighting the comparatively higher potential of the mobile phone diffusion for global development in the poorest contexts.

Focusing on experiences of intimate partner violence, some evidence indicates that mobile phones may help women overcome physical boundaries, especially women who are separated from support networks and are bound within their husbands' social spheres. A recent study covering 10 low-income countries and employing instrumental-variable and nonparametric matching techniques found that women's independent (e.g., independent of women's male partners) ownership of mobile phones was associated with a 9–12% lower likelihood of emotional, physical, and sexual violence over the previous 12 months, even after controlling for characteristics proxying for socioeconomic status, household resources, and local development within the community (Pesando, 2022). The study also showed that mobile phone ownership was positively associated with women's decision-making power within the household and male partners' lower acceptability of intimate partner violence. Importantly, this was not observed in all countries, with Angola emerging as an exception—here, women's mobile phone ownership was associated with higher likelihood of experiencing intimate partner violence. This evidence is consistent with the idea that, in some contexts—especially where digital gender gaps are still wide, independent device use is limited, and shared device use is still the norm—mobile phones may serve as "disempowering" devices: independent (or even concealed) use of mobile phones may in fact trigger violent reactions from male partners, who feel threatened by "new" status imbalances within the household unsettling norms of male dominance. Large-scale comparative studies (McDougal et al., 2019) as well as qualitative research in selected low-income countries support this possibility (Mpiima et al., 2019; Uduji & Okolo-Obasi, 2018). In line with the above disempowering scenario, technology and media may also spread gender-traditional ideas and strengthen gender stereotypes, thus reinforcing backlash effects, as shown by Forsyth and Ward (2022) in Honduras and Gray (2014) in Malawi.

A comprehensive overview of the implications of mobile phone expansion for dynamics of gender equality in areas such as health, agriculture, education, food security, labor markets, business, and participation in politics can be found in Pesando and Rotondi (2020). One central tenet of this expanding scholarship is that the full potential of mobile phone technology cannot be reached if digital divides by gender persist. Women are still far less likely to own mobile phones on their own, use them less often when they have access, and have poorer information and communication technology skills compared to men, thus creating second-level (skill-related) digital divides on top of first-level (access-related) divides (Blumenstock & Eagle, 2010; Fatehkia et al., 2018), and therefore highlighting a key area for policy intervention.

Access to healthcare has also been found to be a significant contributor to women's empowerment and agency, illustrating the reciprocal nature of empowerment and healthcare access. Asaolu et al. (2018) analyzed DHS data from 19 countries in Sub-Saharan Africa, defining women's empowerment as attitudes toward violence, labor force participation, education, and access to healthcare. In this study, access to care was described as the distance to health facilities, ability to afford services, and the permission to access services. The study concluded that removing healthcare barriers can empower women by providing resources that allow women to exercise their agency.

Other studies show an association between women's empowerment and antenatal and postnatal service utilization. In an analysis of four rounds of Ethiopia DHS data of 61,635 women ages 15–49 years from 2000–2016, Shibre et al. (2023) found that highly empowered women used more antenatal and postnatal care services than poorly empowered women did. This study utilizes empowerment, defined as decision making, social independence, and attitudes toward violence, as an equity stratifier to assess inequalities in the uptake of maternal child health (MCH) services, including early antenatal care and four or more antenatal care and postnatal care services. Similarly, a cross-sectional study with 200 women in Bangladesh aimed to identify the patterns between women's empowerment, in terms of mobility and decision making, and health-seeking behavior (Mainuddin et al., 2015). This study found that only 12% of women were empowered or had the agency to make their own decisions about seeking healthcare, and that women's empowerment could enhance decision-making authority related to health-seeking behavior. Additional studies using DHS data from LMICs showed that enhanced decision making could increase chances of attending antenatal care visits during pregnancy, receiving skilled antenatal care, making the first prenatal visit during the first three months of pregnancy, and delivery in a hospital (Fawole & Adeoye, 2015; Mokam & Zamo Akono, 2022; Sripad et al., 2019).

An analysis of DHS data in Bangladesh evaluated dimensions of women's empowerment alongside the continuum of care (CoC) for maternal health (including pregnancy, delivery, and postpartum care) among 4,942 married women of reproductive age who had at least one live birth in the past three years (Rahman et al., 2021). After adjusting for individual-, household-, and community-level variables, women with higher social independence were found to have more antenatal care visits, higher retention of skilled birth attendants, and higher completion of full CoC than women with low social independence. Indicators under the social independence domain, including frequency of reading newspapers or magazines, education, age at first cohabitation, and age at first birth, were found to be important predictors of CoC.

Finally, Nieuwenhuijze and Leahy-Warren (2019) systematically reviewed 97 primary research articles (qualitative, quantitative, and mixed methods) from LMICs and high-income countries, focused on empowerment in the areas of birth experience, maternal and newborn health outcomes, use of maternity services, participation in care, and satisfaction with care. This review identified four consequences of women's empowerment in pregnancy and childbirth, finding that women's empowerment based on decision-making indicators during pregnancy and childbirth could increase women's satisfaction with the birth experience, deeming it positive, exuding a sense of accomplishment, and providing an opportunity to heal from a previous traumatic birth. Empowerment was also found to contribute to the woman's overall health as well as the health of her baby and family, enhancing self-confidence and emotional well-being, increasing self-advocacy in terms of more assertive interactions with providers, and contributing to a sense of control over choice and decision making.

WOMEN'S EMPOWERMENT AND HEALTH OUTCOMES

Maternal Health

Associations between women's empowerment and a broader range of women's physical, mental, and maternal health outcomes have also been studied, though the evidence base is generally less robust than it is for healthcare access and service utilization. For example, a few recent studies found that women's empowerment was associated with better maternal and newborn health outcomes. Kabir et al. (2020) analyzed DHS data from Bangladesh, including data from 27,357 women and 9,234 mother-child pairs. This study measured empowerment using the Women's Empowerment Index (WEI), including indicators related to education, access to sociofamilial decision making, economic contribution and access to economic decision making, attitudes toward domestic violence, and mobility. The study found that women with WEI scores in the highest quartile, when compared to women with WEI scores in the lowest quartile, had 32% lower adjusted odds of having a low-birth-weight baby. Moreover, the WEI is moderated by household income, with women in the highest WEI quartile experiencing 54% lower odds of undernutrition in the highest wealth quartile group and 18% lower odds in the lowest wealth quartile group when compared to women in the lowest WEI quartiles within the respective wealth quartile groups. This study concluded that the likelihood of a woman being malnourished or delivering a low-birth-weight baby decreased as levels of empowerment increased.

A few studies also found associations between women's empowerment and select mental health outcomes, most often in the context of pregnancy and parenting. A longitudinal analysis in rural Burkina Faso by Leight et al. (2022) analyzed the association between the project-level Women's Empowerment in Agriculture Index and outcomes of stress and maternal depression. The study found that maternal distress was negatively correlated with women's empowerment scores. Women with high self-efficacy had a 6 percentage point decline in the probability of high maternal stress, and women reporting respect among household members had an 11 percentage point decline in the probability of postpartum depression. A qualitative study in Pakistan of 19 symptomatic pregnant women aged 18–37 years found that autonomy, specifically decision-making power and peer/family support, was an important protective factor against prenatal maternal anxiety and an enabling resource for maternal mental health (Rowther et al., 2020). More generally, a longitudinal study by Richardson et al. (2019) analyzing baseline and follow-up interviews with 2,859 women in rural India found that one standard deviation increase in agency was associated with a 7% reduction relative to the mean in psychological distress symptoms.

Women's Morbidity and Gender Gaps in Morbidity

Morbidity data need to be considered along with mortality data, as morbidities increase risk for years of life lost. Women experience more morbidity than men, and women lose more years of life due to disability than men (James et al., 2018). Nutritional deficiencies and neurological, mental, and musculoskeletal disorders account for the bulk of this pattern, but maternal morbidities also contribute to these differences (James et al., 2018).

Women's Empowerment and Women's Morbidity

At the individual level, women with greater agency tend to exhibit lower morbidity. A study of five African countries found that women with greater influence over household decisions and women less accepting of domestic violence had higher body mass index (Jones et al., 2020a). Another study of 26 African countries found that women were less likely to be anemic or underweight in couples that agreed that the wife played at least an equal role in major household purchase decisions (Annan et al., 2021). Similarly, a study in India found that exposure to domestic violence raised the risk of anemia and underweight in women (Ackerson & Subramanian, 2008). These differences in morbidity may in part relate to the greater use of healthcare, especially reproductive healthcare, by women with greater autonomy and decision-making power (Allendorf, 2007; Bloom et al., 2001; Pratley, 2016) or in areas that have been more exposed to local female leadership (Dupas & Jain, 2024).

Child Health

An array of evidence—correlational and causal, at multiple levels of analysis—suggests that women's empowerment improves the health of their children. In individual-level data, children of women with greater agency have been shown less likely to be malnourished and more likely to survive. Systematic reviews of studies from low-income contexts demonstrated that greater maternal agency was associated with better healthcare and health among their children (Abreha & Zereyesus, 2021; Carlson et al., 2015; Pratley, 2016), including complete childhood immunizations coverage (Thorpe et al., 2016). The most common outcome in the literature is nutritional status, but studies also found associations of autonomy with increased antenatal care, skilled birth attendance, and vaccination, as well as decreased child mortality.

Associations suggest multiple ways through which women's empowerment could matter for child health, reflecting the multiple components of women's empowerment. A study of five African countries found that women with more intrinsic agency, measured by attitudes about domestic violence, had taller and heavier children; women with greater instrumental agency, measured by influence over household decisions, had children who were less anemic (Jones et al., 2020a). Other studies focused on concordance in spouses' reports of who makes household decisions. For example, a study of 26 African countries found that children were less likely to have low height-for-age, low weight-for-height, or incomplete vaccination status when their mothers and fathers agreed that the mother had at least equal say in household decisions or when their mothers claimed more power than their fathers (Annan et al., 2021). Other studies focused on the distinction between community- and individual-level agency. For example, a study of 12 African, Latin American, and South Asian countries found that women's decision-making power predicted children's immunization status, nutritional status, and survival more consistently across communities than across women within communities (Desai & Johnson, 2005).

India stands out for having especially large and statistically significant associations between women's decision-making power and children's health across all outcomes and all levels of analysis (Desai & Johnson, 2005). As seen for research on women's agency and women's health, India also provides a great deal of insight into the relationship between women's positioning in the family and child health. In joint Indian households, in which multiple adult brothers live in the same household, the children of lower-ranking wives were shown to have higher neonatal mortality and lower height-for-age (Coffey et al., 2022).

Lower fertility can also improve children's health and mortality if, due to smaller family size, parents can invest more in each child's health and development. Yount et al. (2014) examined how fertility decline affected girls' well-being and gender gaps in children's well-being in poor countries, using several years of DHS data. They found that fertility decline and women's later first birth were associated with gains in girls' survival at ages 1–4 years, vaccination coverage at ages 12–23 months, and nutrition at 0–36 months. The study demonstrated that the gender gaps in child health reduced as women's median age at first birth increased.

Causal evidence for this so-called "quantity-quality" tradeoff is lacking, however—it is unclear whether factors that cause delayed childbearing (e.g., greater education) also cause improvements in child health, or whether health improvements stem from lower/delayed fertility itself. However, earlier work on child survival, birth spacing, and birth order for nearly 3,000 low-income women in Ecuador demonstrated the negative impact of high birth order and closely spaced births on the survival of infants and young children (Wolfers & Scrimshaw, 1975).

Effects of Women's Socioeconomic Development on Women's and Children's Health via Women's Empowerment

Several studies have shown that multilevel interventions that strengthen women's empowerment through addressing socioeconomic development can improve women's healthcare access and health outcomes (Das et al., 2023; Fawole & Adeoye, 2015; Mokam & Zamo Akono, 2022; Yeo et al., 2022). Key socioeconomic development programs designed to impact healthcare access and outcomes through women's empowerment include increased access to educational opportunities, media exposure, employment and socioeconomic mobility, healthcare payment participation, household decision making and autonomy, and reduced gender-based violence and child marriage (Bamiwuye et al., 2013; Das et al., 2023; Fawole & Adeoye, 2015; Htun et al., 2021; Khatiwada et al., 2020; Mokam & Zamo Akono, 2022; Ntoimo et al., 2022; Shibre et al., 2023; Shimamoto & Gipson, 2019; Woldemicael, 2007; Yaya et al., 2018; Yeo et al., 2022). For example, community health worker interventions including home visits, cash transfers, and participatory women's groups were shown to promote equity in MCH (Blanchard et al., 2019).

A survey designed by de Brauw and Peterman (2020) evaluated the impact of a conditional cash transfers (CCT) program in El Salvador on maternal health service utilization outcomes, including prenatal care, skilled attendance at birth, birth in health facilities, and postnatal care. This study found that CCTs could reduce barriers to healthcare by providing financial incentives and enhancing women's decision-making agency and empowerment. The treatment group receiving CCTs had an increase in skilled attendance at birth following the intervention.

Exploratory research conducted in southeast Nigeria by Ezenwaka et al. (2021) utilized qualitative interviews and thematic analysis of service utilization pre- and post-program to explore how CCTs influence the uptake of MCH services. Results from this study showed that pregnant women who received CCT were more motivated to attend health facilities, resulting in improved utilization of maternal health services, with increased utilization among CCT participants from 2012 to 2015 in the areas of antenatal attendance, antenatal first visit, antenatal fourth visit, delivery by a skilled birth attendant, pregnant women receiving their second dose of tetanus toxoid, and the number of children under one year of age who were fully immunized. Another RCT by Vanhuyse et al. (2022) included 2,522 women in the intervention group who received CCTs and 2,922 women in the control group. The study found that those receiving the intervention attended a significantly higher proportion of antenatal care appointments than those in the control group.

Effects of Policy and Community Interventions
for Women's Empowerment on Health Outcomes

In terms of the role of policies in maternal and child health outcomes, a study that leveraged variation in the gender composition of state legislatures after close elections between male and female candidates found that increased women's representation was associated with reduced neonatal mortality in India (Bhalotra & Clots-Figueras, 2014). Antenatal visits, skilled and institutional birth delivery, nutritional supplementation in pregnancy, tetanus injection in pregnancy, and early breastfeeding also increased—as did the presence of a health center, dispensary, or hospital—suggesting public health investment as a mechanism. At the local level in India, reserved spots for women on village councils—which were randomly assigned to one-third of villages—increased spending on improved drinking water facilities (Chattopadhyay & Duflo, 2004), which can improve children's health. However, spending did not increase on education and sanitation, which surveys suggested were less important to female constituents than drinking water. In other words, women's political agency can elevate the interests of children but not uniformly.

The historical United States provides further evidence of a policy-level effect of women's agency on child health. A classic study focused on the staggered expansion of women's suffrage across states in the early 20th century. Tracking the evolution of state child mortality rates and public health spending during this expansion, Miller (2008) estimated that enfranchising women raised public health spending by one-third and reduced child mortality by 8–15%, principally due to decreases in diarrheal disease and other hygiene-related causes.

Community-based interventions were also shown to increase health awareness and service utilization among women, while being cost effective. Sharma et al. (2020) evaluated a peer-educator intervention in India focused on transfer of knowledge about various aspects of MCH, which aimed to create a supportive environment within the household and community. Via a nonexperimental, post-test evaluation of the treatment group using a mixed-methods approach via qualitative interviews and thematic analysis of 37,324 women, both of which included indicators related to women's awareness and utilization of MCH services (Sharma et al., 2020), the authors found that the intervention increased women's awareness of MCH services, shifted the attitudes of family members toward maternal health, and educated women on saving money to use for emergencies or other health services, such as transportation to the hospital at the time of delivery. In a mixed-methods study of a participatory women's group intervention focused on women's health, nutrition, and family planning, the authors interviewed and surveyed 5,355 women before the intervention and

5,128 following the intervention (Harris-Fry et al., 2016). They found that women's participatory groups could significantly improve women's health knowledge, including improvements in women's dietary diversity scores and participation in healthcare decision making, as well as knowledge regarding contraception, treatment and prevention of sexually transmitted infections, nutrition, and anemia prevention. Other interventions aimed at mitigating domestic violence (Krishnan et al., 2012), improving community health and nutrition (Pradhan et al., 2023), and addressing upstream causes of food insecurity all showed promise in enhancing women's empowerment and reducing negative health outcomes.

Using a clustered RCT design, Handa et al. (2014, 2015, 2017) evaluated a national poverty program named *Kenyan Cash Transfer for Orphans and Vulnerable Children*, an unconditional transfer of US $20 per month to eligible households. The program aimed to positively affect sexual and reproductive health outcomes and socioeconomic development of women, girls, and their families by improving household-level economic stability, investing in educational opportunities, promoting equitable household and community gender norms, and increasing young women's life aspirations and reproductive agency. The program reduced the odds of early initiation of sexual activity by 31%, yet it had no effects on outcomes such as condom use, number of partners, and transactional sex. Additional findings indicated that, while the program reduced the likelihood of pregnancy by 5 percentage points, there was no significant impact on likelihood of early marriage. Program impacts on pregnancy appeared to work through increasing the enrollment of young women in school, financial stability of the household, and delayed age at first sexual encounter. Another randomized cash transfer, conditional on girls' monthly high school attendance in South Africa, decreased the risk of physical intimate partner violence by delaying girls' sexual initiation and reducing the number of sexual partners (Kilburn et al., 2018).

SUMMARY AND CONCLUSIONS

As described in this chapter, a significant body of largely descriptive and associational survey research exists to support relationships between women's empowerment and healthcare access, service utilization, and outcomes. The areas that received the greatest attention (and that have causal evidence) include interventions and programs designed to improve sexual and reproductive health access, family planning use, antenatal health, and infant to young child health outcomes, in part by affecting women's agency or also by affecting indicators of socioeconomic development. Notably, interventions designed to address educational and economic opportunities and social capital have shown positive effects on family planning outcomes (e.g., decreased early marriage, older age at sexual debut, reduced unintended pregnancy, and improved healthcare access) in LMICs, most notably in Sub-Saharan Africa. This work has mainly focused on measuring agency at the individual level and through indicators of self-efficacy, reproductive autonomy, and householding decision making.

Beyond the RCT and quasi-experimental designs cited in this chapter, a larger portion of the existing work has relied upon DHS data and/or secondary analyses of cross-sectional data, has been conducted in limited and specific geographical and clinical settings, and has used empowerment indicators based on somewhat narrow definitions or unidimensional measures. As noted in Chapter 4, associations between health outcomes, women's empowerment, and socioeconomic development are often bidirectionally framed in the literature. As such, our new conceptual framework considers health fundamental to population dynamics and socioeconomic development. Finally, the greatest body of work reviewed focused on individual-level conceptualizations and targets for empowerment, with less overall evidence existing for measurements and interventions designed to affect agency and subsequently the health of women and girls at community and societal levels.

Overall, future research is warranted to expand the evidence base, to further illuminate causal associations between women's empowerment and health and healthcare access using primary data collection, longitudinal and prospective designs, quasi-experimental RCTs, and mixed-methods policy-evaluation approaches. Studies are warranted using a broader range of multidimensional measures of both empowerment indicators and priority outcomes that relate to patient-/woman-/community-centered health and healthcare experiences, importantly of quality and respectful care and both within and outside the formal healthcare sectors. Additionally, studies focused on a holistic set of physical, mental, reproductive, and behavioral health conditions most salient to women and their families and communities, across the life course (including beyond reproductive and economically productive years) and across generations, are critically important.

6

Women's Empowerment and Socioeconomic Development

This chapter reviews the state of knowledge on the relationship between women's empowerment (e.g., an expansion in women's resources, choice, agency, or achievements) and various socioeconomic development outcomes. Similar to the preceding chapters, while the committee acknowledges the bidirectional nature of the relationship, as indicated in our new conceptual framework shown in Figure 6-1, this chapter places greater emphasis on how women's empowerment—at various levels of the social ecology—impacts socioeconomic development. As described in Chapter 2, by socioeconomic development we mean the sustained improvement in the social and economic well-being of the population. We operationalize socioeconomic development as consisting of multiple dimensions of well-being, such as human development (e.g., education, nutrition, skills development, health outcomes, and access to quality care); material standard of living (e.g., access to decent work and sustainable livelihoods); social capital and cohesion; social protection; governance and the quality of public services; peace, security, and safety from violence (especially intimate partner violence [IPV]); and climate resilience. The chapter is organized around these topics, with health outcomes primarily discussed in Chapter 5. We recognize that reducing the breadth and depth of inequality in achieving these outcomes, including along gender lines, is a core component of socioeconomic development. We also acknowledge that important dimensions of socioeconomic development with links to women's agency, such as maternal and child health and sexual and reproductive health, overlap with population dynamics and have thus been covered in previous chapters. Furthermore, we are aware of the large body of literature that relates population dynamics

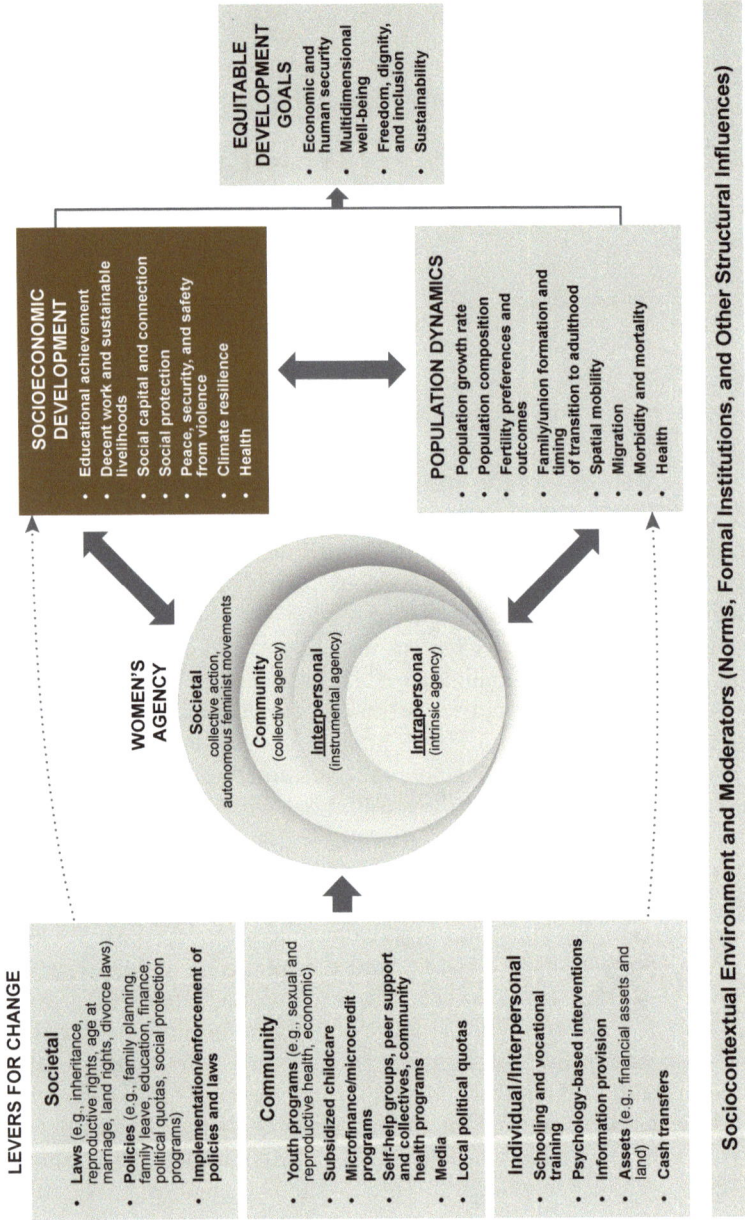

FIGURE 6-1 New conceptual framework of women's empowerment, population dynamics, and socioeconomic development, highlighting this chapter's area of emphasis.
SOURCE: Developed by the committee.

to the socioeconomic outcomes listed above, but in this report, we opt to emphasize the arrow that links women's empowerment to socioeconomic development.

As discussed in prior chapters, literature on the role of women's empowerment faces several methodological challenges, in part due to the variety of ways this concept is measured and its context-specific nature. These challenges are related to the difficulty of finding exogenous variation that drives women's empowerment. In the area of socioeconomic development, studies that attempt a causal identification use legal or institutional changes that enhance women's control over assets or their access to income as natural experiments; or they use programmatic interventions, such as conditional cash transfers, in the context of randomized controlled trials (RCTs). Some of the studies we reviewed directly measured women's empowerment (e.g., through household bargaining or decision-making measures) and identified empowerment as a mediator for impacts of socioeconomic outcomes. However, because of the challenges of operationalizing and measuring empowerment, many of the studies did not explicitly measure the effects of the legal changes or interventions on women's agency but instead examined their effects on the socioeconomic development outcomes of interest, such as female labor force participation or social protection. These studies then implicitly attributed the effects to the mediating role of women's empowerment or resorted to theoretical models of household bargaining and decision making to make the case.

In addition to examining the links between women's empowerment and various socioeconomic development outcomes, this chapter briefly reviews the state of knowledge about the relationship between women's empowerment and macroeconomic outcomes, such as sectoral allocation of resources, productivity, and economic growth. Much of this literature used theory-based computable general equilibrium models to quantify the effects of women's empowerment (or gender equality more broadly) on macroeconomic outcomes. These studies examined potential effects on macroeconomic outcomes through three main channels: an investment channel, in which women's increased decision making affects the allocation of investments into human versus physical capital; a labor-allocation channel, in which lifting barriers to entry for women in various occupations and sectors can increase economic growth; and a fertility channel, in which women's empowerment can affect economic growth through reduced fertility. These model-based approaches are methodologically distinct from the theory-agnostic statistical approaches discussed elsewhere in this report.

CHILD NUTRITIONAL STATUS AND SCHOOLING

Although educational achievement and health are listed as separate dimensions of socioeconomic development in our new conceptual framework, we opt to discuss child nutritional status and schooling together, since existing literature often treats them together as indicators of parental investment in child human capital. Several broad reviews of the association of women's agency, autonomy, and empowerment with child nutritional status have been conducted (Carlson et al., 2015; Ruel & Alderman, 2013; Santoso et al., 2019). Carlson et al. (2015) focused on the notion of women's autonomy, which they conceptualized as women's household decision-making control along with women's attitudes about the legitimacy of domestic violence. The authors acknowledged, however, that the literature they reviewed used many proxy measures of what they term "autonomy," which we may view as "agency" in our new conceptual framework, impeding cross-national and cross-cultural comparability. Nonetheless, this review strongly suggests that improving maternal agency is conducive to improving children's nutritional status. Ruel and Alderman's review (2013) of the impact of agriculture, social safety nets, early child development, and schooling interventions on nutritional outcomes holds similar recommendations but highlights that much of what we see in the value of women's empowerment in this realm is specific to what has been done with agricultural programs.

Santoso et al. (2019) conducted an even broader review of 62 associational studies linking women's empowerment to child nutritional outcomes, using 200 indicators of empowerment and testing 1,316 associations with various child nutrition outcomes. This review did not find a conclusive relationship between women's empowerment and child nutrition, with 82% of associations with stunting outcomes and 84% of associations with wasting outcomes being statistically insignificant. The authors attributed this result to limitations in study design related to poor selection of empowerment indicators, exclusive reliance on cross-sectional rather than longitudinal data, and improperly controlling for pathway variables that may mediate the relationship. Jones et al. (2020a) attempted to distinguish between the domains of empowerment and to account for pathways of influence using structural equation modeling in their study of the relationship between women's empowerment and child nutrition in five African countries. They found that assets, intrinsic agency (which they measured via attitudes accepting of domestic violence), and instrumental agency (which they measured as women's decision-making control) were positively associated with maternal body mass index (BMI). In turn, maternal BMI was positively associated with both the height-for-age and weight-for-height z-scores of their children. The authors also found that their attitudinal measure was associated directly with several indicators of child nutritional status as well as indirectly, through improved maternal nutrition.

Using a novel operationalization of women's empowerment based on a comparison of a woman's perception of her own decision-making power relative to her husband's perception, Annan et al. (2021) studied associations with various household well-being outcomes, including children's health and education, in 23 Sub-Saharan countries. The study found that women assigning themselves higher decision-making power than their husbands assign them, which the authors refer to as "taking power," is as effective as agreement between women and their husbands in terms of reducing girls' stunting and wasting measures and increasing boys' likelihood of receiving a full course of vaccinations. Generally, the authors found that women "taking power" was better for child outcomes than was being "given power," but women who took power were subjected to significantly higher incidence of emotional violence.

Several studies attempted to identify a causal relationship between women's agency at the societal or interpersonal levels and children's nutrition and schooling outcomes. We begin with studies that exploited legal changes as natural experiments to identify causal effects. At the community level, laws that reserve leadership positions for women, such as a 1993 law in India, were shown to increase girls' career aspirations and educational attainment (Beaman et al., 2012) and women's economic empowerment through public work programs and access to financial services (Deininger et al., 2020). At the interpersonal level, researchers studied the impact of changes in divorce laws on household decisions, through their effect on women's bargaining power (Corradini & Buccione, 2023; Roff, 2017; Stevenson, 2007). A law that enhanced women's unilateral divorce rights in Egypt—a context in which divorce laws strongly favor men—was shown to increase investment in child human capital (Corradini & Buccione, 2023). The extension of alimony rights and obligations to cohabiting couples in Brazil was shown to increase hours worked by adult females and to increase investments in the education of children (Rangel, 2006). Kumar and Quisumbing (2012) examined how women's perceptions of the division of household assets upon divorce affected women's well-being and child schooling outcomes in rural Ethiopia. The authors found that in households that perceived divorce allocations to favor men, children's schooling was negatively affected, more so for girls than boys.

There is considerably more research on the role of women's agency as a mediating factor in the relationship between women's economic empowerment and socioeconomic development outcomes. A longstanding result in the international development literature is that household spending decisions depend on the gender of the income recipient, and that when income accrues to women rather than men, it is more likely to be spent on children's nutrition and education rather than on privately consumed items, such as tobacco and alcohol (Doss, 1996; Duflo, 2003; Hoddinott & Haddad, 1995; Quisumbing, 2003). It has long been recognized that this result is at odds with a household decision model in which the household makes decision as a unit (also called the unitary household model). This discrepancy can only be explained by a model of the household in which decisions are a result of a bargaining process between two or more individuals with differing preferences, with the decision outcomes depending on their relative bargaining power (the so-called collective household model; Alderman et al., 1995; Chiappori, 1992, 1997). This approach was expanded in the 1990s and early 2000s into a broader research agenda on "gender and intrahousehold decisions and outcomes" (Quisumbing, 2003; Rogers & Schlossman, 1990). Evidence in favor of collective household models showing that assets or income accruing to women result in different household decisions is, therefore, indirect evidence on how shifts in women's bargaining power—or agency—affect household decisions, even if women's bargaining power or agency are not directly measured.

Exploiting a natural experiment related to agricultural reforms in post-Mao China that differentially increased demand for male and female labor depending on the product mixes in each region, Qian (2008) showed that increases in the relative share of income going to female household members in tea-producing regions resulted in higher survival rates for girls and improved educational attainment for all children. Conversely, a 2011 amendment to the Chinese Marriage Law that reduced women's rights to housing property upon divorce led to significant reductions in household spending on children's education, which one study attributed to women's reduced bargaining power after the law was adopted (Li & Sun, 2023).

Using indicators of human and physical capital brought by men and women at marriage as a proxy for bargaining power, Quisumbing and Maluccio (2003) showed that in Bangladesh and South Africa, more assets brought to the marriage by women increased expenditures on children's education, but the opposite was true in Ethiopia. Using the assets brought into the marriage and the distribution of assets upon divorce as proxies for bargaining power, Fafchamps et al. (2009) showed that increases in women's bargaining power had a positive effect on child nutrition and school attendance, but their results did not extend to all dimensions of household welfare. Using a fully elaborated collective household model and data from Mexico, Reggio (2011) explicitly estimated a mother's bargaining power using information on decision making about major household purchases and the age difference between husband and wife. The study found that an increase in a mother's bargaining power was associated with fewer hours of child labor for her daughters, but not for her sons.

Analyses of the impact of the expansion of an old-age pension program to the Black population in South Africa in 1993 showed that benefits accruing to women had a large impact on the nutritional status of their granddaughters, while no similar effect was found for benefits accruing to men. Men's and women's benefits had similar impacts on the nutritional status of grandsons (Duflo, 2003). Lancaster et al. (2006) showed that when power was more evenly distributed in the household, there was a higher tendency to spend on jointly consumed items, like children's education. This and similar results have made it a standard practice to designate women rather than men as the recipients of cash transfers targeted to poor households, to maximize the transfers' socioeconomic benefits (Gitter & Barham, 2008; Molyneux & Thomson, 2011). Evidence also suggests that women's bargaining power mediates the effects of economic shocks on children's human capital. Dovis et al. (2021) showed that the impact of a father's employment shock on the participation of adolescent daughters in intensive domestic work in Egypt was modulated by the mother's bargaining power.

DECENT WORK AND SUSTAINABLE LIVELIHOODS

Few studies examined the impact of women's agency on women's labor force participation or access to decent work. In fact, most existing literature examines the opposing direction of causality, namely the effect of access to work and economic opportunities on women's agency and decision making (De Hoop et al., 2018; Grogan, 2023; Heath, 2014; Heath & Mobarak, 2015; Jensen, 2012; Kabeer, 1997; Kabeer et al., 2018; Pike & English, 2022; Salem et al., 2018).

A few studies examined the relationship between women's intrahousehold bargaining power and their labor supply. Several studies used the Hindu Succession Act of 1956 in India as a natural experiment, which exogenously shifted women's unearned income by improving their ability to inherit property, to show that the passage of the Act positively shifted women's labor supply, contrary to the predictions of the standard labor supply model (Heath & Tan, 2020; Sapkal, 2017). The research attributed the positive effect to increased control over income and bargaining power, and women's increased agency. In contrast, the introduction of unilateral no-fault divorce laws between 2008 and 2018 in all 32 Mexican states, which made it easier for women to obtain a divorce, did not increase women's labor force participation and had a small positive effect on hours worked for employed married women (Hoehn-Velasco & Penglase, 2021). Hallward-Driemeier and Gajigo (2015) examined the effect of a legal reform in Ethiopia that expanded wives' access to marital property and removed restrictions on working outside the home. They found that women exposed to these reforms were significantly more likely to work in occupations that required work outside the home and that employed more educated workers in paid and full-time jobs. Conversely, a 2011 change in the Marriage Law in China that reduced women's rights to housing property upon divorce led to a reduction in women's work outside the home and women's assumption of a higher burden of household chores (Dong, 2022).

A small but growing literature demonstrates that strengthening women's agency over assets can improve livelihoods. For example, Ali et al. (2014) found that a land-regularization program in Rwanda led to large increases in agricultural investment. This effect was particularly pronounced for female-headed households, suggesting that this group suffered from high levels of tenure insecurity, which the program reduced. In Ghana, strengthening women's tenure security led to shifts away from farm work, with large increases in women's business profits (Agyei-Holmes et al., 2020).

In an RCT in India, Field et al. (2021) found that digital financial inclusion could encourage women's labor force participation. They studied an intervention that helped women open their own bank accounts, trained women to use those accounts, and signed them up to receive direct deposit of wage payments for work under India's public workfare program. The evaluation showed that this intervention, by giving women increased control over their wages, increased women's agency and decision-making power in the household and increased their participation in the labor market. Similarly, providing female factory workers with private, blocked savings accounts in Côte d'Ivoire—thereby shielding their income from family and others in their social networks—increased their work attendance by 10% and earnings by 11% (Carranza et al., 2022). Furthermore, changing the way microfinance loans were disbursed from cash to digital accounts enabled women in Uganda to expand their businesses by allowing them to resist social pressures to share money with others in the household (Riley, 2024).

McKelway (2021) conducted an RCT in which women in India were offered a psychological intervention to increase generalized self-efficacy, and its effect on their labor supply was assessed. The study found short-term effects on women's labor supply but no long-term effects on women's employment. In Kenya, Orkin et al. (2023) found that a 60–90-minute workshop aimed at increasing aspirations and encouraging women to set goals and act on them increased their labor supply compared to a placebo workshop. Other research examined the impacts of psychology-based entrepreneurship training, finding positive impacts on women's business income and profits mediated by changes in entrepreneurial self-efficacy, personal initiative, and/ or entrepreneurial locus of control (e.g., Alibhai et al., 2019; Campos et al., 2017; Glaub et al., 2014).

Another strand of the literature examines the impact of engaging men to enhance women's agency—through couples' training or intrahousehold transfers of productive assets or information—on women's livelihoods and well-being. A couples' training in Uganda that shifted decision making and increased women's group participation resulted in increased food security and perceived well-being (Lecoutere & Wuyts, 2021). In a similar context, targeting women versus men with agricultural information increased women's agricultural decision making, women's subsequent adoption of recommended practices and inputs, and yields on fields that were managed by women (Lecoutere et al., 2023). Including wives in an agricultural extension training for men on cash crops in Côte d'Ivoire led to a large increase in joint farm management and, subsequently, to better economic outcomes on the farm (Donald et al., 2022). However, Ambler et al. (2021) found that although the transfer of a productive asset from husbands to wives increased the wives' access to resources and agency, there were no shifts in food security, health, or educational outcomes, though life satisfaction improved for women and their husbands.

Improved access to childcare may free up women's time and increase their time agency, allowing them to participate in earnings and livelihood activities. Although the positive effects of women's access to childcare on their labor force participation are well documented in developed countries (Bick, 2016; Givord & Marbot, 2015), the evidence base in low-income settings is thinner. In Rio de Janeiro, Brazil, de Barros et al. (2013) showed that the odds of a mother having a job improved from 36% to 46% when she won a spot in a lottery for free childcare for low-income families. Household incomes increased by 16%. Clark et al. (2019) examined the effects of childcare in an informal settlement in Nairobi, Kenya. The authors found that women who were offered vouchers for subsidized early childcare were 8.5 percentage points more likely to be employed than those who were not given vouchers and had 24% higher monthly earnings. Martínez and Perticará (2017) randomized applicants to an afterschool program for children ages 6–13 in Chile and found that program participation increased employment by 5% and labor force participation by 7%. In urban Burkina Faso, Ajayi et al. (2022) found that mobile creches increased women's hours worked and monthly income. Bjorvatn et al. (2022) offered childcare subsidies to households in urban and peri-urban Uganda, and found that single mothers offered the subsidy were 29% more likely to be employed and had 45% higher incomes. Across the sample, the childcare subsidy led to a 19% increase in household income. Lastly, Donald et al. (2023) found that opening community-based childcare centers in the rural Democratic Republic of the Congo not only increased women's engagement in commercial agriculture and overall income but also benefited husbands, with large increases in overall agricultural productivity and income for households. Husbands increased their economic participation, for example by starting a business, and increased their income.

SOCIAL CAPITAL AND CONNECTION

Existing literature generally illustrates that groups and even nations with higher levels of social capital are more likely to be cohesive and reciprocally trusting, which in turn can facilitate positive civic engagement and action (Kawachi et al., 2008; Newton, 2001).

In the fields of public health and economics, focus on social capital is typically at the levels of individual and community. Research from these fields demonstrated that social capital was more likely among people with higher levels of education, income, and asset ownership, and tended to be higher for men relative to women and for middle-aged adults relative to younger adults (Kawachi et al., 2008; Villalonga-Olives et al., 2018). A large body of associational research looked at the reverse relationship—how social capital differentially affected men's versus women's advancement. Some of this work documented how the gender homophily of networks could disadvantage women because, relative to men's networks, women's networks tended to have lower social and economic standing and less proximity to power (Groysberg, 2010; Ibarra, 1992, 1993; Lutter, 2015; McPherson et al., 2001). Additionally, an intervention study in Benin, which provided health education with microfinance, found that effects on social capital (measured using questions on group membership, support networks, participation in village meetings and public positions, and influence in the village) were greater for women in single-sex groups compared to mixed-gender groups, suggesting that women-to-women support may be important in some contexts and possibly for specific issues (Karlan et al., 2017).

Overall, causal evidence on approaches designed to increase social capital for health is promising, but studies do not directly include empowerment indicators as an outcome or mediator despite alignment with empowerment theories. From the public health field, longitudinal studies evaluating interventions designed to affect social capital at the individual level (e.g., via building social networks and social support) as well as at the community and institutional levels (e.g., via use of existing social networks to strengthen community or group capacities and assets) showed significant improvements on network connections, strength of connections, and actions including civic participation (Villalonga-Olives et al., 2018). Furthermore, this study demonstrated some effectiveness in healthcare utilization and health outcomes, including those related to mental health, maternal and child health, water and sanitation, and climate concerns (Villalonga-Olives et al., 2018). However, 25 years of public health work in this area have yielded too few intervention trials and some inconsistent findings on health outcomes (Shiell et al., 2020), and no research recognized women's empowerment as part of evaluating social capital interventions.

Research on social capital interventions has also been conducted in the field of political science, with mixed results. Historically, the field was called to view social capital as endogenous and not as a means nor an outcome for intervention (Jackman & Miller, 1998). However, evidence regarding the importance of social networks as a means of trust building and cohesion at the national level (Newton, 2001) led to greater work on interventions to promote social capital, though these studies remain few. One such example is a randomized field experiment of a participatory development intervention conducted in rural Sudan with 24 communities (16 treatment communities and 8 control communities). This study measured norms and network density in the communities by surveying select residents, and it assessed perceptions of local governance and civic participation via household surveys (Avdeenko & Gilligan, 2015). No effects were seen on social networks or norms, but civic participation and perceptions of a more open local governing body increased. These findings suggested that the impact of this intervention may have come from its effect on governing institutions more than its effect on networks. In contrast, a qualitative analysis of an intervention designed to improve social capital to reduce violence among youth in Cali, Colombia, suggested that drawing on the strong internal bonds of pre-existing groups and linking these groups to the wider community and municipal institutions was useful in reducing public and domestic violence (Snoxell et al., 2006).

Intervention studies have also focused on life skills and cash transfers for women and girls, to assess the impact of these interventions on social capital in post-conflict and conflict settings. These studies also yielded mixed findings. A multicomponent intervention for "ultra-poor" women in Afghanistan offered training and linkage to sustainable livelihoods, asset transfers (often cows), unconditional cash transfers, and coaching (Bedoya et al., 2023). A two-armed RCT was used to evaluate the program, and significant effects included improved social capital for women. Furthermore, these effects were largely sustained even after U.S. troop withdrawal from Afghanistan, showing the improved resiliency for women receiving the intervention. A three-armed cluster RCT conducted in Liberia (post-Ebola and post-conflict) evaluated three groups: Group 1—Girls' Empowerment (GE), a mentor-facilitated life skills intervention for 13–14-year-old girls; Group 2—Girls' Empowerment Plus (GE+), which added cash transfers to GE; and Group 3—a control condition (Özler et al., 2020). The GE interventions had no impact on girls' social capital. A two-armed cluster RCT evaluated a safe-spaces plus life skills intervention for South Sudanese adolescent girls recruited from refugee camps in Ethiopia (Lindsay et al., 2018). The intervention showed a significant effect on girls' social supports and connections; however, observed effects only held true for girls in communities that were not severely affected by conflict (Buehren et al., 2017). Finally, a two-armed cluster RCT evaluated effects of a group intervention offering microfinance with IPV prevention and support counseling for women in South Africa (Pronyk et al., 2008). This intervention showed significant effects on community participation; strength of networks; and collective reciprocity, solidarity, and action two years subsequent to the intervention initiation. A review of evaluations testing the effect of cash transfers on risk for IPV revealed some mixed findings, but many indicated reduced risk for IPV and none indicated increased risk for IPV (Buller et al., 2018). Buller et al. (2018) proposed that cash transfers reduce women's risk for IPV by increasing their emotional security and well-being, as well as their empowerment in terms of decision-making control. Research also suggests that cash transfers can reduce mental health stress, though findings are mixed depending on country context (Maara et al., 2023).

In the above review of interventions to affect social capital, we could find no causal evidence specifically focused on women's empowerment to increase social capital, nor could we find any studies that assessed whether observed effects on social capital were mediated by women's agency. This is an important area for further inquiry.

SOCIAL PROTECTION

As defined in Chapter 3, as an outcome, social protection captures food security, resilience to shocks, smooth income (or consumption), and a safety net for the poorest residents. Studies have found that women absorb household shocks by reducing their own nutrient intake before that of their children (Bhutta et al., 2009; Christian, 2010) and by selling off female assets like jewelry (Rao et al., 2019). This pattern of women as "shock buffers" was also found during the recent COVID-19 pandemic, during which women took on a greater share of the increase in domestic and care work and suffered economically as a consequence (e.g., Goldstein et al., 2022). Another pathway identified in the literature explores how women's lack of access to information and communications technology (ICT) could affect social protection. Such technology is crucial for information acquisition on upcoming shocks and in post-disaster situations, for maintaining familial and social ties, and for receiving cash remittances—which are important sources of resilience (Bernier & Meinzen-Dick, 2014; Frankenberger et al., 2013; Mukoya, 2020). Bridging the "digital divide" and increasing women's ownership and control over ICT may thus be a pathway for increased social protection.

A wide-ranging literature documents associations between women's agency and social protection, and describes how certain resources are implicitly linked to greater social protection through women's agency. As mentioned earlier in this chapter in the discussion on child nutrition and schooling, women's increased bargaining power was associated with increased household expenditures on child health and education, which can increase resilience in the long run (e.g., Quisumbing & Maluccio, 2003). Households headed by women with higher economic agency, physical capital empowerment, psychological empowerment, and farm financial management skills empowerment were found to be more food secure (e.g., Sharaunga et al., 2016). Moreover, women's access to land was correlated with household food security across contexts (e.g., Alemu, 2015). Some literature demonstrates that increasing women's land rights and knowledge of their rights could lead to adoption of practices that increase resilience, such as soil and water conservation practices and agroforestry on agricultural lands (Meinzen-Dick et al., 2019; Quisumbing & Kumar, 2014).

A recent systematic review (Perera et al., 2022) looked at studies that evaluated the effects of social protection programs on socioeconomic development outcomes (e.g., education, health, safety) and empowerment indicators (e.g., economic empowerment, voice, agency) in low- and middle-income countries (LMICs). Evaluated programs included social assistance (77%), labor market programs (40%), social insurance interventions (11%), and social care interventions (9%). The authors found that, overall, these programs were more effective for women than men in affecting socioeconomic development and empowerment outcomes, but family support was important for women to benefit from the programs. Furthermore, the study found that the social assistance and social insurance programs supported women's savings and investments (e.g., economic empowerment). Evidence on the value of social care interventions was limited.

Levels of women's agency were found to predict whether women were insured and by how much—for example, through women's willingness to pay for index insurance-based products (Akter et al., 2016; Bageant & Barrett, 2017; Clarke & Kumar, 2016). Some studies documented a relationship between women's inclusion in decision making over water and better-functioning water systems with expanded access to water, which could lead to strengthened resilience to shocks (e.g., United Nations Development Programme, 2006). One study in Tanzania found that women share water more equitably than men do, especially in times of scarcity (Lecoutere et al., 2015). Lastly, women's self-help groups have been recognized internationally as central to social protection efforts (e.g., Asaki & Hayes, 2011), due to their role as platforms for distributing, targeting, and advocating for resources by communities, and as sources of mutual aid for their members. Notably, however, a tension may exist between social protection for households and for women. While lending to women likely reduces household vulnerability, the benefits to women are not as certain, because loans procured by women can be diverted into enhancing the household's assets and income (Garikipati, 2008). This tension highlights the importance of women controlling the resource in question—and the importance of considering the potential backlash she might face from doing so.

A growing literature also documents causal relationships between women's empowerment and greater social protection. Graduation programs designed to increase the agency of extremely poor women led to higher levels of total consumption and food security and stronger social and financial support (e.g., Bossuroy et al., 2022). Similar livelihood programs for adolescent girls also affected household-level food security (Adoho et al., 2014). Women's financial inclusion—through products as simple as savings lockboxes—helped households cope with adverse health shocks by allowing them to smooth their consumption through self-insurance rather than shedding livestock assets (Aker et al., 2020; Dupas & Robinson, 2013). Lastly, though insurance tends to be more effective than savings at managing food insecurity and shocks, field experiments showed that female farm managers were less likely to purchase agricultural insurance and more likely to invest in savings for emergencies (Delavallade et al., 2015).

POLITICAL PARTICIPATION AND GOOD GOVERNANCE

As discussed, a growing body of research focuses on the role of technology, and specifically mobile phones, in women's empowerment and shifting attitudes. For example, Varriale et al. (2022) conducted an analysis using micro-level data from the *AfroBarometer* covering 36 African countries and estimated that regular mobile phone use was associated with more positive attitudes of women toward women's participation in politics.

Women's greater agency in politics—defined here as the increased capacity for women to influence political decision making—can influence socioeconomic outcomes in two main ways. First, to the extent that women have distinct priorities from men, an increase in the consideration given to women's priorities could change the types of programs or policies put in place. Second, to the extent that women behave differently than men when in political positions (e.g., if they are less likely to be corrupt or more responsive to voters' priorities), an increase in women's representation in politics could alter the effectiveness of public spending. There is descriptive evidence for gender gaps in both priorities and behavior. Turning first to priorities, Clayton's (2021) review listed a series of studies from across the globe showing how women tended to report more concern about healthcare and poverty while men reported more concern for national safety and infrastructure. A national study in India also suggested that the gender and caste of women state legislative representatives may matter for district-level investments in child schooling (Halim et al., 2016). Concerning behavior, both a cross-country analysis and a within-country, across-time analysis by Swamy et al. (2001) showed that corruption was less severe in locations where women held a larger share of parliamentary seats and senior positions in the government bureaucracy and comprised a larger share of the labor force. Survey evidence also suggested that Indian female leaders elected under the reservation system were less corrupt than male leaders (Beaman et al., 2010).

Establishing the causal impact of increased women's political agency on policy outcomes is difficult because countries with more women in leadership positions, or countries where women's votes are more likely to be pivotal, may differ from countries where women have less political agency. To credibly establish causality, studies have exploited sudden changes in laws or rules governing women's suffrage or representation. For example, Miller (2008) exploited the sharp timing of state-level women's suffrage laws in the late 19th-/early 20th-century United States to document how the increase in female suffrage led directly to an increase in healthcare spending: politicians were immediately responsive to the fact that the composition of the electorate had changed. Similarly, Fujiwara (2015) showed that a technology-induced decrease in de facto de-enfranchisement of the poor in Brazil led to a shift in government spending toward healthcare that was particularly beneficial to the poor. Since women were disproportionately poor, they disproportionately benefited. The same study found positive downstream effects of political inclusion on both the utilization of health services (e.g., prenatal visits) and newborn health (e.g., low-weight births) for less-educated mothers. This finding is consistent with Kudamatsu's (2012) cross-country evidence on democracy's effect on health outcomes in Sub-Saharan Africa.

As discussed in Chapter 4, introduction of gender quotas in politics is a common tool to increase women's representation in government. Evidence from India, where gender quotas at various levels of government are often not imposed consistently across geographies, showed that quotas influenced policy outcomes in ways that benefitted women and children in particular (Beaman et al., 2010; Chattopadhyay & Duflo, 2004; Clots-Figueras, 2011). A recent review of the evidence on quotas by Clayton (2021) concluded that by making gender issues salient to legislators as well as by increasing the share of legislators who are women, quotas typically increase "legislative attention to issues related to women's rights, public health (particularly children's health), poverty alleviation, and, in agrarian rural contexts, access to potable water" (p. 239). Whether this increase is a net "positive" for socioeconomic development depends, of course, on whether legislative attention is zero sum. In that case, an increased focus on issues that are of greater relevance for women's well-being may decrease attention given to other issues that are of greater concern to men. This shift, in turn, may lead to backlash or retaliation for nonadherence to prevailing gender norms (Raj et al., 2024).

PEACE, SECURITY, AND SAFETY FROM VIOLENCE

This section reviews the evidence on how women's empowerment impacts security and safety from violence at both a societal level (e.g., the avoidance of war) and at the individual or household levels (e.g., reducing IPV). Starting with the societal level, some studies suggested that greater societal gender equality had a pacifying effect on the willingness of political leaders to use violence to achieve political goals (Hudson et al., 2012), but causality was difficult to establish. Some scholars argued that greater representation of women in state/national legislatures increased the likelihood that a conflict would terminate in a negotiated settlement (Best et al., 2019), but here again, causality was difficult to establish.

At the individual and community levels, studies showed that women holding less decision-making control and having attitudes more accepting of IPV were more likely to report IPV (Dalal et al., 2022; García-Moreno et al., 2013; Garg et al., 2021; Mootz et al., 2022; Muluneh et al., 2021; Sardinha et al., 2022). Family contexts and community norms of violence against women also affected women's risk for IPV. Cross-national research showed that women who have witnessed IPV in their parents' relationships, experienced abuse in childhood, and who reside in contexts with attitudes accepting of IPV were more likely to report a history of IPV in their current relationships (Mootz et al., 2022; Muluneh et al., 2021; Shakya et al., 2022).

Research showed mixed associations between women's agency and risk for IPV. For example, in Bangladesh, women's participation in microfinance was not significantly associated with their experiences of physical, psychological, sexual, or economic IPV; however, their participation was significantly positively associated with other agency outcomes, including their intrinsic voice/mobility; instrumental agency (e.g., using financial services, voice with husband, voice/mobility outside the home); and collective agency (Yount et al., 2021). A 2016 systematic review of the effects of microfinance (e.g., savings and credit) programs, which included controlled trials, observational studies, and panel data analyses, showed mixed effects on IPV and mostly null effects on decision-making ability and mobility (Gichuru et al., 2019). Considering digital technology as a proxy for women's agency, using cross-national Demographic and Health Surveys (DHS) data, Pesando (2022) found that women's independent ownership of mobile phones was associated with a 9–12% decreased likelihood of emotional, physical, and sexual violence over the previous 12 months (except in Angola)—a result that was robust to the use of matching techniques and instrumental variable estimates.

Causal evidence generally finds that increases in women's agency lead to decreases in women's experiences of IPV. Through a cluster RCT in Uganda, Chioda et al. (2023) found that a school-based upper-secondary life skills intervention expanded women's agency and reduced the incidence of IPV. Shah et al. (2023) found that an intervention to improve girls' goal setting regarding their sexual and reproductive health and a soccer intervention, which "educates and inspires young men to make better sexual and reproductive health choices" both reduced IPV through different mechanisms; notably, the intervention showed no impact on contraceptive use despite increasing supply access (Shah et al., 2022). An RCT of facilitated group discussions for men around gender relations in the Democratic Republic of the Congo found that the program led to a decrease in the probability and severity of physical IPV but only among women who experienced high physical and moderate sexual violence at baseline (Gurbuz Cuneo et al., 2023). In Rwanda, the Bandebereho intervention, which involved couples in a curriculum focused on topics such as gender and power, couple communication and decision making, IPV, and reproductive and maternal health, led to large reductions in physical and sexual IPV, along with more equitable decision making (Doyle et al., 2018), and impacts were sustained up to six years later (Doyle et al., 2023).

Eggers del Campo and Steinert (2022) conducted a meta-analysis of 19 RCTs assessing the impact of economic empowerment interventions on women's exposure to IPV. The analysis showed that women's economic empowerment led to a significant reduction in the pooled measure of emotional, sexual, and physical IPV. The authors found tentative evidence that these effects may be amplified when gender sensitization training is included in the interventions. Some studies included in the meta-analysis, however, showed increases in IPV, often in the form of controlling behavior and economic coercion.

Lastly, increasing the availability of justice centers and police stations, in which female officers provide policing and legal services to reduce gender-based violence, appeared to be associated with increased reporting and prosecutions (Natarajan & Babu, 2020; Sviatschi & Trako, 2024). Research from Peru exploited the gradual rollout of women's justice centers across districts and villages and found a 10% reduction in self-reported domestic violence, female deaths due to aggression, and hospitalizations due to mental health after a women's justice center opened (Sviatschi & Trako, 2024). Women living near an all-women's justice center were more likely to report shared decision making with partners.

Fewer studies have examined policy and intervention effects on sexual violence, sex trafficking, female genital cutting (FGC), and other forms of violence against women. There is a dearth of literature, particularly from LMICs, demonstrating significant reductions in sexual violence and sex trafficking. Much of the existent work is either with adolescents and focused on dating violence, or with college students and focused on rape (DeGue et al., 2014; Rivera et al., 2021; Vladutiu et al., 2011). These programs, largely conducted in school contexts, showed that education, normative shifts, bystander behavior (e.g., "see something, say something"), and role models such as coaches as educators and supports can reduce sexual violence and dating violence. There is a lack of rigorous evaluation of interventions to affect sex trafficking, sexual exploitation, and sexual harassment, highlighting the need for greater focus on these pervasive gendered risks.

Evidence on effective interventions to prevent FGC shows more promise. Regression discontinuity analysis with DHS data from Burkina Faso showed a significant reduction in FGC following policy changes, but the authors recognize that the policy change happened simultaneously with community-level intervention efforts, suggesting that both top-down and bottom-up approaches may be important (Crisman et al., 2016). It should also be noted that these types of policies show greater effect in the Global North than the Global South, likely because of laws in national contexts where FGC is not normative (Boyle & Corl, 2010; Njue et al., 2019). Largely, across Africa, policies on FGC have little effect, both because these laws often do not co-occur with social norm change efforts and because the laws may not be strictly implemented (Muthumbi et al., 2015). Community-level social norm change interventions show some success in Africa (Berg & Denison, 2012; Diop & Askew, 2009; McChesney, 2015; Parvez Butt, 2020).

CLIMATE RESILIENCE

Much of the literature on women's empowerment and climate resilience examines gender differences in exposure to climate shocks and differences in preferences and capacity in terms of response. Women tend to have less access to resources necessary to respond to climate change, such as assets, land and water, human capital, and technologies. Gender-specific constraints related to time, wealth, norms, and skills can hamper women's adaptation and resilience (Food and Agriculture Organization, 2023). Easing these constraints could improve climate resilience, though rigorous evidence is scarce.

In addition, associations between women's agency and mechanisms that could lead to greater climate resilience have been documented across countries. In particular, increased women's agency was linked to higher adoption of climate adaptation strategies that involved increased agricultural information and knowledge, such as climate-smart agriculture (e.g., Mittal, 2016) and higher investment and planting (e.g., Madajewicz et al., 2013). A systematic review of studies conducted in Sub-Saharan Africa found conservation agriculture to be associated with women's increased participation in agricultural decisions, increased income, and increased food security—but also with increased workloads and health risks (Wekesah et al., 2019). Moreover, a documented relationship was found between women's bargaining power in the household and the extent of diversification and commercialization of agricultural and livestock systems (Tavenner et al., 2019). Some evidence of differential investment also exists, for example higher farm investment than off-farm investment among women, resulting in less diversification (Andrews et al., 2012). Other studies found that women were more likely to adopt crop and livelihood diversification strategies important for reducing climate risks (De Pinto et al., 2020; Mersha & Van Laerhoven, 2016).

The importance of women's groups and collective action emerges strongly in the literature on climate resilience. Women's groups can function as effective avenues for conveying climate change and weather information, thereby enhancing awareness of practices that promote resilience to climate-related challenges (Dey et al., 2018; Farnworth et al., 2017). Establishment of community development councils and civic education leadership training was shown to increase women's decision-making authority and the adoption of drought-preparedness measures by households (Grillos, 2018). Activism by women's organizations has played a role in international climate policy processes, such as the establishment of the Women and Gender Constituency at the United Nations Framework Convention on Climate Change's Convention of the Parties (Picard, 2021; Resurrección, 2013). Another channel emerges at the macro level, when gender-specific preferences regarding the environment are empowered through women's leadership: greater female representation in governing bodies was associated with a lower climate footprint across contexts (Altunbas et al., 2022; Mavisakalyan & Tarverdi, 2019; McKinney & Fulkerson, 2015).

Causal evidence directly relating increased women's agency to increased climate security and resilience is very thin. Gender-responsive approaches are rarely incorporated into "shock-sensitive" social protection programs, and research is lacking on how gender-responsive strategies within social protection intersect with climate change, providing limited insight into the effectiveness of such approaches in mitigating gender inequality in the context of climate change impacts (Bryan et al., 2023; Holmes, 2019).

MACROECONOMIC CONSIDERATIONS

So far, this chapter has detailed research on the effects of women's empowerment on socioeconomic development outcomes at the levels of the individual, household, community, and society. But for many, the topic invokes macroeconomic considerations that have so far been outside the scope of inquiry. How does empowering women affect investment, sectoral allocation, productivity, and economic growth?

One strand of literature on these questions compares the economic growth experiences of countries that exhibit differing extents of structural gender inequality, using cross-country growth regressions (Kabeer,

2016). Many studies focus on gender gaps in education and labor force participation. A meta-analysis of studies on education, which included cross-country studies and single-country studies, found that greater gender inequality in average educational attainment predicted lower economic growth (Minasyan et al., 2019). Similarly, studies on women's work found that gender inequality in labor force participation predicted lower economic growth (Klasen, 2002; Klasen & Lamanna, 2009). Other aspects of societal-level measures of women's agency, including those directly related to women's agency, are harder to measure in a consistent way for many countries and thus have received less attention. However, a recent extension of the literature investigated measures of women's political empowerment— indices of women's civil liberties, civil society participation, and political participation—finding positive associations with economic growth (Dahlum et al., 2022). These exercises are useful for identifying correlates of economic growth, but specific causal mechanisms are difficult to disentangle.

Because of this difficulty, research on macroeconomic consequences of increasing women's empowerment necessarily relies more on economic theory and less on theory-agnostic statistical tools. Macroeconomists have worked toward quantifying specific mechanisms by specifying general-equilibrium models that embed various aspects of women's empowerment and calibrating those models to the data (Cuberes & Teignier, 2014; Santos Silva & Klasen, 2021). Some of these models directly study pathways involving conventional factors of production: investment in physical capital, investment in human capital, and the size and sectoral allocation of the labor force. Others study indirect demographic pathways, especially the decline of fertility and consequent changes in the age structure of the population (e.g., the demographic dividend; Bloom et al., 2003).

The sections that follow review model-based approaches to understanding macroeconomic consequences of women's empowerment. These model-based approaches are methodologically distinct from research cited in other sections of this report, and they lay out interesting economic mechanisms in specific terms. The work does not always focus specifically on women's agency but instead on diverse forms of gender inequality, from control over household economic resources, to wage discrimination, to arranged marriage. We cast a wide net and try to draw out the implications for women's agency, even for models of other forms of women's empowerment and disempowerment. However, we narrowed the scope by including only quantitative models that are fit to data in a way that is relevant to contemporary LMICs. We omitted purely theoretical exercises and quantitative exercises that used less-relevant data.

Investment Channel

Investment is a classic starting point for considering the determinants of economic growth. How do aggregate saving and investment depend on women's empowerment? Two quantitative macroeconomic models explore this issue in a way that offers insights into the effects of women's agency.

The first model studies the macroeconomic effects of empowering women to have more control over household economic resources (Doepke & Tertilt, 2019). The authors highlighted a tradeoff between investment in physical and human capital. Household savings went toward the former, while spending on children's health and education went toward the latter. To study these mechanisms, they built a model in which women and men exert differing control over household decisions. Incorporating the empirical finding that money in the hands of women rather than men is more likely to be spent on children (Duflo, 2012), they used the model to compare the effects of cash transfers targeting either gender.

Doepke and Tertilt found that the economic development consequences of gender-targeted transfers depended on the economy's production technology. When the most important factor of production is human capital, money in the hands of women is more likely to boost economic growth because women spend it on their children's human capital development. However, when physical capital or land are more important, money in the hands of men is more likely to boost growth because men put it in savings. Consistent with their theoretical claims, Doepke and Tertilt found that in the experimental evaluation of Mexico's cash transfer program *Progresa*, transfers to women raised spending on children but reduced the savings rate. Although the authors specifically studied the allocation of cash, other drivers of women's agency are likely to have similar effects in their model.

An earlier model by Tertilt (2005) offered other insights into women's empowerment and investment. Tertilt studied how two marriage institutions that are thought to restrict women's agency—polygyny and bride price in Sub-Saharan Africa—may reduce savings and economic growth. She developed a macroeconomic model incorporating these institutions, illuminating how they incentivize a father to have many daughters and profit from their marriages. The resulting overinvestment in the number of children crowds out saving and, consequently, investment in physical capital. The model looks at the role of marriage laws, rules, and norms, and finds that enforcing monogamy reduces fertility and increases savings and output per capita. Notably, economic models like Tertilt's ignore the cultural embeddedness of polygyny and related institutions. As such, these models are more useful in their ability to illuminate macroeconomic mechanisms rather than in guiding policy. Consistent with the proposed mechanism, Tertilt documented that investment rates and capital-output ratios were much higher in predominantly monogamous economies than in predominantly polygynous economies. The original analysis focused on the impact of enforcing monogamy rather than specifically promoting women's agency. However, in follow-up work, Tertilt (2006) found that transferring consent from fathers to daughters had similar effects. Such a transfer of consent could directly improve women's agency.

Labor Allocation Channel

In many LMICs, women face barriers to working, especially in certain occupations and industries. How do these barriers affect economic growth? Three quantitative models of sectoral choice shed light on this question. In all three cases, the key insight is that barriers to women's work, either in specific sectors or overall, lead to the misallocation of talent, thereby shrinking the economy.

One thread in the literature on this topic explores the consequences of barriers to women working as managers or entrepreneurs. Cuberes and Teignier (2016) specify a model of occupational choice in which women face restrictions of increasing strictness on working, on working in self-employment, and on working as managers. These restrictions lead to the misallocation of female talent. Many women who would be productive in self-employment or managing others are prevented from doing so. Calibrating their model to data from many countries, the authors found that restrictions on the type of work women do caused substantial losses in per capita income in developing countries.

Chiplunkar and Goldberg (2023) noted that barriers to female management and entrepreneurship have ripple effects for female labor force participation more broadly, due to the greater tendency of female entrepreneurs to hire female workers. To quantify this effect, they developed a model with gender differences in economic frictions faced at multiple levels, as in Cuberes and Teignier (2016), and included an informal sector—a key feature of many low- and middle-income economies. Estimating the model using data from India, they found that policies supporting female entrepreneurship raised female labor force participation, female earnings, and aggregate output. Consistent with the channel emphasized by Cuberes and Teignier, one key mechanism for the increase in aggregate output was the reallocation of workers from firms owned by unproductive men to higher-productivity firms owned by productive women.

Another thread in the literature on labor misallocation focuses on industry rather than occupation. Lee (2024) built and calibrated an economic model to study the effects of the misallocation of women's labor across industries on aggregate economic development. He documented that women were underrepresented in nonagricultural relative to agricultural jobs, especially in lower-income countries, and used this fact to motivate an economic model in which women faced greater barriers to working in services or manufacturing. The model extended a well-known framework developed by Hseih et al. (2019) to quantify the effects of employment barriers faced by women and racial minorities in the United States. In Lee's application to lower-income countries, the barriers to nonagricultural work led to a pernicious form of misallocation: women better suited for services or manufacturing instead had to work in agriculture or not at all. This mismatch of skills reduced labor productivity, both within agriculture and across the economy at large.

Fertility Channel

A final set of quantitative macroeconomic models explored how fertility affects the macroeconomy and, to a more limited extent, how it may mediate the effect of women's empowerment. A large body of literature explores the first link, with early contributions featuring prominently in the National Academies of Sciences, Engineering, and Medicine's precursor to this report (National Research Council [NRC], 1986). Model-based efforts to understand how the link mediates the effect of women's empowerment are more limited.

Cavalcanti and Tavares (2016) recently attempted to understand this mediating role by analyzing the consequences of gender wage discrimination in a model that includes saving, labor force participation, and fertility. The modeling of wage discrimination and labor force participation mirrors the labor misallocation literature, but the addition of saving and fertility distinguishes this work. Applying their model to data from the United States and around the world, the authors found that reductions in gender wage discrimination increased market participation by women, which directly increased output per capita. But an indirect fertility channel turned out to be nearly as important quantitatively, with the increase in women's work leading to lower fertility, which raised the capital-labor ratio, which raised output per capita.

That study aside, many macroeconomic studies that aim to quantify the economic growth consequences of fertility decline take fertility decline as exogenous. In other words, they disregard its root causes, including women's empowerment. Nevertheless, insofar as expansions in women's agency contribute to fertility decline, these studies can help shed light on how women's empowerment may affect macroeconomic outcomes through the fertility channel. In the mid-20th century, Coale and Hoover (1958) pioneered the classic approach to quantifying the macroeconomic consequences of exogenous fertility decline.

Ashraf et al. (2013) updated Coale and Hoover's approach, specifying a macroeconomic accounting framework and simulating it under various fertility trajectories. Their framework quantified seven channels through which reduced population growth can affect per capita economic growth: (a) by raising land per worker, (b) by raising physical capital per worker, (c) by reducing the number of dependents per working-age adult, (d) by raising the average experience of workers, (e) by raising labor force participation rates by working-age adults, (f) by raising investment in children's human capital, and (g) by freeing parents from childcare responsibilities. Coale and Hoover emphasized channels (a) and (b), but the previous National Academies report on this topic (NRC, 1986) argued that these channels were quantitatively modest at best. Channel (c), involving favorable changes in the age structure, is known as the "demographic dividend" (Bloom et al., 2003). Notably, over the long run, sustained fertility decline causes population aging, which brings new economic challenges (Kotschy & Bloom, 2023). So, the framework's implications depend heavily on its parameterization.

Ashraf et al. (2013) parameterized their framework using data and projections for Nigeria, finding that meaningfully large reductions in fertility—moving from the medium to low variant of the United Nation's fertility projection for Nigeria—moderately boosted output per capita, by 6% at a 20-year horizon and 12% at a 50-year horizon. Early on, reduction in the number of dependents per working-age adult was the primary channel, and freedom from childcare responsibilities was the next-most important. At 50 years, increases in land, physical capital, and human capital per worker became important, while the childcare channel mattered less. Karra et al. (2017) extended Ashraf et al.'s framework to allow for multiple sectors of economic activity and for the effect of lower fertility on women's schooling. These additional channels doubled the economic growth benefits calculated by Ashraf et al.

Taking Stock of Macroeconomic Considerations

Quantitative economic models suggest nuanced effects of women's empowerment on macroeconomic dynamics. Alleviating constraints on women's work, both overall and in specific occupations and industries, may reduce the misallocation of talent and raise output per capita. Giving young women greater control over marriage may raise saving and output per capita, at least in polygynous societies. Increasing women's control over household economic resources may have ambiguous effects, depending on the importance of physical and human capital in production. Also, fertility decline may moderately increase output per capita in high-fertility populations, but external validity is unclear for populations that have already undergone substantial fertility decline.

SUMMARY AND CONCLUSIONS

Overall, a great deal of evidence suggests that exogenous shifts in the determinants of women's bargaining power, such as women's access to assets or income, significantly affect household decision making in favor of investments conducive to long-term socioeconomic development, such as children's education and nutrition. Household spending decisions depend on the gender of the income recipient. When income accrues to women, it is more likely to be spent on children's nutrition and education rather than on privately consumed items, such as tobacco and alcohol.

Strengthening women's control over assets, including secure vehicles for savings, can improve livelihoods by increasing women's labor force participation and business profits. Such changes can also occur by directly strengthening women's sense of agency through psychosocial interventions, though impacts are not always sustained over time. The positive effects of women's access to childcare on their labor force participation are well documented in developed countries, with a slowly growing evidence base in low-income countries documenting large income benefits for women and men alike (though, interestingly, further improvements in women's agency are not observed to result from childcare utilization).

Laws that reserve political leadership positions for women have been shown to increase girls' career aspirations and educational attainment and women's economic empowerment through public work programs and access to financial services. Though effects vary across studies and contexts, women's economic empowerment appears to be associated with reductions in IPV in some contexts. In contrast, little to no research looks at how investments that increase women's agency impact women's social capital and connections. In addition, causal evidence directly relating increased women's agency to increased climate security and resilience is very thin. Lastly, fertility decline may moderately increase output per capita in high-fertility populations, but it is unclear whether the findings can be generalized to populations that have already undergone substantial fertility decline.

Comparing available empirical evidence to theoretical pathways at the individual, interpersonal, community, and societal levels, a few patterns emerge. First, many measured impacts of individual agency and choice on socioeconomic development outcomes result from women's differential preferences, yet these preferences are seldom measured directly. The individual agency construct for which the most direct empirical evidence exists is self-efficacy, though studies are limited. Even less empirical evidence exists for awareness of rights, locus of control, goal setting, and internal motivation, despite their theoretical importance. In terms of interpersonal agency, women's decision-making ability is by far the most measured construct. However, the evidence review shows that the specific type of decision making measured is not always in line with potential theoretical pathways. In terms of community-level agency, causal evidence is lacking on how shifting agency at this level (e.g., through changes in broader norms or community-mobilization efforts to expand and to strengthen women's social networks, shared awareness of historical gender inequities and women's rights, shared goal setting, and collective action) impacts socioeconomic development outcomes, especially given their theoretical relevance. Lastly, the evidence on how societal-level changes to women's agency affect socioeconomic development outcomes is strikingly thin. Beyond legal changes, levers to be explored include women's collective action and the formation and impacts of autonomous feminist movements at the societal level.

7

Levers for Change: Evidence on Programs and Policies to Increase Women's Agency in the Empowerment Process

As presented in prior chapters, evidence suggests the utility of programs and policy approaches that provide women with resources or a more enabling environment to help them achieve their goals. While this work presumes significant impacts on women's lives via agency, causal evidence from this research rarely includes measures of women's agency as an outcome. This chapter focuses on studies that evaluate the impact of programs and policies on women's agency. These programs and policies can be described as the "levers for change" in the committee's new conceptual framework (Figure 7-1).

This review focuses on causal evidence generated from randomized controlled trials (RCTs) and regression discontinuity analyses, but we consider some studies with associational evidence to help contextualize and clarify findings. Broadly, this review includes evidence of impact on women's agency outcomes from (a) economic empowerment programs for women, (b) women's collectives and self-help groups, (c) maternal child health and family planning interventions, (d) youth and girls' development programming, and (e) social and legal protections and policies. In this chapter, we consider the evidence base from these broad areas of program and policy.

FINANCIAL AND EMPLOYMENT PROGRAMS FOR WOMEN

Cash Transfers

Cash transfers involve the direct payment of money into a household or to an eligible person, typically with the goal of alleviating poverty or as part

LEVERS FOR CHANGE

Societal

- Laws (e.g., inheritance, reproductive rights, age at marriage, land rights, divorce laws)
- Policies (e.g., family planning, family leave, education, finance, political quotas, social protection programs)
- Implementation/enforcement of policies and laws

Community

- Youth programs (e.g., sexual and reproductive health, economic)
- Subsidized childcare
- Microfinance/microcredit programs
- Self-help groups, peer support and collectives, community health programs
- Media
- Local political quotas

Individual/Interpersonal

- Schooling and vocational training
- Psychology-based interventions
- Information provision
- Assets (e.g., financial assets and land)
- Cash transfers

WOMEN'S AGENCY

Societal
collective action, autonomous feminist movements

Community
(collective agency)

Interpersonal
(instrumental agency)

Intrapersonal
(intrinsic agency)

SOCIOECONOMIC DEVELOPMENT

- Educational achievement
- Decent work and sustainable livelihoods
- Social capital and connection
- Social protection
- Peace, security, and safety from violence
- Climate resilience
- Health

POPULATION DYNAMICS

- Population growth rate
- Population composition
- Fertility preferences and outcomes
- Family/union formation and timing of transition to adulthood
- Spatial mobility
- Migration
- Morbidity and mortality
- Health

EQUITABLE DEVELOPMENT GOALS

- Economic and human security
- Multidimensional well-being
- Freedom, dignity, and inclusion
- Sustainability

Sociocontextual Environment and Moderators (Norms, Formal Institutions, and Other Structural Influences)

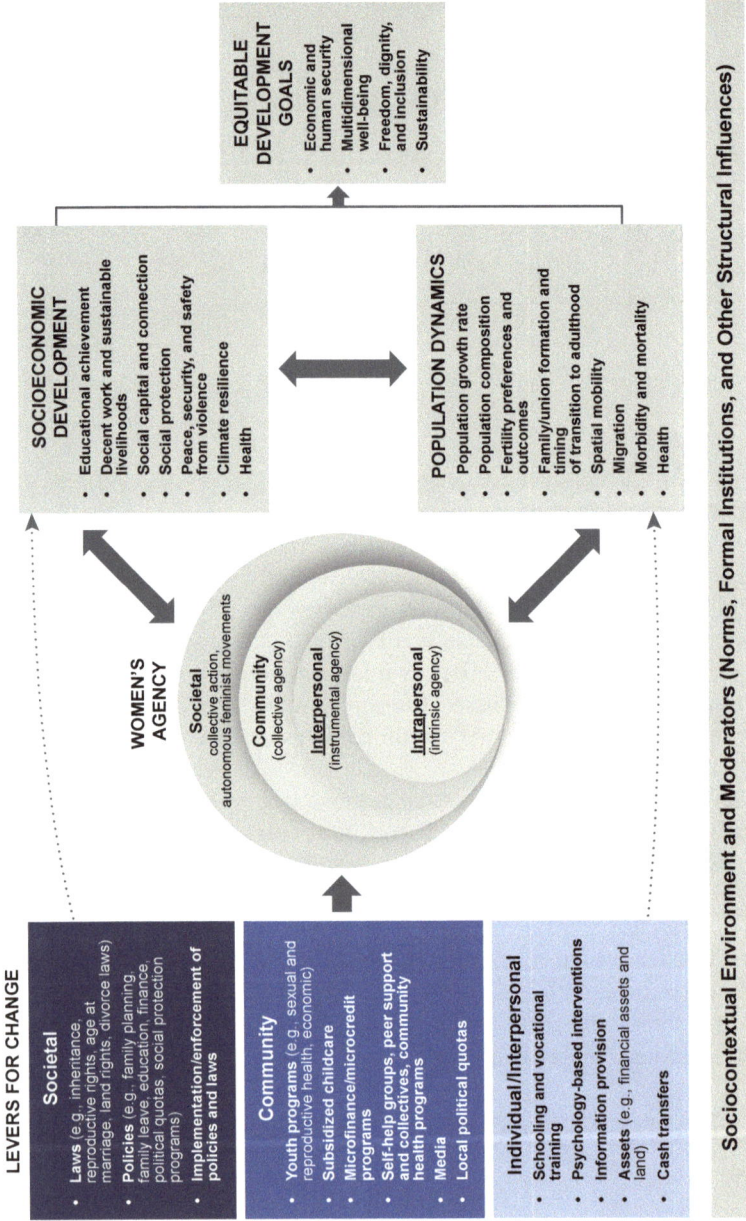

FIGURE 7-1 New conceptual framework of women's empowerment, population dynamics, and socioeconomic development, highlighting this chapter's area of emphasis.
SOURCE: Developed by the committee.

of humanitarian response in times of crisis. Cash transfers can be unconditional or conditional, with the latter provided only if specified provisions are met, such as children in the household attending school or a pregnant person attending antenatal care. In addition to evidence regarding the effects of cash transfers on population and development outcomes discussed in prior chapters, some evidence exists regarding effects of cash transfers on direct measures of women's agency.

Several studies evaluated effects of cash transfer programs to women in Latin America, conditional on child education or healthcare attendance, and showed positive impacts on women's agency (Bergolo & Galván, 2018; Chang et al., 2020; de Brauw et al., 2014; Feldman et al., 2009; Handa et al., 2009; Molyneux & Thomson, 2011). A qualitative study involving narratives with mothers examined conditional cash transfer (CCT) programs conducted in Peru, Ecuador, and Bolivia, in which women received the transfers conditional on their children's school attendance or their attendance at maternal and pediatric appointments (Molyneux & Thomson, 2011). This program demonstrated improvements in women's household decision-making control, bargaining power, and freedom of movement. Using propensity score weighting, an evaluation of *Bolsa Família,* a nationwide cash transfer program in Brazil that provided an unconditional transfer to "extremely poor" households and a CCT (predicated on child's school attendance and maternal and child healthcare attendance) to "poor" households with children below the age of 16, showed an increase in women's decision-making power regarding contraception use, household durable goods purchases, as well as children's school attendance and health expenses (de Brauw et al., 2014). However, these effects were largely driven by households in urban areas. In rural areas, the study found no increases, and possible reductions, in women's decision-making power.

Other CCT studies from Latin America focused on children's education alone, and these showed mixed effects. Another nationwide cash transfer program, the *Oportunidades* program in Mexico, increased women's decision-making control over food expenditures and financial investments in children, likely because of the transfer going to the women, but there was no change in their decision-making control over children's education, healthcare, and household repairs (Feldman et al., 2009; Handa et al., 2009). A similar program in Uruguay, evaluated via a regression discontinuity design, found an increase in women's decision making on expenditures for the household (Bergolo & Galván, 2018). The findings from this study also suggested a possible increase in women's responsibility for decisions related to some areas of household expenditures.

Research on cash transfers from other world regions shows some promise but appears to be more affected by social norms maintaining men's economic control in households. Researchers conducted a cluster RCT evaluation of the Government of Zambia's *Child Grant Program*, which randomized the arms for mothers with children younger than six years to either receive an unconditional cash transfer or not receive the transfer. Families were then followed over four years. Women in households that received the cash transfer were more likely to be involved in a broader array of areas for household decision making, including household investments, though qualitative evidence indicated that men remained the primary decision makers (Bonilla et al., 2017). Studies from Uganda and Afghanistan also offered a cash and asset transfer intervention, combined with microenterprise training and psychosocial support, and these indicated significant effects on hope, aspirations, self-efficacy, and, in Afghanistan, aspirations for their daughters (Bedoya et al., 2019; Sedlmayr et al., 2018). A livestock transfer study from Bangladesh, focused on rural, "ultra poor" households, showed some complexity in findings related to women's empowerment. While women retained ownership of the transferred livestock, they did not gain from new investments in mobilized resources and they actually showed a reduction in freedom of movement following gain in resources (Roy et al., 2015). Nonetheless, beneficiary women reported an increase in social capital, and results suggested that lower mobility aligned with not having to work outside the home, a preference of the beneficiary women. In sum, these studies again showcase the role of restrictive gender norms in affecting broader decision-making control and women's preferences and choices regarding economic empowerment.

Microfinance and Entrepreneurship

Financial inclusion programs for women are designed to engage them with financial systems, such as banking and savings accounts, credit, money transfers, and insurance. Substantial research, some with causal evidence, exists in this area, including a systematic review of 32 reviews conducted on the topic. This research, while extensive, did not reveal clear and consistent findings regarding the value of financial inclusion on women's agency (Duvendack & Mader, 2020; Saluja et al., 2023). The absence of clear and consistent findings may have been due to the focus on women's entry into financial systems, so evidence regarding longer-term effects was lacking. Agency often was not measured, as the programs were designed to sway women toward the use of financial systems rather than to assess women's desire for financial inclusion based on its value for their lives (Duvendack & Mader, 2020). Furthermore, key structural barriers persist in many contexts, compromising women's uptake of and benefit from financial inclusion. These barriers include persistent male dominance in banking structures, unequal and low wages for women, gendered social norms that affect women's financial literacy and feelings of competency, and structural barriers based on class and ethnicity (Hoover et al., 2024). Nonetheless, some evidence suggests that the following types of financial inclusion programs are most useful for supporting women's financial engagement and decision-making agency: microfinance, savings accounts, cash and asset transfer, and digital inclusion. This work also highlights the value of women's self-help groups or collectives to support these types of financial-inclusion endeavors (Saluja et al., 2023; Yount et al., 2021).

Microfinance programs, particularly microcredit, have received much attention as a means to support women's empowerment, but evaluations have yielded mixed results regarding impact on women's agency outcomes (Alibhai et al., 2019; Chang et al., 2020; Gichuru et al., 2019; Kabeer, 2001; Orton et al., 2016). For example, Tarozzi et al. (2015) found no effect of access to microcredit on women's agency, and Field et al. (2010) found that, in India, while women's entrepreneurships benefitted from training for microcredit programs, these effects were observed for Hindu but not Muslim (i.e., religious minority) women.

An RCT evaluation of the *Gender and Entrepreneurship Together* (GET Ahead) program, developed by the International Labour Organization and now implemented worldwide, indicated important positive effects on women's choice and agency (Huis et al., 2019). This evaluation, conducted in North Vietnam, demonstrated significant effects on female microfinance borrowers regarding their perceptions of choice and self-efficacy as well as household decision-making power for larger expenditures. Household conflicts or frictions also decreased over time. Interestingly, these effects were seen at the 12-month follow-up but not in earlier follow-ups, indicating that choice and agency may take time to develop in microfinance programs. A study from Nigeria similarly evaluated a rural microcredit scheme for women using a regression discontinuity design. The study compared women who were able and unable to obtain microcredit from the bank and found that obtaining microcredit increased women's household decision making (Ikenwilo et al., 2016).

While these findings highlight the value of financial inclusion programs for women, another study, conducted in Burkina Faso, suggested that context matters with these types of programs. The research team evaluated the effects of economic interventions on a range of outcomes, including women's agency in terms of decision-making control (Karimili et al., 2021). The study involved a three-armed RCT with the following treatment conditions. Intervention Arm 1 included four components: (a) a self-help savings group, (b) financial and entrepreneurial skills training, (c) cash transfer with training on effective investment of the cash for the business, and (d) monthly coaching and support. Intervention Arm 2 included the same components as Arm 1 but also included gender norm discussions with the family as well as discussion of child protection issues, such as early marriage and trafficking.

Intervention Arm 3 was a control group. Findings documented that Arms 1 and 2 both led to an increase in women's decision making regarding their children's health and well-being compared to the control group, but effects were stronger for Arm 2, which included gender norms and child protections coaching for families.

A study on microfinance participation in Bangladesh used propensity score matching to study the association between microfinance and key outcomes for married women. This study found that, in Matlab, women's participation was associated with higher levels of agency, as measured by confidence in and use of voice and mobility with family and in the community, and in use of financial services and collective agency (Yount et al., 2021). Another study involved a cluster randomized trial to evaluate a five-day business training program in post-conflict Uganda, which also included a US $150 cash transfer along with management supervision and advising. At the 16-month follow-up, intervention participants reported improvements in women's household decision making and perceived marital quality, as well as increases in women's business ownership and incomes (Green et al., 2015). However, the inclusion of men mitigated the observed effects of the intervention on women's household decision making.

Savings and savings accounts are another important element of financial inclusion, but these programs have received less study regarding their effects on women's agency. We found one RCT evaluating women's access to and use of a commitment savings product, conducted in the Philippines. Savings account withdrawal was allowed only when the account balance reached a pre-specified amount, making women less vulnerable to pressures from partners or others to withdraw the money. Women receiving these accounts reported an increase in decision-making control over a wide range of areas, including purchasing and investments, children's education, fertility, and family planning. Effects were strongest for women with below-median decision-making power at baseline, suggesting the value of these types of products for vulnerable women (Ashraf et al., 2010).

Women's Employment and Job Training

Women's employment is associated with agency in many contexts, but not in all contexts and not across all types of agency indicators (Anderson & Eswaran, 2009; Grogan, 2023; Jensen, 2012; Kabeer et al., 2018; Salem et al., 2018). Using structural equations models for panel data and propensity score adjustment, Salem et al. (2018) found that women's market and subsistence work was associated with women's increased freedom of movement but not with gender role beliefs and household decision making. Different contexts and populations may yield different findings. For example, Dharmalingam and Philip Morgan (1996) suggested that women's employment led to greater agency only in communities in which most women held jobs.

Nonetheless, women who have an independent income or some savings do appear to have greater freedom of movement and decision-making authority in their households (Acharya et al., 2010), whereas women without independent funds appear to have lower household bargaining power (Anderson & Eswaran, 2009). RCTs suggest that employment and job training programs strengthen women's agency. An intervention in rural India increased awareness of and access to jobs with the help of recruiters, and found increases in women's aspirations, with women reporting wanting to work more steadily throughout their lives (Jensen, 2012). McKelway (2018) also conducted an experimental trial in India to assess the causal impact of employment on women's general self-efficacy by randomly assigning job offers to women enrolled in an employment placement program. The study found that those who received an employment offer reported significantly higher self-efficacy than those who did not receive an employment offer, with effects retained over time regardless of employment at follow-up assessment. Research from Kenya also showed increases in self-efficacy among young women as a result of a skills training program that provided internships and job placement support (de Azevedo et al., 2013).

Women's Agricultural Development Interventions

Agricultural development programs are the cornerstone of maintaining a global food supply. These programs support farmers by providing them with better seeds, soil, and irrigation systems to strengthen production and improve their products; building farmers' entrepreneurial and financial capacities to move their products to market effectively; and linking farmers to markets to maximize access to their products. While women make up a substantial portion of the agricultural labor force globally, due to gender discrimination, they are often left out of agricultural development programs and the production value chain. Women's focused agricultural development interventions show some promise in improving women's choice, agency, and benefit as agricultural workers.

Quisumbing et al. (2024) synthesized mixed-methods findings of the effects of 11 agricultural development programs across nine countries in South Asia and Africa using rigorous RCTs and measures of choice and agency in the Women's Empowerment in Agriculture Index. The authors found largely null results, though somewhat stronger findings in South Asia compared with Africa. Collective efficacy effects were more likely to be observed than were household agency impacts. Women's critical consciousness and choice were more likely to be raised in programs that also addressed gender norms as part of agricultural development.

When extending the program with a nutrition-sensitive approach for women agricultural workers and children in Bangladesh, findings were strengthened. Waid et al. (2022) evaluated the impact of a three-year home-stead food production program using a similar above-described agricultural development program for women and men but with additional nutritional training. Using a two-armed cluster RCT, the study found that, by the four-year follow-up, women in the intervention group demonstrated improve-ments in self-efficacy, asset ownership, and group membership, though again, household decision making was not affected. Inclusion of male partners may have reduced the intervention's effectiveness with respect to women's bargaining power and decision making. An experimental study conducted with agricultural workers in Uganda found that targeting women alone for training on agricultural development led to their having a greater role in agricultural decision making than did working with both men and women in the same household (Lecoutere et al., 2023). An RCT among sugarcane farmers in Uganda showed that an intervention that relied on in-trahousehold transfers of productive assets to women as well as a behavior change intervention substantially increased women's agency, measured as group membership, self-confidence, and decision making regarding house-hold, financial, and agricultural decisions (Ambler et al., 2021).

Results from women's empowerment programs in agriculture do not always yield positive findings. A study evaluating provision of motor pumps for irrigation to farmers in northern Ghana assessed outcomes on women's empowerment and found no effect (Bryan & Mekonnen, 2023). The study, which compared matched treatment and control villages, with a subgroup of farmer groups from treatment villages receiving the pumps, used differ-ence-in-difference analyses to assess both effects on farmers and, within the treatment villages, potential spillover effects on those who did not receive the pumps. While there was no effect of the intervention, there were in fact negative spillover effects on those who did not receive pumps. These findings show the sensitivity needed when engaging in empowerment and development intervention efforts to avoid adverse study effects.

WOMEN'S COLLECTIVES

Emerging evidence supports the value of women's collectives for their role in increasing collective efficacy and collective action, but this literature primarily focuses on health or economic outcomes, not on agency outcomes (Brody et al., 2015; Farnsworth et al., 2014; Minckas et al., 2020). Still, literature review on women's collectives shows their favorable effects on key aspects of women's collective agency (Evans & Nambiar, 2013):

- *Collective problem-solving* to ensure access to and safety for shared environmental resources, such as rivers and forests;

- *Collective decision making* on how to access and use financial assets and resources within families and communities; and
- *Collective challenging of gender norms* that restrict women's full and safe participation in society.

However, findings with respect to women's collectives are mixed, and evaluations of transformative outcomes arising from these collectives are rare. Inadequate assessments of contextual considerations (e.g., the presence of functioning infrastructures, inadequate follow-up periods to see transformative impacts) may have contributed to these limited outcomes. Other studies suggested that the collective's functionality and "cooperative infrastructure" may affect women's perceptions of its value and consequently their participation, as well as its agency-related effects (Ostrom, 2000). Nonetheless, it has been argued that women's collective action is central to create women's empowerment (Evans & Nambiar, 2013; Ostrom, 2000).

The strongest work on the impact of women's collectives on economic outcomes and health outcomes has focused on self-help groups in India. A natural experiment evaluating effects of expanding women's social networks via women's entry into women-only credit self-help groups favorably affected women's political agency and participation, their household decision making, and their collective efficacy (Prillaman, 2023). Another study using a neighbor-matching system to evaluate the effect of self-help group membership on women's empowerment in India included assessments on empowerment of women and men. The study found that women's empowerment improved without concurrent reduction in men's empowerment, suggesting that women's empowerment need not be a zero-sum game (Kumar et al., 2021). Women participating in self-help groups showed greater control over income and decision making over credit, with more active participations associated with stronger outcomes. Importantly, effects on domestic violence and respect in the household were not seen, indicating that effects were limited to economic empowerment.

A pre-post evaluation of a women's self-help group program, which combined gender-transformative education and financial skills training delivery for women in a group setting, showed improvements in women's financial decision making regarding their health and the household (Jejeebhoy et al., 2017). Evaluation of self-help groups for women sex workers in India, when integrated with HIV-prevention training (Guha et al., 2012), showed positive effects on condom use and collective efficacy; however, effects varied by city, with stronger effects observed in areas where sex worker self-help groups were stronger. Women's self-help groups in India were also used in a maternal-neonatal behavior change health intervention in a quasi-experimental study, in which the intervention arm received an eight-session health intervention and the control arm received a standard microcredit intervention (Saggurti et al., 2018). Women reporting a birth in the past 12 months were followed. Intervention participants showed better behavioral health outcomes, greater support from group members for care and transport, and greater collective self-efficacy. Findings suggested that salient health needs supported by women's groups may yield stronger collective efficacy findings than what are seen for microcredit self-help groups.

Studies on women's collectives in Africa also focused on economic and health outcomes. A cluster RCT evaluated the effects of a community-based, savings-led microfinance program for women's self-help groups in poor and rural communities in Ghana, Malawi, and Uganda. The program, which involved pooling savings and turn-taking access, increased women's household decision making, especially in households in which women started with lower-than-median household decision-making levels; and improved decision making led to more durable goods purchased for the household (Karlan et al., 2017). A study in Burkina Faso used a cluster RCT to evaluate an integrated agriculture and health program for women, with two treatment arms that varied on who delivered information—a woman elder or a health committee member. Both arms were compared to a control condition. Women in the treatment groups had the opportunity to work with other women on model farms and participate in meetings focused on nutrition and health. In addition to showing positive health effects on children (Olney et al., 2016), structural equation modeling of empowerment indicators as a mediator of observed health effects also revealed significant effects of the intervention on spouse communication, financial decision making, healthcare decision making, and family planning decision making (Heckert et al., 2019).

WOMEN'S HEALTH INITIATIVES

Sexual and Reproductive Health and Family Planning Interventions

A vast literature on family planning interventions incorporates gender-transformative approaches that are designed to alter restrictive gender norms and gender roles for women and men to support women's reproductive agency and contraceptive use, in both clinical and community-based settings (Hay et al., 2019; Heymann et al., 2019). Evaluation studies, most of which involved gender-transformative family planning interventions, showed favorable effects on women's contraceptive self-efficacy (Babalola et al., 2019; Begay et al., 2023; Lee & Yen, 2007; Raj et al., 2022). Finlay and Lee (2018) reviewed and synthesized studies exploring the causal effect of family planning on women's economic empowerment and showed the effects of family planning services on women's reproductive decision making. The authors highlighted a study by Ashraf et al. (2014), which demonstrated that access to concealable contraceptives can empower women to better achieve their desired fertility level but also can lead to their lower subjective well-being, suggesting a psychosocial cost of making contraceptives more concealable. Chang et al. (2020) reviewed interventions designed to affect women's and girls' agency and highlighted programs that supported girls' self-efficacy in Kenya and India (Baiocchi et al., 2017; Leventhal et al., 2015), though other research using a similar model of gender-transformative programing for girls in Kenya did not show effects on agency (Decker et al., 2018).

Robinson et al. (2017) conducted a systematic review of longitudinal studies and evaluation trials that examined the effectiveness of sexual and reproductive health interventions for women with HIV. The review reported mixed findings regarding self-efficacy to use condoms and other contraceptives, likely due to high levels of condom use and condom self-efficacy at baseline in many contexts. Moore et al.'s (2014) review of community empowerment-focused sexual and reproductive health interventions with female sex workers in Sub-Saharan Africa found that the interventions produced largely nascent levels of collective engagement and action, with only a few interventions progressing to community ownership and sustainability of the collective. Women in interventions that did progress to a sustained and stable collective were more likely to report improved sexual negotiation power with clients and community solidarity. In a one-arm longitudinal study, Gourlay et al. (2022) used collectives to support sexual and reproductive health, inclusive of HIV prevention, for adolescent girls and young adult women in HIV hotspots in Kenya and South Africa. All girls received the *DREAMS* intervention, which included sexual and reproductive health education and access to health services, family strengthening, peer group support, mentors and safe spaces, and community mobilization to change gender norms. The evaluation found weak effects on self-efficacy but favorable effects on social support, though these effects diminished over time as networks dissipated. Taken together, these findings do not indicate strong effects on women's agency.

Community Health Worker-Delivered Maternal
and Child Interventions

Community health workers (CHWs) are a low-cost, community-based approach used by clinics to ensure proximal reach to patients (Masis et al., 2021). CHWs are often women who provide the first point of contact for community members to enter care in low-resource settings in low- and middle-income countries (LMICs). Maternal and child healthcare and nutrition (MCHN), as well as women's reproductive healthcare, are often a priority of CHW services, but these services are also central to infectious disease management in cases of outbreaks and epidemics (Bhutta et al., 2013; Masis et al., 2021; Questa et al., 2020). Studies of CHW interventions and women's agency are limited, but a recent RCT in Tanzania that evaluated a CHW-delivered MCHN intervention found increased decision-making power and choice in domestic labor among women in the intervention arm (which included men in the sessions with the CHW) than women in the control condition (in which CHWs only spoke to women; Galvin et al., 2023). Like the aforementioned family planning interventions, this inclusive-of-men approach can also change norms, as it is not normative for men to participate in CHW sessions.

Peer Support Interventions for Women's Mental Health

Burke et al. (2019) reviewed the evidence from evaluation trials on peer support interventions to assess their effects on empowerment (as measured by the Rogers' Empowerment Scale [Rogers et al., 1997], Personal Empowerment Scale [Segal et al., 1995], and Dutch Empowerment Scale [Boevink et al., 2016]), self-efficacy, and internalized stigma. The study found that much of the research focused on mental health interventions, and those interventions were offered as peer-led groups, one-on-one peer support, and a peer-run service model. Peer-led group interventions were the most common, and these showed small but significant positive effects on self-efficacy and self-regulation.

YOUTH DEVELOPMENT INTERVENTIONS

Early Marriage Prevention and School Retention Interventions

Causal studies document the value of child marriage prevention interventions in supporting girls' agency to pursue education and develop aspirations beyond marriage. A systematic review of child marriage prevention interventions highlighted evidence, largely from experimental studies, that life skills and school voucher programs for girls and cash transfer programs for girls and their households could significantly impact girls' choice and agency to remain in school as well as their aspirations for employment (Kalamar et al., 2016). A review of reviews extracted 13 intervention studies to reduce child marriage and identified the most promising empowerment-related intervention components to be skill-building to enhance voice/agency, strengthening social networks, providing women role models outside the family, and community engagement to change restrictive social and gender norms (Yount et al., 2017).

Consistent with these reviews, several programs in Africa, specifically in Liberia, Zimbabwe, and Zambia, focused on the ability of skills training, mentoring, safe spaces, and tutoring to keep girls in school and reduce child marriage and adolescent pregnancies. These programs demonstrated significant effects on aspirations, self-confidence, self-efficacy, and self-reliance, as well as social skills (Adhoho et al., 2014; Ashraf et al., 2020; Hallfors et al., 2011). Often, these programs were offered after school and included assets such as school supplies.

A more recent cluster RCT study evaluating child marriage in Nepal included a three-arm comparison of (a) a girls' intervention, providing economic and social supports as well as skill building (the *Tipping Point Intervention*); (b) a group that received the same intervention plus a community-based social norms program involving community and girl leaders (*Tipping Point Plus*); and (c) a control group (Yount et al., 2023). This study included a comprehensive set of choice and agency indicators at the individual (e.g., personal awareness/knowledge of sexual and reproductive health, aspirations for schooling and marriage, self-efficacy), interpersonal (e.g., communication with parents), and community (e.g., collective participation and action) levels. Despite COVID-19-related disruptions to programming, favorable effects at an eight-month follow-up were observed for the *Tipping Point Plus* arm on girls' personal awareness of sexual and reproductive health and collective participation outcomes.

While these programs may be promising for agency indicators related to averting child marriage or to remaining in school, they may not lead to career or even employment aspirations. A review of programs designed to keep girls in school found that most of the evaluated interventions demonstrated increases in self-efficacy and confidence but not in aspirations in areas such as marriage, childbearing, education, and jobs (Adoho et al., 2014; Baiocchi et al., 2017; Bandiera et al., 2020; Chang et al., 2020; Decker et al., 2018; Leventhal et al., 2015; Rodella et al., 2015; Scales et al., 2013). Therefore, while girls' education is important, it is not necessarily a panacea for all dimensions of women's empowerment identified in the committee's new conceptual framework. In Bangladesh, for example, research indicated that women who received formal education may have had more decision-making control, but that control did not appear to correlate with greater freedom of movement (Hussain & Smith, 1999); moreover, women who received higher education reported greater recognition of their *choice* to attain a career but not their actual attainment of a professional position (Ahmed & Hyndman-Rizk, 2020). Finally, education does not always lead to aspirational wage earning and employment, as seen in India (Chatterjee et al., 2018). These findings suggest that programs designed to keep girls in school may be more impactful on girls' aspirations and actions when paired with concurrent efforts to change community norms and opportunities.

Life Skills Interventions

More general life skills interventions (i.e., not specifically focused on preventing child marriage and/or school retention) are household, community, or school-based programs that support people to manage aspects of everyday life, including social interactions, time management, and basic functioning. These are the skills people need to function effectively within general society, as well as in school and work environments. As such, these skills can help women and girls navigate spaces in which they lack or have been denied exposure, and they can facilitate women's and girls' choice and agency across domains of influence. A systematic review of life skills interventions documented that many interventions focused on girls and produced small yet significant positive effects on a number of choice and agency indicators, including self-worth and self-efficacy; but collective agency effects were not seen (Singh et al., 2022b).

Recent work integrated life skills with entrepreneurial skills training for youth. A recent study involved a three-armed cluster RCT evaluation of the *Skills for Effective Entrepreneurship Development* program, a three-week mini master of business administration program for high school students in Uganda. Treatment arms were (a) a 75% hard skills and 25% soft skills program, and (b) a 75% soft skills and 25% hard skills program; both were compared with a control condition. Over the 3.5-year follow-up, researchers found that the group with greater soft-skills training was more likely to demonstrate improved self-efficacy, persuasion, and negotiation, though both treatment conditions were more likely to see positive entrepreneurship and income outcomes compared with the control condition (Chioda et al., 2023). Pre-post evaluation of *The Economic Empowerment of Adolescent Girls and Young Women* project in Liberia similarly provided livelihood and life skills training for young people and, over the two-year follow-up period, found that women reported increases in self-confidence corresponding to increases in employment (Adoho et al., 2014). Rodella et al. (2015) evaluated the *Haiti Adolescent Girl Initiative*, which also offered skills training and job placement support, and found that recipients reported an increase in decision making related to finances, work, education, and relationships.

SOCIAL AND LEGAL PROTECTIONS AND POLICIES

Structural interventions are those designed to operate at scale across communities and to address structural oppressions thought to be caused by poverty and discrimination. While evaluation of programs and interventions can offer important causal evidence, social and legal protections and policies are less amenable to controlled trial designs. Nonetheless, some evidence suggests that these protections and policies may impact women's agency.

Social Protections

A systematic review (Perera et al., 2022) of studies evaluating the effects of social protection programs on socioeconomic development outcomes and empowerment indicators in LMICs found that the programs were more effective for women than men and in some cases increased women's agency. For example, livelihood programs increased self-confidence and empowerment but not confidence regarding future work opportunities.

A difference-in-difference study on women's justice centers in Peru (reviewed in Chapter 6) found that women living near an all-women's justice center were more likely to report shared decision making with husbands (Kavanaugh et al., 2019).

Land Registration and Inheritance Rights

Research on agency-related effects of making land registration and inheritance rights more gender equitable is limited but promising. A study from Holden et al. (2011) showed that after a process of community land registration in the Tigray region in Ethiopia, female heads of household were more likely to rent out land. This was a capability they could enact thanks to increased tenure security. Absent the land certificate, women faced a greater risk of losing their land than did men. While this was the only study we could identify providing causal evidence on the value of land registration on women's agency in land management, the findings suggest that land registration may be a meaningful lever for change. Adequate causal evidence on land registration from other contexts (and on assets more broadly) is lacking, despite the above-noted review on assets as a correlate of women's choice and agency.

Heath and Tan (2020) studied another policy lever—inheritance rights. Between 1976 and 2005, a series of amendments to the Hindu Succession Act equalized inheritance rights between men and women in several Indian states. Comparing outcomes for women who were exposed to these reforms versus those who were not, the authors showed positive correlations of women's inheritance rights at the state level with women's say in household decisions and their autonomy to travel away from the home by themselves.

Gender Quotas

Gender quotas can increase women's representation in government and corporate boards and increase policies that support women and families

(Clayton, 2021; Hughes et al., 2017; Krook & Zetterberg, 2014). However, these effects are context-specific. Furthermore, evidence is limited on the effects of gender quotas on agency indicators. Research from India indicated that gender quotas for women increased parental aspirations for daughters and aspirations among adolescent girls themselves, possibly by viewing the leaders as role models and/or by improvement of policies to support women's employment and opportunities (Beaman et al., 2012). Gender quotas also increased public perceptions regarding women candidates' capacities to win and to lead, and this change in public perception was associated with women's collective agency in terms of their participation in political or community decision making (Allen & Cutts, 2018; Beaman et al., 2009; Bhavnani, 2009).

Subsidized Childcare

Global evidence documents the importance of quality childcare and early childhood education for both women's employment and child development, but subsidized or free childcare remains limited across many countries (Chaturvedi, 2019). In many contexts, women's employment relies on grandparent and extended family engagement for childcare, and studies document the value of grandparent involvement for child education, health, and development (Anderson et al., 2018; Coall & Hertwig, 2010; Pulgaron et al., 2016; Sear & Coall, 2011; Sear & Mace, 2008). However, even when grandparent involvement is an option, it is not ensured childcare, as grandparents might have more say over women's employment, compromising women's economic agency. To determine whether subsidized childcare for children under five would be of interest to women and would support their employment, an RCT in Nairobi demonstrated a potential increase in household decision making related to children's healthcare, though no effects were seen on other decision-making variables (Clark et al., 2019). However, other childcare interventions (e.g., Ajayi et al., 2022) found no impacts on women's decision making.

SUMMARY AND CONCLUSIONS

This chapter reviewed programs and policies from a wide variety of LMIC settings that showed impacts on women's and girls' agency via (a) *financial interventions*, including cash transfers, microfinance, and job training and placement; (b) interventions to expand and strengthen *women's collectives*, to support women's economic and health status and build collective agency; (c) *health interventions*, including sexual and reproductive health programs, CHW programs for maternal and child health, and peer programs for mental health; (d) *youth development interventions*, to prevent early marriage, to promote education, and to strengthen life skills for other more general purposes; and (e) *social and legal protections and policies*, particularly those related to gender-equal opportunity and safety from gender-based violence. This literature shows that these approaches can have favorable effects on women's and girls' aspirations, self-efficacy, and influence in decision making. These program and policy approaches align with those that show significant changes in delayed marriage, health and family planning, and positive socioeconomic development outcomes, as discussed in previous chapters. However, additional research is necessary to better understand the pathways and contexts for the changes observed, including reasons for inconsistent findings.

Notably, one cannot assume that the same impacts would be observed in contexts outside of the intervention sites. Tailoring interventions to the local context, population, needs, and culture is a critical step for program effectiveness. Participation of community members in intervention design and evaluation is also essential for success and sustainment. Furthermore, while evidence is available for these levers, other theoretically important levers, particularly in the policy sphere, lack adequate evidence, such as divorce and custody laws, wage equality laws, and family leave policies. Evidence is also lacking from LMIC contexts regarding the impacts of programs on community efficacy and action-related outcomes. Impacts of women's self-help groups on these outcomes were notable and suggest the importance of women's collectives as an intervention strategy. More robust evidence on agency-related impacts of autonomous feminist movements is also necessary to draw more definitive conclusions about these relationships.

8

Conclusions and Recommendations

This report synthesized available theoretical frameworks and empirical evidence regarding the relationships of women's empowerment with population dynamics and socioeconomic development. Given the committee's charge, we have prioritized evidence that provides insight into the relationships of investments in enabling resources for women (levers for change), impacts of these investments on direct measures of women's agency, and effects on conceptually grounded measures of population dynamics and socioeconomic development. We recognize the reciprocal nature of these relationships and have acknowledged them throughout.

Our review of existing frameworks of women's empowerment revealed general agreement on key dimensions, especially those related to the importance of resources, the centrality of women's agency in the empowerment process, and the importance of an enabling structural and normative context for women's agency to be fully realized at lower levels of the social ecology. Conceptual gaps in these frameworks were also notable. For example, frameworks tended to focus on resources and agency at the individual and interpersonal levels, with less attention to collective resources and agency at the community and societal levels. Also, the powerful roles of formal institutions and sociocultural norms in maintaining the status quo of women's disempowerment received less attention, and conceptualizing change processes within a multilevel socioecological framework was generally lacking. To integrate and expand upon this conceptual work, our new conceptual framework underscores the multilevel and multidimensional nature of both resources and agency, as well as the unignorable conditioning influence of restrictive gender norms along with the formal institutions and the social, cultural, and structural factors that underlie these norms.

We also observed notable gaps in frameworks for understanding how changes in women's empowerment may, in theory, be related to changes in population dynamics and socioeconomic development, which are also defined as multilevel processes. Specifically, frameworks focused on population dynamics were lacking or focused narrowly on singular aspects, most notably changes in fertility. We found that while frameworks tended to address aspects of empowerment at the individual and collective levels, the roles of structures and organizations were mentioned less often, and multilevel ecological considerations were generally missing. Additionally, most of the frameworks were designed for specific sectors and therefore focused on sector-specific outcomes rather than on socioeconomic development generally. Furthermore, while frameworks tend to suggest that the expansion of enabling resources could shape and foster the empowerment process (from expanded choice to agency to achievements), none were explicit in offering guidance on opportunities to create change (e.g., via enforcement of existing policies and laws, or via creation of new policies).

The new conceptual framework developed by the committee (Figure 3-1) builds on existing frameworks and illustrates the role of population dynamics as a potential mechanism through which empowerment can operate to further socioeconomic development. The new conceptual framework also identifies ways in which resources can support empowerment. Within empowerment, the construct of agency emerged as an important lens through which to view women's empowerment and women's ability to act. The new conceptual framework considers multiple levels of agency: the individual, family, community, and societal levels.

Our review of the research on the impact of women's empowerment—and particularly agency—on a range of population dynamics identified studies that point to causal evidence in the realms of family formation and fertility, associated with interventions such as cash transfers, skills training, and education subsidies. These studies suggest that impacts on family and fertility outcomes flow through women's agency, but findings were often inconsistent across studies and geographies. Reasons for the inconsistencies include differences in definitions and measurement of women's empowerment, a paucity of measures focused on mechanisms through which the relationships operate, and lack of longitudinal data. Research in this area is typically focused on individual-level empowerment, with a lack of attention to the structural and gender context, such as the norms that shape women's and men's roles within a given culture. In addition, the interventions studied are often limited to single geographies and relatively homogenous cultural contexts. Causal studies on the role of women's empowerment in mortality and morbidity are limited, and such studies are largely lacking when it comes to migration.

A significant body of work focuses on the relationships between women's empowerment and healthcare access, utilization, and outcomes—almost entirely in the areas of access to family planning and sexual and reproductive, maternal, and newborn/early child health. Opportunities for healthcare, access to health information and autonomous decision making, and healthy behaviors are all required for achieving well-being and ultimately health and gender equity. Yet access to these conditions is not distributed equally. While the manifestations and magnitude of impact of social influences on health vary across settings and populations, many factors influence vulnerabilities to illness and contribute to higher rates of adverse health and social outcomes for women and girls versus men and boys. These include differential power relationships; control over resources including medical services, technologies, and treatments; lack of access to and receipt of quality health services; clean water, hygiene, and sanitation; an overly narrow focus on women's reproductive health with little attention to other critical and interrelated dimensions of well-being (e.g., noncommunicable diseases, mental health); gender-based violence, including forced marriage, sex trafficking, and female genital cutting; marginalization, discrimination, disrespect, and abuse occurring at the health system and community levels; and decreased opportunities for social mobility (e.g., education and employment). Women experience a significant share of the global burden of infectious diseases (e.g., HIV/AIDS, malaria, tuberculosis, hepatitis), sexually transmitted infections, cervical and breast cancers, unintended pregnancy, trauma, intimate partner violence, injury/homicide/suicide, substance use, pregnancy-related death and disability, malnutrition, and chronic conditions including depression, cardiovascular disease, diabetes, cancer, and overall morbidity and mortality.

Much of the work on the role of empowerment in the health area relies on cross-sectional data and uses unidimensional or otherwise narrowly defined empowerment indicators, which limits understanding of the complex causal relationships between women's empowerment and health outcomes. Studies are critically important to further illuminate causal associations between women's empowerment and health and healthcare access using primary data collections, longitudinal and prospective designs, and quasi-experimental, randomized controlled trial, and mixed-methods policy-evaluation approaches. Research using a broader range of multidimensional measures of both empowerment indicators and outcome measures is also important.

Evidence suggests that shifts in the determinants of women's bargaining power, such as women's access to assets or income, lead to investments associated with long-term socioeconomic development, such as children's education and nutrition. We also found that increases in women's control over assets can lead to livelihood improvements by increasing women's labor force participation and business profits. However, there is insufficient causal evidence on how land registration, and assets more broadly, impact women's agency specifically. Furthermore, women's access to childcare tends to be associated with increased labor force participation and large income benefits, but we found no evidence of childcare utilization leading to further improvements in women's agency.

Other areas of socioeconomic development that research has linked to women's empowerment include increases in girls' career aspirations and educational attainment because of laws that reserve political leadership positions for women, and a reduction in intimate partner violence associated with women's economic empowerment.

In terms of areas in which evidence is lacking, little to no research examines the impact of investments that increase women's agency on broader levels of social capital. In addition, causal evidence directly relating increased women's agency to increased climate security and resilience is very thin. Lastly, fertility decline may moderately increase output per capita in high-fertility populations, but external validity is unclear for populations that have already undergone substantial fertility decline.

We found that measured impacts of individual agency on socioeconomic development outcomes result from women's differential preferences, yet these preferences are seldom measured directly. Some studies show that self-efficacy is the individual agency construct with the most direct empirical evidence. Even less empirical evidence exists for goal setting, awareness of rights, and locus of control, despite their theoretical importance. In terms of interpersonal agency, women's decision-making ability is by far the most measured construct. However, the specific type of decision making measured is not always in line with potential theoretical pathways. In terms of community-level agency, there is a dearth of causal evidence on how shifting agency at this level (e.g., through changes in broader norms or expansion of women's networks) impacts socioeconomic development outcomes. Lastly, evidence is particularly lacking on the effects on socioeconomic development outcomes in response to societal-level changes to resources that play a role in women's agency. Beyond legal changes, policy levers such as collective action and formation of autonomous feminist movements have also not been adequately explored.

Our review of evaluations of specific policies and programs that impact women's agency identified several areas in which interventions have been found to influence women's aspirations, self-efficacy, self-confidence, and decision-making control. These areas include (a) financial programs, including cash transfers, microfinance, and job training and placement; (b) women's collectives to support women's economic and health status and build collective efficacy; (c) health interventions, including family planning and sexual and reproductive health programs, community health worker programs for maternal and child health, and peer programs for mental health; (d) youth development interventions, including those focused on early marriage prevention and education promotion, as well as life skills training; and (e) social and legal protections and policies, particularly those related to gender-equal opportunity and safety from gender-based violence. These program and policy approaches align with those that show significant improvements in delayed marriage, increased health and family planning, and positive socioeconomic development outcomes. While studies often show robust impacts of these programs, the evidence cannot be generalized to geographies and cultural contexts that differ from those in which the research was conducted.

Policies and programs for which there appear to be inadequate evidence include the areas of divorce and custody laws, wage equality laws, and family leave policies, possibly because implementation of these policies varies and few studies measure implementation. Additionally, inadequate evidence is available from low- and middle-income countries regarding the role of agency at levels beyond the individual and interpersonal. Evidence on collective efficacy as an outcome is limited, except in the case of women's self-help groups, likely because these groups themselves operate as collectives. Evidence is also limited on the impact of social movements (e.g., women's movements) on agency across various levels.

RECOMMENDATIONS

While the roles of some of the concepts and dynamics described in our new conceptual framework are well supported by evidence, other areas would benefit from further research. Our review also revealed a great deal of variation in disciplinary approaches to measuring and analyzing women's empowerment, population dynamics, and socioeconomic development, emphasizing the importance of harmonizing measures and approaches. Our recommendations for ways to advance the work in this area are summarized below.

Measuring Women's Empowerment and Associated Concepts

While the committee was not specifically tasked with conducting a systematic review of data-collection and measurement approaches, our review of the existing research on women's empowerment identified inconsistencies, limitations, and gaps in definitions, as well as the operationalization and measurement of terms to be among the main barriers to better understanding the role of women's empowerment in population dynamics and socioeconomic development. Data limitations often mean that concepts and relationships that appear to be important based on theoretical pathways are not well understood, and that findings are not comparable across diverse social contexts, making it difficult to eliminate confounding effects. The committee's statement of task includes a request to set an agenda for future research and data collection, and many of our recommendations are in this area.

> RECOMMENDATION 1: Data collection on women's empowerment should be expanded to include the range of measures necessary to fully capture elements of women's empowerment, as well as the dynamics and pathways in the committee's new conceptual framework that remain poorly understood. Many of these aspects are multidimensional and should be understood as such. These include
> - Sociocultural norms and structures as conditioning factors in the sociocontextual environment.
> - Structural dynamics and sexism.
> - The role of men, including structural gender inequalities, inequitable gender norms, and masculine dominance.
> - Barriers to empowerment.
> - Effective methods to reduce gender inequality in productivity, earnings, and profits.
> - Effective methods to address norms surrounding women's domestic work.
> - Effective methods to eliminate occupational segregation.
> - Effective methods to build resilience for women in the face of climate change and other shocks.
> - Women's access to health programs (e.g., social protection, insurance, contraception, prenatal and childbirth care, infant and child healthcare, women's healthcare).
> - Girls' and women's education and skill building.
> - Girls' and women's social networks and supports.
> - Couple dynamics.
> - Perceptions of rights.
> - Time allocation and control over time.

> RECOMMENDATION 2: Researchers and government data-collection entities studying women's empowerment should identify opportunities to collect longitudinal data from large-scale studies to better understand change over time, including the determinants of sustained gains in women's empowerment and the long-term effects of women's empowerment on socioeconomic development.

Measuring Women's Agency

In addition to improving measurement of women's empowerment, this report also highlighted work that is important for developing better measures of women's agency and areas in which a better understanding of the role of agency is critical.

RECOMMENDATION 3: Research should prioritize the development of direct multidimensional, construct-specific, and multilevel measures of agency. To the extent that proxy measures are used, researchers should strive for consistency and clarity on how such measures are defined and used, and should be clear that the role of women's agency is assumed and not directly measured. Particular attention should be paid to defining, operationalizing, and assessing the reliability and validity of the following dimensions of women's agency in diverse contexts, leveraging the newest research:
- Individual awareness of rights, aspirations and preferences, goal setting and choice, and internal motivation.
- Control and decision making, including economic and reproductive decision making, at the individual and interpersonal levels.
- Collective agency in formal groups and informal networks at the community and societal levels (e.g., shared goals, collective efficacy, collective action toward shared goals).

Studies of agency would benefit from a life-course perspective—in other words, from recognizing that there are trajectories and turning points as people grow and change across life stages and are influenced by their lived experiences. Agency around life transition points and opportunities, such as fertility or wage earning, can be particularly important to support women to achieve their life goals.

RECOMMENDATION 4: Research on agency should include studies of women's agency across the entire life course and at key life stages and milestones, with consideration of the socioecological and cultural context and intergenerational influences on key life stages, milestones, and inflection points.

Enhancing Study Designs

While this report prioritized the discussion of existing research pointing to the causal influences on women's agency, and in turn the causal effects of women's agency on population dynamics and socioeconomic development, the literature we reviewed included a wide variety of methods, including qualitative research such as community-participatory and community-engaged research. Considerable gaps exist in some areas in which study designs able to establish causality are lacking, or in which further insight on underlying dynamics could be gained through in-depth qualitative exploration.

> RECOMMENDATION 5: Research on women's empowerment and agency should prioritize study designs that:
> - Test causal relationships between dimensions of women's empowerment and population dynamics and socioeconomic development, and that better elucidate the role of relevant concepts as causal factors or outcomes. These designs include randomized controlled trials, quasi-experiments, natural experiments, and longitudinal designs to establish causality; to examine reciprocal, temporal relationships; and to distinguish effects related to the mode of intervention delivery and quality of implementation from the content of the intervention.
> - Include qualitative data collection to contextualize theories of change, to inform intervention and research design, and to aid in the interpretation of findings that offer causal evidence.
> - Are informed by the perspectives of the women and communities being studied.
> - Examine multiple intervention points along the theoretical pathways of interest.
> - Provide understanding of life-course trajectories and inflection points.

RECOMMENDATION 6: Research funders should support studies designed to examine the effects of programs and policies intended to enhance women's empowerment and, thereby, socioeconomic development. Study designs should include sufficient follow-up time to examine sustainability of impacts, as well as measures that permit assessment of unintended adverse effects of interventions, including outcomes (both intended and unintended) that may not be immediate.

RECOMMENDATION 7: To establish external validity, more attention should be devoted to understanding the role of interventions and the specific role of women's agency as a mechanism for social change—at the institutional and societal levels, as well as across diverse cultural settings. Also, more attention should be paid to understanding the feasibility, acceptability, and sustainability of, as well as engagement with, these interventions.

RECOMMENDATION 8: Studies are needed to better understand the impacts of integrated approaches to women's empowerment (e.g., cash transfers to women alongside efforts to address restrictive social and gender norms) and integrated women's healthcare (e.g., service-delivery models that can address women's sexual and reproductive health as well as psychosocial care needs).

The committee's review primarily focused on the empirical evidence regarding how women's empowerment influences population dynamics and socioeconomic development, and not on the cost effectiveness of programs. Very little information is available about the cost implications of various interventions or about the best ways to scale up and integrate promising findings into policies or practice. Looking ahead, it is important to systematically track program-implementation data and for more research to be performed to guide decisions about implementation.

RECOMMENDATION 9: Research funders should support cost analyses and implementation science studies to provide guidance on scaling up efficacious interventions. Such efforts should include systematic tracking of program-implementation data. As evidence from experimental studies continues to grow, comparative effectiveness studies may provide best-practice guidance to government officials and civil society organizations regarding the most cost-effective empowerment approaches in specific country contexts.

Collaboration and Harmonization

The extremely interdisciplinary nature of this field and the challenges associated with generalizing research findings beyond limited geographic and cultural contexts highlight the importance of collaboration to set priorities, coordinate research efforts, and refine measurement approaches to expedite insights into these questions.

RECOMMENDATION 10: Research funders should establish an international, multidisciplinary group to increase coordination and priority setting for the work in this area. The advisory group could include representatives of funding organizations and other experts and stakeholders, and it would be charged with
- Developing and publishing standards and best practices for development and validation of measures for empowerment, so researchers and implementers can better distinguish among the array of measures in use.

- Coordinating work on psychometric assessment of measures of empowerment and related concepts, and evaluating the possibility of (and recommended processes for) harmonizing measures and global indicators of women's agency and empowerment that would be suitable for comparative use cross-culturally and with various populations.
- Identifying questions and measures that improve measurement of specific empowerment constructs in specific cultures and languages.
- Setting priorities for development of experimental studies to generate causal evidence on relationships that currently are not well understood.

RECOMMENDATION 11: Government, program, and researcher data collections should be better coordinated and aligned. The international group named in Recommendation 10 could facilitate efforts to enhance coordination and alignment across these groups.

References

Abada, T., & Tenkorang, E. Y. (2012). Women's autonomy and unintended pregnancies in the Philippines. *Journal of Biosocial Science, 44*(6), 703–718. https://doi.org/10.1017/S0021932012000120

Abbink, K., Islam, A., & Nguyen, C. (2020). Whose voice matters? An experimental examination of gender bias in intra-household decision-making. *Journal of Economic Behavior & Organization, 176*, 337–352. https://doi.org/10.1016/j.jebo.2020.02.003

Abreha, S. K., & Zereyesus, Y. A. (2021). Women's empowerment and infant and child health status in Sub-Saharan Africa: A systematic review. *Maternal and Child Health Journal, 25*, 95–106. https://doi.org/10.1007/s10995-020-03025-y

Abubakar, N. H., & Dasuki, S. I. (2018). Empowerment in their hands: Use of WhatsApp by women in Nigeria. *Gender, Technology, and Development, 22*(2), 164–183. https://doi.org/10.1080/09718524.2018.1509490

Acharya, D. R., Bell, J. S., Simkhada, P., van Teijlingen, E. R., & Regmi, P. R. (2010). Women's autonomy in household decision-making: A demographic study in Nepal. *Reproductive Health, 7*, Article 15. https://doi.org/10.1186/1742-4755-7-15

Ackerson, L. K., Kawachi, I., Barbeau, E. M., & Subramanian, S. V. (2008). Effects of individual and proximate educational context on intimate partner violence: A population-based study of women in India. *American Journal of Public Health, 98*(3), 507–514. https://doi.org/10.2105%2FAJPH.2007.113738

Ackerson, L. K., & Subramanian, S. V. (2008). Domestic violence and chronic malnutrition among women and children in India. *American Journal of Epidemiology, 167*(10), 1188–1196. https://doi.org/10.1093%2Faje%2Fkwn049

Adoho, F., Chakravarty, S., Korkoyah, D. T., Lundberg, M. K., & Tasneem, A. (2014). *The impact of an adolescent girls employment program: The EPAG project in Liberia* (The World Bank Policy Research Working Paper No. 6832). The World Bank. https://ssrn.com/abstract=2420245

Agarwal, B. (1997). "Bargaining" and gender relations: Within and beyond the household. *Feminist Economics, 3*(1), 1–51. https://doi.org/10.1080/135457097338799

Agyei-Holmes, A., Buehren, N., Goldstein, M. P., Osei, R. D., Osei-Akoto, I., & Udry, C. (2020). *The effects of land title registration on tenure security, investment and the allocation of productive resources* (Global Poverty Research Lab Working Paper No. 20–107). Global Poverty Research Lab, Buffet Institute for Global Studies. https://doi.org/10.2139/ssrn.3694776

Ahmed, R., & Hyndman-Rizk, N. (2020). The higher education paradox: Towards improving women's empowerment, agency development and labour force participation in Bangladesh. *Gender and Education*, *32*(4), 447–465. https://doi.org/10.1080/09540253.2018.1471452

Ahmed, S., Ahmed, S., McKaig, C., Begum, N., Mungia, J., Norton, M., & Baqui, A. H. (2015). The effect of integrating family planning with a maternal and newborn health program on postpartum contraceptive use and optimal birth spacing in rural Bangladesh. *Studies in Family Planning*, *46*(3), 297–312. https://doi.org/10.1111/j.1728-4465.2015.00031.x

Ahmed, S., Creanga A. A., Gillespie, D. G., & Tsui, A. O. (2010). Economic status, education and empowerment: Implications for maternal health service utilization in developing countries. *PLOS One*, *5*(6), Article e11190. https://doi.org/10.1371/journal.pone.0011190

Ajayi, K. F., Dao, A., & Koussoube, E. (2022). *The effects of childcare on women and children: Evidence from a randomized evaluation in Burkina Faso* (The World Bank Policy Research Working Paper No. 10239). The World Bank. https://documents1.worldbank.org/curated/en/099215111282254210/pdf/IDU09ee54b690865904f71089a60d76ad621601c.pdf

Aker, J. C., Ksoll, C., & Lybbert, T. J. (2012). ABC, 123: Can mobile phones improve learning? Evidence from a field experiment in Niger. *American Economic Journal: Applied Economics*, *4*(4), 94–120. https://doi.org/10.1257/app.4.4.94

Aker, J. C., & Mbiti, I. M. (2010). Mobile phones and economic development in Africa. *Journal of Economic Perspectives*, *24*(3), 207–232. https://doi.org/10.1257/jep.24.3.207

Aker, J. C., Sawyer, M., Goldstein, M., O'Sullivan, M., & McConnell, M. (2020). Just a bit of cushion: The role of a simple savings device in meeting planned and unplanned expenses in rural Niger. *World Development*, *128*, Article 104772. http://dx.doi.org/10.1016/j.worlddev.2019.104772

Akter, S., Krupnik, T. J., Rossi, F., & Khanam, F. (2016). The influence of gender and product design on farmers' preferences for weather-indexed crop insurance. *Global Environmental Change*, *38*, 217–229.

Al Akash, R. A., & Chalmiers, M. A. (2021). Early marriage among Syrian refugees in Jordan: Exploring contested meanings through ethnography. *Sexual and Reproductive Health Matters*, *29*(1). https://doi.org/10.1080/26410397.2021.2004637

Alam, A., Baez, J., & Del Carpio, X. V. (2021). *Does cash for school influence young women's behavior in the longer term? Evidence from Pakistan* (IZA Discussion Paper No. 5703). IZA Institute of Labor Economics. https://www.iza.org/pub/2tYyeF3t

Alderman, H., Chiappori, P.-A., Haddad, L., Hoddinott, J., & Kanbur, R. (1995). Unitary versus collective models of the household: Is it time to shift the burden of proof? *The World Bank Research Observer*, *10*(1), 1–19. https://doi.org/10.1093/wbro/10.1.1

Alemu, G. T. (2015). Women's land use right policy and household food security in Ethiopia. *International Journal of African and Asian Studies*, *12*, 56–65. https://www.iiste.org/Journals/index.php/JAAS/article/viewFile/24781/25384

Ali, D. A., Deininger, K., & Goldstein, M. (2014). Environmental and gender impacts of land tenure regularization in Africa: Pilot evidence from Rwanda. *Journal of Development Economics*, *110*(September), 262–275. https://doi.org/10.1016/j.jdeveco.2013.12.009

Alibhai, S., Buehren, N., Frese, M., Goldstein, M., Papineni, S., & Wolf, K. (2019). *Full esteem ahead? Mindset-oriented business training in Ethiopia* (The World Bank Policy Research Working Paper No. 8892). The World Bank. https://doi.org/10.1596/1813-9450-8892

Alkema, L., Chou, D., Hogan, D., Zhang, S., Moller, A.-B., Gemmill, A., Fat, D. M., Boerma, T., Temmerman, M., Mathers, C., Say, L., Ahmed, S., Ali, M., Amouzou, A., Braunholtz, D., Byass, P., Carvajal-Velez, L., Gaigbe-Togbe, V., ... Suzuki, E. (2016). Global, regional, and national levels and trends in maternal mortality between 1990 and 2015, with scenario-based projections to 2030: A systematic analysis by the UN Maternal Mortality Estimation Inter-Agency Group. *The Lancet*, *387*(10017), 462–474. https://doi.org/10.1016/S0140-6736(15)00838-7

Alkire, S. (2008). *Concepts and measures of agency* (OPHI Working Paper No. 09). Oxford Poverty and Human Development Initiative, University of Oxford. https://ophi.org.uk/sites/default/files/OPHI-wp09.pdf

Allen, A. (2008). Power and the politics of difference: Oppression, empowerment, and transnational justice. *Hypatia*, *23*(3), 156–172. https://doi.org/10.1111/j.1527-2001.2008.tb01210.x

Allen, P., & Cutts, D. (2018). How do gender quotas affect public support for women as political leaders? *West European Politics*, *41*(1), 147–168. https://doi.org/10.1080/01402382.2017.1320082

Allendorf, K. (2007). Couples' reports of women's autonomy and health-care use in Nepal. *Studies in Family Planning*, *38*(1), 35–46. https://doi.org/10.1111/j.1728-4465.2007.00114.x

Allendorf, K. (2012). Women's agency and the quality of family relationships in India. *Population Research and Policy Review*, *31*(2), 187–206. https://doi.org/10.1007%2Fs11113-012-9228-7

Altunbas, Y., Gambacorta, L., Reghezza, A., & Velliscig, G. (2022). Does gender diversity in the workplace mitigate climate change? *Journal of Corporate Finance*, *77*, Article 102303. https://doi.org/10.1016/j.jcorpfin.2022.102303

Ambler, K., Jones, K. M., & O'Sullivan, M. (2021). *Increasing women's empowerment: Implications for family welfare* (IZA Discussion Paper No. 14861). IZA Institute of Labor Economics. https://www.iza.org/publications/dp/14861/increasing-womens-empowerment-implications-for-family-welfare

Amin, S., Ahmed, J., Saha, J., Hossain, M. I., & Haque, E. (2016). *Delaying child marriage through community-based skills-development programs for girls: Results from a randomized controlled study in rural Bangladesh*. Population Council. https://knowledgecommons.popcouncil.org/departments_sbsr-pgy/557/

Amirapu, A., Asadullah, M. N., & Wahhaj, Z. (2022). Social barriers to female migration: Theory and evidence from Bangladesh. *Journal of Development Economics*, *158*, Article 102891. https://doi.org/10.1016/j.jdeveco.2022.102891

Anderson, L., Sheppard, P., & Monden, C. (2018). Grandparent effects in educational outcomes: A systematic review. *Sociological Science*, *5*, 114–142. https://doi.org/10.15195/v5.a6

Anderson, L. M., Scrimshaw, S. C., Fullilove, M. C., Fielding, J. E., & Task Force on Community Preventive Services. (2003). The Community Guide's model for linking the social environment to health. *American Journal of Preventive Medicine*, *24*(3S), 12–20. https://doi.org/10.1016/s0749-3797(02)00652-9

Anderson, S., & Eswaran, M. (2009). What determines female autonomy? Evidence from Bangladesh. *Journal of Development Economics*, *90*(2), 179–191. https://doi.org/10.1016/j.jdeveco.2008.10.004

Anderson, S., & Ray, D. (2010). Missing women: Age and disease. *Review of Economic Studies*, *77*, 1262–1300. https://doi.org/10.1111/j.1467-937X.2010.00609.x

Andrews, C., Backiny-Yetna, P., Garin, E., Weedon, E., Wodon, Q., & Zampaglione, G. (2011). *Liberia's cash for work temporary employment project: Responding to crisis in low income, fragile countries* (SP Discussion Paper No. 1114). The World Bank. http://documents.worldbank.org/curated/en/836781468263674274

Andriano, L., & Monden, C. W. S. (2019). The causal effect of maternal education on child mortality: Evidence from a quasi-experiment in Malawi and Uganda. *Demography*, *56*(5), 1765–1790. https://link.springer.com/article/10.1007/s13524-019-00812-3

Annan, J., Donald, A., Goldstein, M., Gonzalez Martinez, P., & Koolwal, G. (2021). Taking power: Women's empowerment and household well-being in Sub-Saharan Africa. *World Development*, *140*, Article 105292. https://doi.org/10.1016/j.worlddev.2020.105292

Asaki, B., & Hayes, S. (2011). Leaders, not clients: Grassroots women's groups transforming social protection. *Gender & Development*, *19*(2), 241–253. https://doi.org/10.1080/13 552074.2011.592634

Asaolu, I. O., Alaofè, H., Gunn, J. K. L., Adu, A. K., Monroy, A. J., Ehiri, J. E., Hayden, M. H., & Ernst, K. C. (2018). Measuring women's empowerment in sub-Saharan Africa: Exploratory and confirmatory factor analyses of the demographic and health surveys. *Frontiers in Psychology*, *9*. https://doi.org/10.3389/fpsyg.2018.00994

Ashraf, N. (2009). Spousal control and intra-household decision making: An experimental study in the Philippines. *American Economic Review*, *99*(4), 1245–1277. https://doi.org/10.1257/aer.99.4.1245

Ashraf, N., Bau, N., Low, C., & McGinn, K. (2020). Negotiating a better future: How interpersonal skills facilitate intergenerational investment. *Quarterly Journal of Economics*, *135*(2), 1095–1151. https://doi.org/10.1093/qje/qjz039

Ashraf, N., Field, E., & Lee, J. (2014). Household bargaining and excess fertility: An experimental study in Zambia. *American Economic Review*, *104*(7), 2210–2237. https://doi.org/10.1257/aer.104.7.2210

Ashraf, N., Karlan, D., & Yin, W. (2010). Female empowerment: Impact of a commitment savings product in the Philippines. *World Development*, *38*(3), 333–344. https://doi.org/10.1016/j.worlddev.2009.05.010

Ashraf, Q. H., Weil, D. N., & Wilde, J. (2013). The effect of fertility reduction on economic growth. *Population and Development Review*, *39*(1), 97–130. https://doi.org/10.1111/j.1728-4457.2013.00575.x

Atake, E.-H., & Ali, P. G. (2019). Women's empowerment and fertility preferences in high fertility countries in Sub-Saharan Africa. *BMC Women's Health*, *19*, 1–14. https://doi.org/10.1186/s12905-019-0747-9

Athey, S., Bergstrom, K., Hadad, V., Jamison, J. C., Özler, B., Parisotto, L., & Sama, J. D. (2023). Can personalized digital counseling improve consumer search for modern contraceptive methods? *Science Advances*, *9*(40). https://doi.org/10.1126/sciadv.adg4420

Austrian, K., Soler-Hampejsek, E., Behrman, J. R., Digitale, J., Jackson Hachonda, N., Bweupe, M., & Hewett, P. C. (2020). The impact of the Adolescent Girls Empowerment Program (AGEP) on short and long term social, economic, education and fertility outcomes: A cluster randomized controlled trial in Zambia. *BMC Public Health*, *20*(1), Article 349. https://doi.org/10.1186/s12889-020-08460-0

Austrian, K., Soler-Hampejsek, E., Kangwana, B., Maddox, N., Diaw, M., Wado, Y. D., Abuya, B., Muluve, E., Mbushi, F., Mohammed, H., Aden, A., & Maluccio, J. A. (2022). Impacts of multisectoral cash plus programs on marriage and fertility after 4 years in pastoralist Kenya: A randomized trial. *Journal of Adolescent Health*, *70*(6), 885–894. https://doi.org/10.1016/j.jadohealth.2021.12.015

Avdeenko, A., & Gilligan, M. J. (2015). International interventions to build social capital: Evidence from a field experiment in Sudan. *American Political Science Review*, *109*(3), 427–449. https://doi.org/10.1017/S0003055415000210

Averbach, S., Johns, N. E., Ghule, M., Dixit, A., Begum, S., Battala, M., Saggurti, N., Silverman, J., & Raj, A. (2023). Understanding quality of contraceptive counseling in the CHARM2 gender-equity focused family planning intervention: Findings from a cluster randomized controlled trial among couples in rural India. *Contraception*, *118*, Article 109907. https://doi.org/10.1016/j.contraception.2022.10.009

Babalola, S., Loehr, C., Oyenubi, O., Akiode, A., & Mobley, A. (2019). Efficacy of a digital health tool on contraceptive ideation and use in Nigeria: Results of a cluster-randomized control trial. *Global Health: Science and Practice, 7*(2), 273–288. https://doi.org/10.9745/ghsp-d-19-00066

Bageant, E. R., & Barrett, C. B. (2017). Are there gender differences in demand for index-based livestock insurance? *The Journal of Development Studies, 53*(6), 932–952. https://doi.org/10.1080/00220388.2016.1214717

Baiocchi, M., Omondi, B., Langat, N., Boothroyd, D. B., Sinclair, J., Pavia, L., Mulinge, M., Githua, O., Golden, N. H., & Sarnquist, C. (2017). A behavior-based intervention that prevents sexual assault: The results of a matched-pairs, cluster-randomized study in Nairobi, Kenya. *Prevention Science, 18*(7), 818–827. https://doi.org/10.1007/s11121-016-0701-0

Baird, S., Chirwa, E., de Hoop, J., & Özler, B. (2016). Girl power: Cash transfers and adolescent welfare. Evidence from a cluster-randomized experiment in Malawi. In S. Edwards, S. Johnson, & D. Weil (Eds.), *African successes, Volume II: Human capital* (pp. 139–164). University of Chicago Press.

Baird, S., Ferreira, F. H. G., Özler, B., & Woolcock, M. (2013), Relative effectiveness of conditional and unconditional cash transfers for schooling outcomes in developing countries: A systematic review. *Campbell Systematic Reviews, 9*, 1–124. https://doi.org/10.4073/csr.2013.8

Baird, S., McIntosh, C., & Özler, B. (2011). Cash or condition? Evidence from a cash transfer experiment. *The Quarterly Journal of Economics, 126*(4), 1709–1753. https://doi.org/10.1093/qje/qjr032

___. (2019). When the money runs out: Do cash transfers have sustained effects on human capital accumulation? *Journal of Development Economics 140*, 169–185. https://doi.org/10.1016/j.jdeveco.2019.04.004

Balaj, M., York, H. W., Sripada, K., Besnier, E., Vonen, H. D., Aravkin, A., Friedman, J., Griswold, M., Jensen, M. R., Mohammad, T., Mullany, E. C., Solhaug, S., Sorensen, R., Stonkute, D., Tallaksen, A., Whisnant, J., Zheng, P., Gakidou, E., & Eikemo, T. A. (2021). Parental education and inequalities in child mortality: A global systematic review and meta-analysis. *Lancet, 398*(10300), 608–620. https://doi.org/10.1016/S0140-6736(21)00534-1

Bamiwuye, S. O., Wet, N. D., & Adedini, S. A. (2013). Linkages between autonomy, poverty and contraceptive use in two sub-Saharan African countries. *African Population Studies, 27*(2). https://doi.org/10.11564/27-2-438

Bandiera, O., Buehren, N., Burgess, R., Goldstein, M., Gulesci, S., Rasul, I., & Sulaiman, M. (2020). Women's empowerment in action: Evidence from a randomized control trial in Africa. *American Economic Journal: Applied Economics, 12*(1), 210–259. https://doi.org/10.1257/app.20170416

Bandura, A. (2001). Social cognitive theory: An agentic perspective. *Annual Review of Psychology, 52*(1), 1–26. https://doi.org/10.1146/annurev.psych.52.1.1

Bapolisi, W. A., Ferrari, G., Blampain, C., Makelele, J., Kono-Tange, L., Bisimwa, G., & Merten, S. (2020). Impact of a complex gender-transformative intervention on maternal and child health outcomes in the eastern Democratic Republic of Congo: Protocol of a longitudinal parallel mixed-methods study. *BMC Public Health, 20*(1), Article 51. https://doi.org/10.1186/s12889-019-8084-3

Baraka, J., Lawson, D. W., Schaffnit, S. B., Wamoyi, J., & Urassa, M. (2022). Why marry early? Parental influence, agency and gendered conflict in Tanzanian marriages. *Evolutionary Human Sciences, 4*, Article e49. https://doi.org/10.1017/ehs.2022.46

Barbieri, M., & Hertrich, V. (2005). Age difference between spouses and contraceptive practice in sub-Saharan Africa. *Population, 60*(5-6), 617–654. https://doi.org/10.2307/4148187

Barcellos, S. H., Carvalho, L. S., & Lleras-Muney, A. (2014). Child gender and parental investments in India: Are boys and girls treated differently? *American Economic Journal: Applied Economics, 6*(1), 157–189. https://doi.og/10.1257/app.6.1.157

Basu, A. M., & Koolwal, G. B. (2005). *Two concepts of female empowerment: Some leads from DHS data on women's status and reproductive health*. The DHS Program. https://dhsprogram.com/pubs/pdf/od32/3.pdf

Basu, K. (2006). Gender and say: A model of household behaviour with endogenously determined balance of power. *The Economic Journal, 116*(511), 558–580. https://doi.org/10.1111/j.1468-0297.2006.01092.x

Batyra, E., & Pesando, L. M. (2024). Increases in child marriage among the poorest in Mali: "Reverse policies" or data quality issues? *Population Studies, 78*(1), 93–111. https://doi.org/10.1080/00324728.2023.2181383

Bazzi, S., Cameron, L. A., Schaner, S., & Witoelar, F. (2021). *Information, intermediaries, and international migration* (NBER Working Paper No. 29588). National Bureau of Economic Research. http://dx.doi.org/10.2139/ssrn.3989597

Beaman, L., Chattopadhyay, R., Duflo, E., Pande, R., & Topalova, P. (2009). Powerful women: Does exposure reduce bias? *Quarterly Journal of Economics, 124*(4), 1497–1540. https://doi.org/10.1162/qjec.2009.124.4.1497

Beaman, L., Duflo, E., Pande, R., & Topalova, P. (2010). Political reservation and substantive representation: Evidence from Indian Village Councils. *India Policy Forum*. https://www.ncaer.org/wp-content/uploads/2022/09/4_Lori-Beaman_Esther-Duflo_Rohini-Pande_Petia-Topalova.pdf

___. (2012). Female leadership raises aspirations and educational attainment for girls: A policy experiment in India. *Science, 335*(6068), 582–586. https://doi.org/10.1126/science.1212382

Becchetti, L., & Pelloni, A. (2013). What are we learning from the life satisfaction literature? *International Review of Economics, 60*, 113–155. https://doi.org/10.1007/s12232-013-0177-1

Beckwith, K. (2000). Beyond compare? Women's movements in comparative perspective. *European Journal of Political Research, 37*(4), 431–468. https://doi.org/10.1111/1475-6765.00521

Bedoya, G., Belyakova, Y., Coville, A., Escande, T., Isaqzadeh, M., & Ndiaye, A. (2023). *The enduring impacts of a big push during multiple crises: Experimental evidence from Afghanistan* (Policy Research Working Paper No. 10596). The World Bank Group. https://documents.worldbank.org/curated/en/099837211062311087

Bedoya, G., Coville, A., Haushofer, J., Isaqzadeh, M., & Shapiro, J. (2019). *No household left behind: Afghanistan targeting the ultra poor impact evaluation* (Policy Research Working Paper No. 8877). The World Bank Group. https://documents.worldbank.org/en/publication/documents-reports/documentdetail/855831560172245349/no-household-left-behind-afghanistan-targeting-the-ultra-poor-impact-evaluation

Begay, J. L., Chambers, R. A., Rosenstock, S., Kemp, C. G., Lee, A., Lazelere, F., Pinal, L., & Tingey, L. (2023). Assessing the effectiveness of the respecting the circle of life project on condom and contraception self-efficacy among American Indian youth. *Prevention Science, 24*(2), 283–291. https://doi.org/10.1007/s11121-023-01514-4

Behrman, J. A. (2019). Contextual declines in educational hypergamy and intimate partner violence. *Social Forces, 97*(3), 1257–1282. https://doi.org/10.1093/sf/soy085

Berg, R. C., & Denison, E. (2012). Effectiveness of interventions designed to prevent female genital mutilation/cutting: A systematic review. *Studies in Family Planning, 43*(2), 135–146. https://doi.org/10.1111/j.1728-4465.2012.00311.x

Bergenfeld, I., Cislaghi, B., Yount, K. M., Essaid, A., Sajdi, J., Taleb, R. A., Morrow, G. L., D'souza, J. S., Spencer, R. A., & Clark, C. J. (2021). Diagnosing norms surrounding sexual harassment at a Jordanian university. *Frontiers in Sociology, Gender, Sex and Sexualities, 6*. https://doi.org/10.3389/fsoc.2021.667220

Bergolo, M., & Galván, E. (2018). Intra-household behavioral responses to cash transfer programs. Evidence from a regression discontinuity design. *World Development, 103*, 100–111. https://doi.org/10.1016/j.worlddev.2017.10.030

Bernheim, B. D., & Whinston, M. D. (1985). Common marketing agency as a device for facilitating collusion. *The RAND Journal of Economics, 16*(2), 269–281. https://doi.org/10.2307/2555414

Bernier, Q., & Meinzen-Dick, R. S. (2014). *Resilience and social capital.* International Food Policy Research Institute. http://ebrary.ifpri.org/cdm/ref/collection/p15738coll2/id/128152

Best, R. H., Shair-Rosenfield, S., & Wood, R. M. (2019). Legislative gender diversity and the resolution of civil conflict. *Political Research Quarterly, 72*(1), 215–228. https://doi.org/10.1177/1065912918785459

Beyers, J. M., Bates, J. E., Pettit, G. S., & Dodge, K. A. (2003). Neighborhood structure, parenting processes, and the development of youths' externalizing behaviors: A multilevel analysis. *American Journal of Community Psychology, 31*, 35–53. https://doi.org/10.1023%2Fa%3A1023018502759

Bhalotra, S. (2010). Fatal fluctuations? Cyclicality in infant mortality in India. *Journal of Development Economics, 93*(1), 7–19. https://doi.org/10.1016/j.jdeveco.2009.03.006

Bhalotra, S., Brulé, R., & Roy, S. (2020). Women's inheritance rights reform and the preference for sons in India. *Journal of Development Economics, 146*. https://doi.org/10.1016/j.jdeveco.2018.08.001

Bhalotra, S., Clarke, D., Gomes, J. F., & Venkataramani, A. (2023). Maternal mortality and women's political power. *Journal of the European Economic Association, 21*(5), 2172–2208. https://doi.org/10.1093/jeea/jvad012

Bhalotra, S., & Clots-Figueras, I. (2014). Health and the political agency of women. *American Economic Journal: Economic Policy, 6*(2), 164–197. https://doi.org/10.1257/pol.6.2.164

Bhandari, A. (2017). Women's status and global food security: An overview. *Sociology Compass, 11*(5), 1–17. https://doi.org/10.1111/soc4.12479

Bhavnani, R. R. (2009). Do electoral quotas work after they are withdrawn? Evidence from a natural experiment in India. *The American Political Science Review, 103*(01), 23–35. https://doi.org/10.1017/S0003055409090029

Bhutta, Z. A., Bawany, F. A., Feroze, A., Rizvi, A., Thapa, S. J., & Patel, M. (2009). Effects of the crises on child nutrition and health in East Asia and the Pacific. *Global Social Policy, 9*(Suppl. l), 119–143. https://doi.org/10.1177/1468018109106888

Bhutta, Z. A., Das, J. K., Rizvi, A., Gaffey, M. F., Walker, N., Horton, S., Webb, P., Lartey, A., & Black, R. E. (2013). Evidence-based interventions for improvement of maternal and child nutrition: What can be done and at what cost? *The Lancet, 382*(9890), 452–477. https://doi.org/10.1016/s0140-6736(13)60996-4

Bhuwania, P., Huh, K., & Heymann, J. (2023). Impact of tuition-free education policy on child marriage and early childbearing: Does secondary matter more? *Population and Development Review, 49*(1), 43–70. https://doi.org/10.1111/padr.12538

Biasi, B., & Sarsons, H. (2022). Flexible wages, bargaining, and the gender gap. *The Quarterly Journal of Economics, 137*(1), 215–266. https://doi.org/10.1093/qje/qjab026

Bick, A. (2016). The quantitative role of child care for female labor force participation and fertility. *Journal of the European Economic Association, 14*(3), 639–668. https://doi.org/10.1111/jeea.12143

Bill & Melinda Gates Foundation. (2018). *A conceptual model of women and girls' empowerment.* https://docs.gatesfoundation.org/Documents/BMGF_EmpowermentModel.pdf

Biskupski-Mujanovic, S., & Najjar, D. (2020). *Gender and rural women's collectives literature review.* https://hdl.handle.net/20.500.11766/12394

Bjorvatn, K., Ferris, D., Gulesci, S., Nasgowitz, A., Somville, V., & Vandewalle, L. (2022). *Childcare, labor supply, and business development: Experimental evidence from Uganda* (CEPR Discussion Paper No. DP17243). Centre for Economic Policy Research. https://ssrn.com/abstract=4121426

Blanc, A. K. (2001). The effect of power in sexual relationships on sexual and reproductive health: An examination of the evidence. *Studies in Family Planning*, *32*(3), 189–213. https://doi.org/10.1111/j.1728-4465.2001.00189.x

Blanchard, A. K., Prost, A., & Houweling, T. A. J. (2019). Effects of community health worker interventions on socioeconomic inequities in maternal and newborn health in low-income and middle-income countries: A mixed-methods systematic review. *BMJ Global Health*, *4*(3), Article e001308. https://doi.org/10.1136/bmjgh-2018-001308

Blaydes, L. (2023). Assessing the labor conditions of migrant domestic workers in the Arab gulf states. *ILR Review*, *76*(4), 724–747. https://doi.org/10.1177/00197939221147497

Bloom, D., Canning, D., & Sevilla, J. (2003). *The demographic dividend: A new perspective on the economic consequences of population change.* RAND. https://www.rand.org/pubs/monograph_reports/MR1274.html

Bloom, S. S., Wypij, D., & Das Gupta, M. (2001). Dimensions of women's autonomy and the influence on maternal health care utilization in a north Indian city. *Demography*, *38*, 67–78. https://doi.org/10.1353/dem.2001.0001

Blumenstock, J., & Eagle, N. (2010). Mobile divides: Gender, socioeconomic status, and mobile phone use in Rwanda. *ACM Int Conf Proc Ser. ICTD '10: Proceedings of the 4th ACM/IEEE International Conference on Information and Communication Technologies and Development*, Article 6. https://doi.org/10.1145/2369220.2369225

Boevink, W., Kroon, H., Delespaul, P., & Van Os, J. (2016). Empowerment according to persons with severe mental illness: Development of the Netherlands Empowerment List and its psychometric properties. *Open Journal of Psychiatry*, *7*(01), 18–30. http://dx.doi.org/10.4236/ojpsych.2017.71002

Bongaarts, J., & Guilmoto, C. Z. (2015). How many more missing women? Excess female mortality and prenatal sex selection, 1970–2050. *Population and Development Review*, *41*(2), 241–269. https://doi.org/10.1111/j.1728-4457.2015.00046.x

Bonilla, J., Zarzur, R. C., Handa, S., Nowlin, C., Peterman, A., Ring, H., & Seidenfeld, D. (2017). Cash for women's empowerment? A mixed-methods evaluation of the government of Zambia's Child Grant Program. *World Development*, *95*, 55–72. https://doi.org/10.1016/j.worlddev.2017.02.017

Bossuroy, T., Goldstein, M., Karimou, B., Karlan, D., Kazianga, H., Parienté, W., Premand, P., Thomas, C. C., Udry, C., Vaillant, J., & Wright, K. A. (2022). Tackling psychosocial and capital constraints to alleviate poverty. *Nature*, *605*(7909), 291–297. https://doi.org/10.1038/s41586-022-04647-8

Boyer, K. (2023). Sexual harassment and claiming the right to everyday life. *Activist Feminist Geographies*, *46*(2). http://dx.doi.org/10.1177/03091325211024340

Boyle, E. H., & Corl, A. C. (2010). Law and culture in a global context: Interventions to eradicate female genital cutting. *Annual Review of Law and Social Science*, *6*(1), 195–215.

Brassiolo, P. (2016). Domestic violence and divorce law: When divorce threats become credible. *Journal of Labor Economics*, *34*(2), 443–477. https://www.journals.uchicago.edu/doi/abs/10.1086/683666

Brody, C., De Hoop, T., Vojtkova, M., Warnock, R., Dunbar, M., Murthy, P., & Dworkin, S. L. (2015). Economic self-help group programs for improving women's empowerment: A systematic review. *Campbell Systematic Reviews*, *11*(1), 1–182. https://doi.org/10.4073/csr.2015.19

Bronfenbrenner, U. (1979). *The ecology of human development: Experiments by nature and design.* Harvard University Press.

___. (1986). Recent advances in research on the ecology of human development. In R. K. Silbereisen, K. Eyferth, & G. Rudinger (Eds.), *Development as action in context: Problem behavior and normal youth development* (pp. 287–309). Springer. https://doi.org/10.1007/978-3-662-02475-1_15

Brundtland, G. (1987). *Report of the World Commission on Environment and Development: Our common future* (Document No. A/42/427). United Nations General Assembly. http://www.un-documents.net/ocf-ov.htm

Bryan, E., Alvi, M., Huyer, S., & Ringler, C. (2023). *Addressing gender inequalities and strengthening women's agency to create more climate-resilient and sustainable food systems* (Impact Platform Working Paper No. 13). CGIAR GENDER Impact Platform. https://gender.cgiar.org/publications/addressing-gender-inequalities-and-strengthening-womens-agency-climate-resilient-and

Bryan, E., & Mekonnen, D. (2023). Does small-scale irrigation provide a pathway to women's empowerment? Lessons from Northern Ghana. *Journal of Rural Studies, 97*, 474–484. https://doi.org/10.1016/j.jrurstud.2022.12.035

Buchmann, N., Field, E. M., Glennerster, R., Nazneen, S., & Wang, X. Y. (2021). *A signal to end child marriage: Theory and experimental evidence from Bangladesh* (NBER Working Paper No. 29052). National Bureau of Economic Research. https://www.nber.org/papers/w29052

Buehren, N., Goldstein, M., Gulesci, S., Sulaiman, M., & Yam, V. (2017). *Evaluation of an adolescent development program for girls in Tanzania* (Working Paper No. 7961). The Working Bank. https://ssrn.com/abstract=2913320

Buller, A. M., Peterman, A., Ranganathan, M., Bleile, A., Hidrobo, M., & Heise, L. (2018). A mixed-method review of cash transfers and intimate partner violence in low- and middle-income countries. *The World Bank Research Observer, 33*(2), 218–258. https://doi.org/10.1093/wbro/lky002

Burke, E., Pyle, M., Machin, K., Varese, F., & Morrison, A. P. (2019). The effects of peer support on empowerment, self-efficacy, and internalized stigma: A narrative synthesis and meta-analysis. *Stigma and Health, 4*(3), 337–356. https://psycnet.apa.org/doi/10.1037/sah0000148

Cadenas, G. A., Liu, L., Li, K. M., & Beachy, S. (2022). Promoting critical consciousness, academic performance, and persistence among graduate students experiencing class-based oppression. *Journal of Diversity in Higher Education, 15*(1), 26–36. https://doi.org/10.1037/dhe0000250

Caldwell, J. C. (1979). Education as a factor in mortality decline: An examination of Nigerian data. *Population Studies, 33*(3), 395–413. https://doi.org/10.2307/2173888

Calvès, A. E. (2009). Empowerment: The history of a key concept in contemporary development. *Revue Tiers-Monde, 200*(4). https://www.researchgate.net/publication/282978215_Empowerment_The_History_of_a_Key_Concept_in_Contemporary_Development_Discourse

Calvi, R. (2020). Why are older women missing in India? The age profile of bargaining power and poverty. *Journal of Political Economy, 128*(7), 2453–2501. http://dx.doi.org/10.1086/706983

Campos, F., Frese, M., Goldstein, M., Iacovone, L., Johnson, H. C., McKenzie, D., & Mensmann, M. (2017). Teaching personal initiative beats traditional training in boosting small business in West Africa. *Science, 357*(6357), 1287–1290. https://doi.org/10.1126/science.aan5329

Carlson, G. J., Kordas, K., & Murray-Kolb, L. E. (2015). Associations between women's autonomy and child nutritional status: A review of the literature. *Maternal & Child Nutrition, 11*(4), 452–482. https://doi.org/10.1111/mcn.12113

Carranza, E. (2014). Soil endowments, female labor force participation, and the demographic deficit of women in India. *American Economic Journal: Applied Economics, 6*(4), 197–225. https://doi.org/10.1257/app.6.4.197

Carranza, E., Donald, A., Grosset, F., & Kaur, S. (2022). *The social tax: Redistributive pressure and labor supply* (NBER No. w30438). National Bureau of Economic Research. https://ssrn.com/abstract=4216224

Caruso, B. A., Conrad, A., Patrick, M., Owens, A., Kviten, K., Zarella, O., Rogers, H., & Sinharoy, S. S. (2022). Water, sanitation, and women's empowerment: A systematic review and qualitative metasynthesis. *PLoS Water, 1*, Article e0000026. https://doi.org/10.1371/journal.pwat.0000026

Cassidy, R., Bruinderink, M. G., Janssens, W., & Morsink, K. (2021). The power to protect: Household bargaining and female condom use. *Journal of Development Economics, 153*, Article 102745. https://doi.org/10.1016/j.jdeveco.2021.102745

Castilla, C. (2018). Political role models and child marriage in India. *Review of Development Economics, 22*(4), 1409–1431. https://doi.org/10.1111/rode.12513

Cavalcanti, T., & Tavares, J. (2016). The output cost of gender discrimination: A model-based macroeconomics estimate. *Economic Journal, 126*(590), 109–134. https://doi.org/10.1111/ecoj.12303

Centers for Disease Control and Prevention. (2024). *Improving social connectedness.* https://www.cdc.gov/social-connectedness/about/index.html

Chang, W., Diaz-Martin, L., Gopalan, A., Guarnieri, E., Jayachandran, S., & Walsh, C. (2020). *What works to enhance women's agency: Cross-cutting lessons from experimental and quasi-experimental studies* (J-PAL Working Paper No. 87). Abdul Latif Jameel Poverty Action Lab. https://www.povertyactionlab.org/sites/default/files/research-paper/gender_womens-agency-review_2020-march-05.pdf

Chao, F., Gerland, P., Cook, A. R., & Alkema, L. (2019). Systematic assessment of the sex ratio at birth for all countries and estimation of national imbalances and regional reference levels. *Proceedings of the National Academy of Sciences, 116*(19), 9303–9311. https://doi.org/10.1073/pnas.1812593116

Chatterjee, E., & Desai, S. (2019). Physical versus imagined communities: Migration and women's autonomy in India. *Journal of Ethnic and Migration Studies, 46*(14), 2977–2996. https://doi.org/10.1080/1369183X.2019.1585016

Chatterjee, E., Desai, S., & Vanneman, R. (2018). Indian paradox: Rising education, declining womens' employment. *Demographic Research, 38*, 855–878. https://doi.org/10.4054/DemRes.2018.38.31

Chatterji, S., Johns, N., Ghule, M., Begum, S., Averbach, S., Battala, M., & Raj, A. (2023). Examining the longitudinal relationship between intimate partner violence and couples' marital quality in rural India. *Journal of Family Violence, 38*(1), 139–148. https://doi.org/10.1007/s10896-022-00363-z

Chattopadhyay, R., & Duflo, E. (2004). Women as policy makers: Evidence from a randomized policy experiment in India. *Econometrica, 72*(5), 1409–1443. https://doi.org/10.1111/j.1468-0262.2004.00539.x

Chaturvedi, S. (2019). *Global evidence on the impact of center-based quality childcare on maternal employment and early childhood development outcomes* (IWWAGE Working Paper Series No. 1). Initiative for What Works to Advance Women and Girls in the Economy. https://iwwage.org/wp-content/uploads/2019/12/ChildcareseriesPaper1_compressed.pdf

Chiappori, P.-A. (1992). Collective labor supply and welfare. *Journal of Political Economy, 100*(3), 437–467. https://doi.org/10.1086/261825

———. (1997). Introducing household production in collective models of labor supply. *Journal of Political Economy, 105*(1), 191–209. https://doi.org/10.1086/262071

Chiappori, P.-A., Fortin, B., & Lacroix, G. (2002). Marriage market, divorce legislation, and household labor supply. *Journal of Political Economy, 110*(1), 37–72. https://doi.org/10.1086/324385

Chioda, L., Contreras-Loya, D., Gertler, P., & Carney, D. (2023). *Making entrepreneurs: The return to training youth in hard versus soft business skills* (CEDIL Research Project Paper No. 11). Centre of Excellence for Development Impact and Learning. https://doi.org/10.51744/CRPP11

Chiplunkar, G., & Goldberg, P. K. (2023). *Aggregate implications of barriers to female entrepreneurship* (NBER Working Paper No. 28486). National Bureau of Economic Research. https://ssrn.com/abstract=3790224

Chiplunkar, G., & Weaver, J. (2023). *Marriage markets and the rise of dowry in India* (IZA Discussion Paper No. 16135). IZA Institute of Labor Economics. http://dx.doi.org/10.2139/ssrn.4447097

Cho, S.-Y. (2018). A bride deficit and marriage migration in South Korea. *International Migration*, *56*(6), 100–119. https://doi.org/10.1111/imig.12432

Chowa, G. (2019). The next frontier for social development: Deepening our understanding, discovering new solutions, and forging ahead. *Global Social Welfare*, *6*, 1–3. https://doi.org/10.1007/s40609-019-00145-4

Christian, P. (2010). Impact of the economic crisis and increase in food prices on child mortality: Exploring nutritional pathways. *The Journal of Nutrition*, *140*(1), 177S–181S. https://doi.org/10.3945%2Fjn.109.111708

Clark, S. (2000). Son preference and sex composition of children: Evidence from India. *Demography*, *37*(1), 95–108. https://pubmed.ncbi.nlm.nih.gov/10748992/

Clark, S., Kabiru, C. W., Laszlo, S., & Muthuri, S. (2019). The impact of childcare on poor urban women's economic empowerment in Africa. *Demography*, *56*(4), 1247–1272. https://doi.org/10.1007/s13524-019-00793-3

Clarke, D., & Mühlrad, H. (2021). Abortion laws and women's health. *Journal of Health Economics*, *76*, Article 102413. https://doi.org/10.1016/j.jhealeco.2020.102413

Clarke, D. J., & Kumar, N. (2016). Microinsurance decisions: Gendered evidence from rural Bangladesh. *Gender, Technology and Development*, *20*(2), 218–241. http://dx.doi.org/10.1177/0971852416639784

Clayton, A. (2021). How do electoral gender quotas affect policy? *Annual Review of Political Science*, *24*, 235–252. https://doi.org/10.1146/annurev-polisci-041719-102019

Clemens, M. A. (2011). Economics and emigration: Trillion-dollar bills on the sidewalk? *Journal of Economic Perspectives*, *25*(3), 83–106. https://doi.org/10.1257/jep.25.3.83

Clots-Figueras, I. (2011). Women in politics: Evidence from the Indian States. *Journal of Public Economics*, *95*(7-8), 664–690. https://doi.org/10.1016/j.jpubeco.2010.11.017

Coale, A. J. (1991). Excess female mortality and the balance of the sexes in the population: An estimate of the number of "missing females." *Population and Development Review*, *17*(3), 517–523. https://doi.org/10.2307/1971953

Coale, A. J., & Banister, J. (1994). Five decades of missing females in China. *Demography*, *31*(3), 459–479. https://doi.org/10.2307/2061752

Coale, A. J., & Hoover, E. M. (1958). *Population growth and economic development in low-income countries: A case study of India's prospects*. Princeton University Press.

Coall, D. A., & Hertwig, R. (2010). Grandparental investment: Past, present, and future. *Behavioral and Brain Sciences*, *33*(1), 1–19. https://doi.org/10.1017/S0140525X09991105

Coffey, D., Hathi, P., Khurana, N., & Thorat, A. (2018). Explicit prejudice. *Economic and Political Weekly*, *53*(1), 46–54. https://www.epw.in/journal/2018/1/special-articles/explicit-prejudice.html

Coffey, D., Khera, R., & Spears, D. (2022). Mothers' social status and children's health: Evidence from joint households in rural India. *Demography*, *59*(5), 1981–2002. https://doi.org/10.1215/00703370-10217164

Cools, S., & Kotsadam, A. (2017). Resources and intimate partner violence in sub-Saharan Africa. *World Development*, *95*, 211–230. https://doi.org/10.1016/j.worlddev.2017.02.027

Corno, L., Hildebrandt, N., & Voena, A. (2020). Age of marriage, weather shocks, and the direction of marriage payments. *Econometrica*, *88*, 879–915. https://doi.org/10.3982/ECTA15505

Corno, L., & Voena, A. (2023). Child marriage as informal insurance: Empirical evidence and policy simulations. *Journal of Development Economics*, *162*, Article 103047. https://doi.org/10.1016/j.jdeveco.2023.103047

Crisman, B., Dykstra, S., Kenny, C., & O'Donnell, M. (2016). *The impact of legislation on the hazard of female genital mutilation/cutting: Regression discontinuity evidence from Burkina Faso* (Working Paper No. 432). Center for Global Development. https://www.cgdev.org/publication/impact-legislation-hazard-female-genital-mutilationcutting-regression-discontinuity

Croft, T. N., Allen, C. K., Zachary, B. W., et al. (2023). *Guide to DHS statistics*. ICF. https://dhsprogram.com/data/Guide-to-DHS-Statistics/index.cfm

Cuberes, D., & Teignier, M. (2014). Gender inequality and economic growth: A critical review. *Journal of International Development*, *26*(2), 260–276. https://doi.org/10.1002/jid.2983

___. (2016). Aggregate effects of gender gaps in the labor market: A quantitative estimate. *Journal of Human Capital*, *10*(1), 1–32. https://doi.org/10.1086/683847

Dahl, A. L. (2012). Human development: A vision of well-being. *International Environment Forum*. https://iefworld.org/ddahl12m

Dahlum, S., Knutsen, C. H., & Mechkova, V. (2022). Women's political empowerment and economic growth. *World Development*, *156*, Article 105822. https://doi.org/10.1016/j.worlddev.2022.105822

Dalal, K., Yasmin, M., Dahlqvist, H., & Klein, G. O. (2022). Do electronic and economic empowerment protect women from intimate partner violence (IPV) in India? *BMC Women's Health*, *22*(1). https://bmcwomenshealth.biomedcentral.com/articles/10.1186/s12905-022-02110-4

Das, S., Department of Public Health & Mortality Studies, & Singh, R. R. (2023). Does empowering women influence maternal healthcare service utilization? Evidence from National Family Health Survey-5, India. *Maternal and Child Health Journal*, *28*, 679–690. https://doi.org/10.1007/s10995-023-03823-0

Das Gupta, M. (1987). Selective discrimination against female children in rural Punjab, India. *Population and Development Review*, *13*(1), 77–100. https://doi.org/10.2307/1972121

Das Gupta, M., & Bhat, P. N. M. (1997). Fertility decline and increased manifestation of sex bias in India. *Population Studies*, *51*(3), 307–315. https://doi.org/10.1080/0032472031000150076

Das Gupta, M., Zhenghua, J., Bohua, L., Zhenming, X., Chung, W., & Hwa-Ok, B. (2003). Why is son preference so persistent in East and South Asia? A cross-country study of China, India and the Republic of Korea. *Journal of Development Studies*, *40*(2), 153–187. http://dx.doi.org/10.1080/00220380412331293807

De Azevedo, T. A., Davis, J., & Charles, M. (2013). *Testing "What Works in Youth Employment": Evaluating Kenya's Ninaweza Program*. International Youth Foundation.

de Barros, R. P., Olinto, P., Lunde, T., & Caralho, M. (2013). *The impact of access to free childcare on women's labor market outcomes: Evidence from a randomized trial in low-income neighborhoods of Rio de Janeiro*. EnGender Impact, The World Bank. http://documents.worldbank.org/curated/en/672391468231860498/The-impact-of-access-to-free-childcare-on-womens-labor-market-outcomes-evidence-from-a-randomized-trial-in-low-income-neighborhoods-of-Rio-de-Janeiro

de Brauw, A., Gilligan, D. O., Hoddinott, J., & Roy, S. (2014). The impact of Bolsa Família on women's decision-making power. *World Development*, *59*, 487–504. https://doi.org/10.1016/j.worlddev.2013.02.003

de Brauw, A., & Peterman, A. (2020). Can conditional cash transfers improve maternal health care? Evidence from El Salvador's Comunidades Solidarias Rurales program. *Health Economics, 29*(6), 700–715. https://doi.org/10.1002/hec.4012

Deci, E. L., & Ryan, R. M. (1991). A motivational approach to self: Integration in personality. In R. A. Dienstbier (Ed.), *Nebraska Symposium on Motivation, 1990: Perspectives on motivation* (pp. 237–288). University of Nebraska Press.

Decker, M. R., Wood, S. N., Ndinda, E., Yenokyan, G., Sinclair, J., Maksud, N., Ross, B., Omondi, B., & Ndirangu, M. (2018). Sexual violence among adolescent girls and young women in Malawi: A cluster-randomized controlled implementation trial of empowerment self-defense training. *BMC Public Health, 18*(1), Article 1341. https://doi.org/10.1186/s12889-018-6220-0

DeGue, S., Valle, L. A., Holt, M. K., Massetti, G. M., Matjasko, J. L., & Tharp, A. T. (2014). A systematic review of primary prevention strategies for sexual violence perpetration. *Aggression and Violent Behavior, 19*(4), 346–362. https://doi.org/10.1016/j.avb.2014.05.004

De Hoop, J., Premand, P., Rosati, F., & Vakis, R. (2018). Women's economic capacity and children's human capital accumulation. *Journal of Population Economics, 31*(2), 453–481. https://doi.org/10.1007/s00148-017-0656-x

Deininger, K., Goyal, A., & Nagarajan, H. (2013). *Inheritance law reform and women's access to capital evidence from India's Hindu Succession Act* (The World Bank Policy Research Working Paper No. 5338). The World Bank. https://ssrn.com/abstract=1625154

Deininger, K., Nagarajan, H. K., & Singh, S. K. (2020). Women's political leadership and economic empowerment: Evidence from public works in India. *Journal of Comparative Economics, 48*(2), 277–291. https://doi.org/10.1016/j.jce.2019.12.003

Delavallade, C., Dizon, F., Hill, R. V., & Petraud, J. P. (2015). *Managing risk with insurance and savings: Experimental evidence for male and female farm managers in the Sahel* (The World Bank Policy Research Working Paper No. 7176). The World Bank. http://documents.worldbank.org/curated/en/684751524225397389

Delea, M., Sinharoy, S., Cheong, Y. F., Heckert, J., Seymour, G., Meinzen-Dick, R. S., & Yount, K. M. (2021). *The Group-Related Collective Agency Scales (GCAS 23 and GCAS-12)–Full and short form scales for construct measurement.* https://dx.doi.org/10.2139/ssrn.4004711

De Neve, J.-E., & Sachs, J. D. (2020). Chapter 6: Sustainable development and human well-being. In J. F. Helliwell, R. Layard, J. D. Sachs, & J. E. De Neve (Eds.), *World happiness report 2020.* Sustainable Development Solutions Network. https://worldhappiness.report/ed/2020/sustainable-development-and-human-well-being/

De Pinto, A., Seymour, G., Bryan, E., & Bhandari, P. (2020). Women's empowerment and farmland allocations in Bangladesh: Evidence of a possible pathway to crop diversification. *Climatic Change, 163*, 1025–1043. https://doi.org/10.1007/s10584-020-02925-w

Desai, M. A. (2010). *Hope in hard times: Women's empowerment and human development* (UNDP-HDRO Occasional Papers No. 2010/14). https://ssrn.com/abstract=2351509

Desai, S., & Alva, S. (1998). Maternal education and child health: Is there a strong causal relationship? *Demography, 35*(1), 71–81. https://pubmed.ncbi.nlm.nih.gov/9512911/

Desai, S., & Andrist, L. (2010). Gender scripts and age at marriage in India. *Demography, 47*(3), 667–687. https://doi.org/10.1353%2Fdem.0.0118

Desai, S., & Johnson, K. (2005). Women's decisionmaking and child health: Familial and social hierarchies. In S. Kishor (Ed.), *A focus on gender.* ORC Macro.

Devereux, S. (2001). Livelihood insecurity and social protection: A re-emerging issue in rural development. *Development Policy Review, 19*(4), 507–519. https://library.fes.de/libalt/journals/swetsfulltext/12093123.pdf

Dey, A., Singh, G., & Gupta, A. K. (2018). Women and climate stress: Role reversal from beneficiaries to expert participants. *World Development*, *103*, 336–359. https://doi.org/10.1016/j.worlddev.2017.07.026

Dharmalingam, A., & Philip Morgan, S. (1996). Women's work, autonomy, and birth control: Evidence from two South Indian villages. *Population Studies*, *50*(2), 187–201. https://doi.org/10.1080/0032472031000149296

Diemer, M. A., Rapa, L. J., Park, C. J., & Perry, J. C. (2017). Development and validation of the Critical Consciousness Scale. *Youth & Society*, *49*(4), 461–483. https://doi.org/10.1177/0044118X14538289

Diop, N. J., & Askew, I. (2009). The effectiveness of a community-based education program on abandoning female genital mutilation/cutting in Senegal. *Studies in Family Planning*, *40*(4), 307–318. https://doi.org/10.1111/j.1728-4465.2009.00213.x

Doepke, M., & Tertilt, M. (2019). Does female empowerment promote economic development? *Journal of Economic Growth*, *24*, 309–343. https://doi.org/10.1007/s10887-019-09172-4

Donald, A., Goldstein, M., & Rouanet, L. (2022). *Two heads are better than one: Agricultural production and investment in Côte D'Ivoire* (The World Bank Policy Research Working Paper No. 10047). The World Bank. https://doi.org/10.1596/1813-9450-10047

Donald, A., Koolwal, G., Annan, J., Falb, K., & Goldstein, M. (2017). *Measuring women's agency* (The World Bank Policy Research Working Paper No. 8148). SSRN. https://ssrn.com/abstract=3006222

___. (2020). Measuring women's agency. *Feminist Economics*, *26*(3), 200–226. https://doi.org/10.1080/13545701.2019.1683757

Donald, A., Lowes, S., & Vaillant, J. (2023). *Experimental evidence on rural childcare provision*. https://conference.nber.org/conf_papers/f203417.pdf

Donald, A. A., Goldstein, M., Koroknay-Palicz, T., & Sage, M. (2024). *The fertility impacts of development programs* (Impact Evaluation Series Policy Research Working Paper). The World Bank. http://documents.worldbank.org/curated/en/099518407102437684/IDU1699f7acb16ca614fe4199601d8d3c9a94a76

Donato, K. M., Alexander, J. T., Gabaccia, D. R., & Leinonen, J. (2011). Variations in the gender composition of immigrant populations: How they matter. *International Migration Review*, *45*(3), 495–526. https://doi.org/10.1111/j.1747-7379.2011.00856.x

Dong, X. (2022). Intrahousehold property ownership, women's bargaining power, and family structure. *Labour Economics*, *78*, Article 102239. https://doi.org/10.1016/j.labeco.2022.102239

Doss, C. R. (1996). Testing among models of intrahousehold resource allocation. *World Development*, *24*(10), 1597–1609. https://doi.org/10.1016/0305-750X(96)00063-0

___. (2013). *Intrahousehold bargaining and resource allocation in developing countries* (The World Bank Working Paper No. 6337). The World Bank. https://documents1.worldbank.org/curated/en/701071468155969077/pdf/wps6337.pdf

Dovis, M., Augier, P., & Sadania, C. (2021). Labor market shocks and youths' time allocation in Egypt: Where does women's empowerment come in? *Economic Development and Cultural Change*, *69*(4), 1501–1540. https://doi.org/10.1086/705713

Doyle, K., Levtov, R. G., Barker, G., Bastian, G. G., Bingenheimer, J. B., Kazimbaya, S., Nzabonimpa, A., Pulerwitz, J., Sayinzoga, F., Sharma, V., & Shattuck, D. (2018). Gender-transformative Bandebereho couples' intervention to promote male engagement in reproductive and maternal health and violence prevention in Rwanda: Findings from a randomized controlled trial. *PLOS One*, *13*(4). https://doi.org/10.1371/journal.pone.0192756

Doyle, K., Levtov, R. G., Karamage, E., Rakshit, D., Kazimbaya, S., Sayinzoga, F., Sibomana, H., Ngayaboshya, S., Rutayisire, F., & Barker, G. (2023). Long-term impacts of the Bandebereho programme on violence against women and children, maternal health-seeking, and couple relations in Rwanda: A six-year follow-up of a randomised controlled trial. *eClinicalMedicine*, *64*. https://doi.org/10.1016/j.eclinm.2023.102233

Duflo, E. (2003). Grandmothers and granddaughters: Old-age pensions and intrahousehold allocation in South Africa. *The World Bank Economic Review*, *17*(1), 1–25. https://doi.org/10.1093/wber/lhg013

___. (2012). Women empowerment and economic development. *Journal of Economic Literature*, *50*(4), 1051–1079. https://doi.org/10.1257/jel.50.4.1051

Duflo, E., Dupas, P., & Kremer, M. (2015). Education, HIV, and early fertility: Experimental evidence from Kenya. *American Economic Review*, *105*(9), 2757–2797. https://doi.org/10.1257/aer.20121607

Duflo, E., Dupas, P., Spelke, E., & Walsh, M. (2024). *Intergenerational impacts of secondary education: Experimental evidence from Ghana* (Working Paper). The American Economic Association. https://www.nber.org/papers/w32742

Dupas, P. (2011). Do teenagers respond to HIV risk information? Evidence from a field experiment in Kenya. *American Economic Journal: Applied Economics*, *3*(1), 1–34. https://doi.org/10.1257/app.3.1.1

Dupas, P., & Jain, R. (2024). *Women left behind: Gender disparities in utilization of government health insurance in India* (NBER Working Paper No. 28972). National Bureau of Economic Research. https://ssrn.com/abstract=3875139

Dupas, P., & Robinson, J. (2013). Why don't the poor save more? Evidence from health savings experiments. *American Economic Review*, *103*(4), 1138–1171. https://doi.org/10.1257/aer.103.4.1138

Duvendack, M., & Mader, P. (2020). Impact of financial inclusion in low- and middle-income countries: A systematic review of reviews. *Journal of Economic Surveys*, *34*(3), 594–629. https://doi.org/10.4073/csr.2019.2

Dyson, T., & Moore, M. (1983). On kinship structure, female autonomy, and demographic behavior in India. *Population and Development Review*, *9*(1), 35–60. https://doi.org/10.2307/1972894

Edmeades, J., Hinson, L., Sebany, M., & Murithi, L. (2018). *A conceptual framework for reproductive empowerment: Empowering individuals and couples to improve their health* [Issue Brief]. International Center for Research on Women. https://www.icrw.org/wp-content/uploads/2018/10/ICRW_ReproEmpowerment_ConceptualFramework_Brief_WebReady_v14.pdf

Edmonds, E. V., Feigenberg, B., & Leight, J. (2023). Advancing the agency of adolescent girls. *The Review of Economics and Statistics*, *105*(4), 852–866. https://doi.org/10.1162/rest_a_01074

Eger, C., Miller, G., & Scarles, C. (2018). Gender and capacity building: A multi-layered study of empowerment. *World Development*, *106*, 207–219. https://doi.org/10.1016/j.worlddev.2018.01.024

Eggers del Campo, I., & Steinert, J. I. (2022). The effect of female economic empowerment interventions on the risk of intimate partner violence: A systematic review and meta-analysis. *Trauma, Violence, & Abuse*, *23*(3), 810–826. https://doi.org/10.1177/1524838020976088

Elder, G. H., Jr. (1995). The life course paradigm: Social change and individual development. In P. Moen, G. H. Elder, Jr., & K. K. Lüscher (Eds.), *Examining lives in context: Perspectives on the ecology of human development* (pp. 101–139). American Psychological Association. https://doi.org/10.1037/10176-003

Engle, P. L., Scrimshaw, S. C. M., & Smidt, R. (1984). Sex differences in attitudes towards new-born infants among women of Mexican origin. *Medical Anthropology*, *8*(2), 133–144. https://doi.org/10.1080/01459740.1984.9965897

Evans, A., & Nambiar, D. (2013). *Collective action and women's agency: A background paper* (The World Bank Working Paper No. 92758). The World Bank. https://documents1.worldbank.org/curated/en/511631468154151855/pdf/927580NWP0Wome00Box38535 8B00PUBLIC0.pdf

Ewerling, F., Raj, A., Victora, C. G., Hellwig, F., Coll, C. V., & Barros, A. J. (2020). SWPER Global: A survey-based women's empowerment index expanded from Africa to all low- and middle-income countries. *Journal of Global Health*, *10*(2). https://doi.org/10.7189/jogh.10.020434

Ezenwaka, U., Manzano, A., Onyedinma, C., Ogbozor, P., Agbawodikeizu, U., Etiaba, E., Ensor, T., Onwujekwe, O., Ebenso, B., Uzochukwu, B., & Mirzoev, T. (2021). Influence of conditional cash transfers on the uptake of maternal and child health services in Nigeria: Insights from a mixed-methods study. *Frontiers in Public Health*, *9*. https://doi.org/10.3389/fpubh.2021.670534

Fafchamps, M., Kebede, B., & Quisumbing, A. R. (2009). Intrahousehold welfare in rural Ethiopia. *Oxford Bulletin of Economics and Statistics*, *71*(4), 567–599. https://doi.org/10.1111/j.1468-0084.2009.00553.x

Farnworth, C. R., Hà, T. T., Sander, B. O., Wollenberg, E., De Haan, N. C., & McGuire, S. (2017). Incorporating gender into low-emission development: A case study from Vietnam. *Gender, Technology and Development*, *21*(1-2), 5–30. https://doi.org/10.1080/0971852 4.2017.1385314

Farnsworth, S. K., Böse, K., Fajobi, O., Souza, P. P., Peniston, A., Davidson, L. L., Griffiths, M., & Hodgins, S. (2014). Community engagement to enhance child survival and early development in low-and middle-income countries: An evidence review. *Journal of Health Communication*, *19*, 67–88. https://doi.org/10.1080/10810730.2014.941519

Fatehkia, M., Kashyap, R., & Weber, I. (2018) Using Facebook ad data to track the global digital gender gap. *World Development*, *107*, 189–209. https://doi.org/10.1016/j.worlddev.2018.03.007

Fawole, O. I., & Adeoye, I. A. (2015). Women's status within the household as a determinant of maternal health care use in Nigeria. *African Health Sciences*, *15*(1), 217–225. https://doi.org/10.4314/ahs.v15i1.28

Feldman, B. S., Zaslavsky, A. M., Ezzati, M., Peterson, K. E., & Mitchell, M. (2009). Contraceptive use, birth spacing, and autonomy: An analysis of the Oportunidades program in rural Mexico. *Studies in Family Planning*, *40*(1), 51–62. https://doi.org/10.1111/j.1728-4465.2009.00186.x

Ferrant, G., & Tuccio, M. (2015). South–south migration and discrimination against women in social institutions: A two-way relationship. *World Development*, *72*, 240–254. https://doi.org/10.1016/j.worlddev.2015.03.002

Ferrant, G., Tuccio, M., Loiseau, E., & Nowacka, K. (2014). *The role of discriminatory social institutions in female South-South migration* (OECD Report). The Organisation for Economic Co-operation and Development. https://doi.org/10.1787/45d3a024-en

Fiala, N., Garcia-Hernandez, A., Narula, K., & Prakash, N. (2022). *Wheels of change: Transforming girls' lives with bicycles* (CESifo Working Paper No. 9865). CESifo Group. https://www.cesifo.org/DocDL/cesifo1_wp9865.pdf

Field, E., Jayachandran, S., & Pande, R. (2010). Do traditional institutions constrain female entrepreneurship? A field experiment on business training in India. *American Economic Review*, *100*(2), 125–129. https://doi.org/10.1257/aer.100.2.125

Field, E., Pande, R., Rigol, N., Schaner, S., & Moore, C. T. (2021). On her own account: How strengthening women's financial control impacts labor supply and gender norms. *American Economic Review*, *111*(7), 2342–2375. https://doi.org/10.1257/aer.20200705

Finlay, J. E., & Lee, M. A. (2018). Identifying causal effects of reproductive health improvements on women's economic empowerment through the population poverty research initiative. *The Milbank Quarterly*, *96*(2), 300–322. https://doi.org/10.1111/1468-0009.12326

Flake, D. F. (2005). Individual, family, and community risk markers for domestic violence in Peru. *Violence Against Women*, *11*(3), 353–373. https://doi.org/10.1177/1077801204272129

Fleming, P. J., Silverman, J., Ghule, M., Ritter, J., Battala, M., Velhal, G., Nair, S., Dasgupta, A., Donta, B., Saggurti, N., & Raj, A. (2018). Can a gender equity and family planning intervention for men change their gender ideology? Results from the CHARM intervention in rural India. *Studies in Family Planning*, *49*(1), 41–56. https://doi.org/10.1111/sifp.12047

Folbre, N. (1995). Engendering economics: New perspectives on women, work, and demographic change. In M. Bruno & B. Pleskovic (Eds.), *Proceedings of the Annual World Bank conference on development economics* (pp. 127–153). The World Bank. http://documents.worldbank.org/curated/en/887251468764143753

Foner, N. (2009). Gender and migration: West Indians in comparative perspective. *International Migration*, *47*(1), 3–29. https://doi.org/10.1111/j.1468-2435.2008.00480.x

Food and Agriculture Organization. (2023). *The status of women in agrifood systems*. The United Nations. https://doi.org/10.4060/cc5343en

Forsyth, S., & Ward, K. P. (2022). Media use and men's approval of intimate partner violence in Honduras. *Journal of Interpersonal Violence*, *37*(13–14), NP11541–NP11556. https://doi.org/10.1177/0886260521993926

Frankenberger, T., Mueller, M., Spangler, T., & Alexander, S. (2013). *Community resilience: Conceptual framework and measurement feed the future learning agenda* [Issue Brief]. https://agrilinks.org/sites/default/files/resource/files/FTF%20Learning_Agenda_Community_Resilience_Oct%202013.pdf

Freire, P. (1978). Pedagogy of the oppressed. In J. Beck, C. Jenks, & N. Keddie (Eds.), *Toward a sociology of education*. Routledge. https://www.taylorfrancis.com/chapters/edit/10.4324/9780429339530-34/pedagogy-oppressed-paulo-freire

Friedemann-Sánchez, G. (2006). Assets in intrahousehold bargaining among women workers in Colombia's cut-flower industry. *Feminist Economics*, *12*(1–2), 247–269. https://doi.org/10.1080/13545700500508551

Fujiwara, T. (2015). Voting technology, political responsiveness, and infant health: Evidence from Brazil. *Econometrica*, *83*(2), 423–464. https://doi.org/10.3982/ECTA11520

Fukuda-Parr, S. (2003). The human development paradigm, operationalizing Sen's ideas on capabilities. *Feminist Economics*, *9*(2–3), 301–317. https://doi.org/10.1080/135457002 2000077980

Fukuyama, F. (2001). Social capital, civil society and developme. *Third World Quarterly*, *22*(1), 7–20. https://doi.org/10.1080/713701144

Galiè, A., & Farnworth, C. R. (2019). Power through: A new concept in the empowerment discourse. *Global Food Security*, *21*, 13–17. https://doi.org/10.1016/j.gfs.2019.07.001

Galvin, L., Verissimo, C. K., Ambikapathi, R., Gunaratna, N. S., Rudnicka, P., Sunseri, A., Jeong, J., O'Malley, S. F., Yousafzai, A. K., Sando, M. M., Mosha, D., Kumalija, E., Connolly, H., PrayGod, G., Endyke-Doran, C., & Kieffer, M. P. (2023). Effects of engaging fathers and bundling nutrition and parenting interventions on household gender equality and women's empowerment in rural Tanzania: Results from EFFECTS, a five-arm cluster-randomized controlled trial. *Social Science & Medicine*, *324*, Article 115869. https://doi.org/10.1016/j.socscimed.2023.115869

Gammage, S., Kabeer, N., & van der Meulen Rodgers, Y. (2016). Voice and agency: Where are we now? *Feminist Economics*, 22(1), 1–29. https://doi.org/10.1080/13545701.2015.1101308

García-Moreno, C., Pallitto, C., Devries, K., Stöckl, H., Watts, C., & Abrahams, N. (2013). *Global and regional estimates of violence against women: Prevalence and health effects of intimate partner violence and non-partner sexual violence.* World Health Organization. https://iris.who.int/bitstream/handle/10665/85239/9789241564625_eng.pdf?sequence=1

Gardner, N., Cui, J., & Coiacetto, E. (2017). Harassment on public transport and its impacts on women's travel behaviour. *Australian Planner*, 54(1), 8–15. https://doi.org/10.1080/07293682.2017.1299189

Garg, P., Das, M., Goyal, L. D., & Verma, M. (2021). Trends and correlates of intimate partner violence experienced by ever-married women of India: Results from National Family Health Survey round III and IV. *BMC Public Health*, 21, Article 2012. https://doi.org/10.1186/s12889-021-12028-5

Garikipati, S. (2008). The impact of lending to women on household vulnerability and women's empowerment: Evidence from India. *World Development*, 36(12), 2620–2642. https://doi.org/10.1016/j.worlddev.2007.11.008

Garro, L. (2000). Remembering what one knows and the construction of the past: A comparison of cultural consensus theory and cultural schema theory. *Ethos*, 28, 275–319. https://doi.org/10.1525/eth.2000.28.3.275

Gasper, D. (1997). Sen's capability approach and Nussbaum's capabilities ethic. *Journal of International Development*, 9(2), 281–302. https://doi.org/10.1002/(SICI)1099-1328(199703)9:2%3C281::AID-JID438%3E3.0.CO;2-K

Gewirth, A. (1992). Human dignity as the basis of rights. In M. J. Meyer & W. A. Parent (Eds.), *The constitution of rights* (pp. 10–28). Cornell University Press. https://doi.org/10.7591/9781501737213-003

Ghanotakis, E., Hoke, T., Wilcher, R., Field, S., Mercer, S., Bobrow, E. A., Namubiru, M., Katirayi, L. & Mandera, I. (2017). Evaluation of a male engagement intervention to transform gender norms and improve family planning and HIV service uptake in Kabale, Uganda. *Global Public Health*, 12(10), 1297–1314. https://doi.org/10.1080/17441692.2016.1168863

Ghurye, G. S. (1955). *Family and kin in Indo-European culture.* Oxford University Press. https://archive.org/details/in.gov.ignca.4182/page/n8/mode/1up

Gibbs, A., & Hatcher, A. (2020). Covert family planning as a symbol of agency for young, married women. *EClinicalMedicine*, 23, Article 100393. https://doi.org/10.1016/j.eclinm.2020.100393

Gichuru, W., Ojha, S., Smith, S., Smyth, A. R., & Szatkowski, L. (2019). Is microfinance associated with changes in women's well-being and children's nutrition? A systematic review and meta-analysis. *BMJ Open*, 9(1). https://doi.org/10.1136/bmjopen-2018-023658

Gitter, S. R., & Barham, B. L. (2008). Women's power, conditional cash transfers, and schooling in Nicaragua. *The World Bank Economic Review*, 22(2), 271–290. https://doi.org/10.1093/wber/lhn006

Givord, P., & Marbot, C. (2015). Does the cost of child care affect female labor market participation? An evaluation of a French reform of childcare subsidies. *Labour Economics*, 36, 99–111. https://doi.org/10.1016/j.labeco.2015.07.003

Glaub, M. E., Frese, M., Fischer, S., & Hoppe, M. (2014). Increasing personal initiative in small business managers or owners leads to entrepreneurial success: A theory-based controlled randomized field intervention for evidence-based management. *Academy of Management Learning & Education*, 13(3), 354–379. https://doi.org/10.5465/amle.2013.0234

Goldstein, M., Gonzalez, P., Papineni, S., & Wimpey, J. (2022). *Childcare, COVID-19 and female firm exit: Impact of COVID-19 school closure policies on global gender gaps in business outcomes* (The World Bank Working Paper No. 10012). The World Bank. http://documents.worldbank.org/curated/en/099801504202219533

González, L., & Viitanen, T. K. (2009). The effect of divorce laws on divorce rates in Europe. *European Economic Review, 53*(2), 127–138. https://doi.org/10.1016/j.euroecorev.2008.05.005

Gourlay, A., Floyd, S., Magut, F., Mulwa, S., Mthiyane, N., Wambiya, E., Otieno, M., Kamire, V., Osindo, J., & Chimbindi, N. (2022). Impact of the DREAMS Partnership on social support and general self-efficacy among adolescent girls and young women: Causal analysis of population-based cohorts in Kenya and South Africa. *BMJ Global Health, 7*(3). https://doi.org/10.1136/bmjgh-2021-006965

Graham, L. M., Ranapurwala, S. I., Zimmer, C., Macy, R. J., Rizo, C. F., Lanier, P., & Martin, S. L. (2021). Disparities in potential years of life lost due to intimate partner violence: Data from 16 states for 2006–2015. *PLOS One, 16*(2). https://doi.org/10.1371/journal.pone.0246477

Gram, L., Morrison, J., & Skordis-Worrall, J. (2019). Organising concepts of "women's empowerment" for measurement: A typology. *Social Indicators Research, 143*(3), 1349–1376. https://doi.org/10.1007/s11205-018-2012-2

Gray, J. (2014). Scales of cultural influence: Malawian consumption of foreign media. *Media, Culture & Society, 36*, 982–997. https://doi.org/10.1177/016344371453608

Green, E. P., Blattman, C., Jamison, J., & Annan, J. (2015). Women's entrepreneurship and intimate partner violence: A cluster randomized trial of microenterprise assistance and partner participation in post-conflict Uganda (SSM-D-14-01580R1). *Social Science & Medicine, 133*, 177–188. https://doi.org/10.1016/j.socscimed.2015.03.042

Grépin, K. A., & Bharadwaj, P. (2015). Maternal education and child mortality in Zimbabwe. *Journal of Health Economics, 44*, 97–117. https://doi.org/10.1016/j.jhealeco.2015.08.003

Grillos, T. (2018). Women's participation in environmental decision-making: Quasi-experimental evidence from northern Kenya. *World Development, 108*, 115–130. https://doi.org/10.1016/j.worlddev.2018.03.017

Grogan, L. (2023). Manufacturing employment and women's agency: Evidence from Lesotho 2004–2014. *Journal of Development Economics, 160*, Article 102951. https://doi.org/10.1016/j.jdeveco.2022.102951

Groysberg, B. (2010). *Chasing stars: The myth of talent and the portability of performance.* Princeton University Press. https://archive.org/details/chasingstarsmyth0000groy

Guha, M., Baschieri, A., Bharat, S., Bhatnagar, T., Sane, S. S., Godbole, S. V., Saravanamurthy, P. S., Mainkar, M. K., Williams, J., & Collumbien, M. (2012). Risk reduction and perceived collective efficacy and community support among female sex workers in Tamil Nadu and Maharashtra, India: The importance of context. *Journal of Epidemiology & Community Health, 66*(Suppl. 2), 55–61. https://doi.org/10.1136/jech-2011-200562

Guirkinger, C., Gross, J., & Platteau, J. P. (2021). Are women emancipating? Evidence from marriage, divorce and remarriage in rural northern Burkina Faso. *World Development, 146*, Article 105512. https://doi.org/10.1016/j.worlddev.2021.105512

Gurbuz Cuneo, A., Vaillant, J., Koussoubé, E., Pierotti, R. S., Falb, K., & Kabeya, R. (2023). Prevention, cessation, or harm reduction: Heterogeneous effects of an intimate partner violence prevention program in eastern Democratic Republic of the Congo. *PLOS One, 18*(3). https://doi.org/10.1371/journal.pone.0282339

Gurrieri, L., Prothero, A., Bettany, S., Dobscha, S., Drenten, J., Ferguson, S., Finkelstein, S., McVey, L., Ourahmoune, N., Steinfield, L., & Zayer, L. T. (2022). Feminist academic organizations: Challenging sexism through collective mobilizing across research, support, and advocacy. *Gender, Work & Organization*, 1–22. https://doi.org/10.1111/gwao.12912

Hahn, Y., Islam, A., Nuzhat, K., Smyth, R., & Yang, H. S. (2018). Education, marriage, and fertility: Long-term evidence from a female stipend program in Bangladesh. *Economic Development and Cultural Change, 66*(2), 383–415. http://dx.doi.org/10.1086/694930

Halim, N., Yount, K. M., Cunningham, S. A., & Pande, R. P. (2016). Women's political empowerment and investments in primary schooling in India. *Social Indicators Research*, *125*(3), 813–851. https://doi.org/10.1007/s11205-015-0870-4

Hallfors, D., Cho, H., Rusakaniko, S., Iritani, B., Mapfumo, J., & Halpern, C. (2011). Supporting adolescent orphan girls to stay in school as HIV risk prevention: Evidence from a randomized controlled trial in Zimbabwe. *American Journal of Public Health*, *101*(6), 1082–1088. https://doi.org/10.2105/ajph.2010.300042

Hallward-Driemeier, M., & Gajigo, O. (2015). Strengthening economic rights and women's occupational choice: The impact of reforming Ethiopia's family law. *World Development*, *70*(C), 260–273. https://doi.org/10.1016/j.worlddev.2015.01.008

Handa, S., Halpern, C. T., Pettifor, A., & Thirumurthy, H. (2014). The government of Kenya's cash transfer program reduces the risk of sexual debut among young people age 15-25. *PLOS One*, *9*(1). https://doi.org/10.1371/journal.pone.0085473

Handa, S., Palermo, T., Rosenberg, M., Pettifor, A., Halpern, C. T., & Thirumurthy, H. (2017). How does a national poverty programme influence sexual debut among Kenyan adolescents? *Global Public Health*, *12*(5), 617–638. https://doi.org/10.1080/17441692.2015. 1134617

Handa, S., Peterman, A., Davis, B., & Stampini, M. (2009). Opening up Pandora's box: The effect of gender targeting and conditionality on household spending behavior in Mexico's Progresa program. *World Development*, *37*(6), 1129–1142. https://doi.org/10.1016/j. worlddev.2008.10.005

Handa, S., Peterman, A., Huang, C., Halpern, C., Pettifor, A., & Thirumurthy, H. (2015). Impact of the Kenya cash transfer for orphans and vulnerable children on early pregnancy and marriage of adolescent girls. *Social Science and Medicine*, *141*, 36–45. https://doi. org/10.1016/j.socscimed.2015.07.024

Haque, R., Alam, K., Rahman, S. M., Keramet, S. A., & Al-Hanawi, M. K. (2021). Women's empowerment and fertility decision-making in 53 low and middle resource countries: A pooled analysis of demographic and health surveys. *BMJ Open*, *11*(6). https://doi. org/10.1136/bmjopen-2020-045952

Harris-Fry, H. A., Azad, K., Younes, L., Kuddus, A., Shaha, S., Nahar, T., Hossen, M., Costello, A., & Fottrell, E. (2016). Formative evaluation of a participatory women's group intervention to improve reproductive and women's health outcomes in rural Bangladesh: A controlled before and after study. *Journal of Epidemiology & Community Health*, *70*(7), 663–670. https://doi.org/10.1136/jech-2015-205855

Hathi, P., Coffey, D., Thorat, A., & Khalid, N. (2021). When women eat last: Discrimination at home and women's mental health. *PLOS One*, *16*(3). https://doi.org/10.1371/journal. pone.0247065

Hay, K., McDougal, L., Percival, V., Henry, S., Klugman, J., Wurie, H., Raven, J., Shabalala, F., Fielding-Miller, R., Dey, A., Dehingia, N., Morgan, R., Atmavilas, Y., Saggurti, N., Yore, J., Blokhina, E., Huque, R., Barasa, E., Bhan, N., Kharel, C., ... Gender Equality, Norms, and Health Steering Committee. (2019). Disrupting gender norms in health systems: Making the case for change. *Lancet*, *393*(10190), 2535–2549. https://doi.org/10.1016/ S0140-6736(19)30648-8

Heath, R. (2014). Women's access to labor market opportunities, control of household resources, and domestic violence: Evidence from Bangladesh. *World Development*, *57*, 32–46. https://doi.org/10.1016/j.worlddev.2013.10.028

Heath, R., & Jayachandran, S. (2016). *The causes and consequences of increased female education and labor force participation in developing countries* (NBER Working Paper No. 22766). National Bureau of Economic Research. https://www.nber.org/system/files/ working_papers/w22766/w22766.pdf

Heath, R., & Mobarak, A. M. (2015). Manufacturing growth and the lives of Bangladeshi women. *Journal of Development Economics*, *115*, 1–15. https://doi.org/10.1016/j.jdeveco.2015.01.006

Heath, R., & Tan, X. (2018). Worth fighting for: Daughters improve their mothers' autonomy in south Asia. *Journal of Development Economics*, *135*, 255–271. https://doi.org/10.1016/j.jdeveco.2018.07.003

___. (2020). Intrahousehold bargaining, female autonomy, and labor supply: Theory and evidence from India. *Journal of the European Economic Association*, *18*(4), 1928–1968. https://doi.org/10.1093/jeea/jvz026

Heck, C. J., Grilo, S. A., Song, X., Lutalo, T., Nakyanjo, N., & Santelli, J. S. (2018). "It is my business": A mixed-methods analysis of covert contraceptive use among women in Rakai, Uganda. *Contraception*, *98*(1), 41–46. https://doi.org/10.1016/j.contraception.2018.02.017

Heckert, J., Olney, D. K., & Ruel, M. T. (2019). Is women's empowerment a pathway to improving child nutrition outcomes in a nutrition-sensitive agriculture program? Evidence from a randomized controlled trial in Burkina Faso. *Social Science & Medicine*, *233*, 93–102. https://doi.org/10.1016/j.socscimed.2019.05.016

Heymann, J., Levy, J. K., Bose, B., Ríos-Salas, V., Mekonen, Y., Swaminathan, H., Omidakhsh, N., Gadoth, A., Huh, K., Greene, M. E., Darmstadt, G. L., & Gender Equality, Norms and Health Steering Committee. (2019). Improving health with programmatic, legal, and policy approaches to reduce gender inequality and change restrictive gender norms. *The Lancet*, *393*(10190), 2522–2534. https://doi.org/10.1016/S0140-6736(19)30656-7

Hitlin, S., & Kirkpatrick Johnson, M. (2015). Reconceptualizing agency within the life course: The power of looking ahead. *American Journal of Sociology*, *120*(5), 1429–1472. https://doi.org/10.1086/681216

Hoddinott, J., & Haddad, L. (1995). Does female income share influence household expenditures? Evidence from Côte d'Ivoire. *Oxford Bulletin of Economics and Statistics*, *57*(1), 77–96. https://doi.org/10.1111/j.1468-0084.1995.tb00028.x

Hoehn-Velasco, L., & Penglase, J. (2021). The impact of no-fault unilateral divorce laws on divorce rates in Mexico. *Economic Development and Cultural Change*, *70*(1), 203–236. https://doi.org/10.1086/706826

Holden, S. T., Deininger, K., & Ghebru, H. (2011). Tenure insecurity, gender, low-cost land certification and land rental market participation in Ethiopia. *The Journal of Development Studies*, *47*(1), 31–47. https://doi.org/10.1080/00220381003706460

Holmes, R. (2019). *Promoting gender equality and women's empowerment in shock-sensitive social protection* (ODI Working Paper No. 549). Overseas Development Institute & Australian Aid. https://media.odi.org/documents/20190228_sp_promoting_gender_equality.pdf

Hoover, A., Andes, K., Talukder, A., Naved, R., & Yount, K. M. (2024). Microcredit, gender norms, and women's experiences of economic coercion and agency in Matlab, Bangladesh. *Journal of the Asia Pacific Economy*, 1–21. https://doi.org/10.1080/13547860.2024.2345998

Hornung, C. A., McCullough, B. C., & Sugimoto, T. (1981). Status relationships in marriage: Risk factors in spouse abuse. *Journal of Marriage and the Family*, *43*(3), 675–692. https://doi.org/10.2307/351768

Hsieh, C.-T., Hurst, E., Jones, C. I., & Klenow, P. J. (2019). The allocation of talent and U.S. economic growth. *Econometrica*, *87*, 1439–1474. https://doi.org/10.3982/ECTA11427

Htun, M., & Weldon, S. L. (2012). The civic origins of progressive policy change: Combating violence against women in global perspective, 1975–2005. *American Political Science Review*, *106*(3), 548–569. https://doi.org/10.1017/s0003055412000226

Htun, N. M. M., Hnin, Z. L., & Khaing, W. (2021). Empowerment and health care access barriers among currently married women in Myanmar. *BMC Public Health*, 21(139). https://doi.org/10.1186/s12889-021-10181-5

Hudson, V. M., Ballif-Spanvill, B., Caprioli, M., & Emmett, C. F. (2012). *Sex and world peace.* Columbia University Press.

Hughes, M. M., Paxton, P., & Krook, M. L. (2017). Gender quotas for legislatures and corporate boards. *Annual Review of Sociology*, 43, 331–352. https://doi.org/10.1146/annurev-soc-060116-053324

Huis, M., Lensink, R., Vu, N., & Hansen, N. (2019). Impacts of the gender and entrepreneurship together ahead (GET ahead) training on empowerment of female microfinance borrowers in northern Vietnam. *World Development*, 120, 46–61. https://doi.org/10.1016/j.worlddev.2019.04.001

Hulme, D., & Shepherd, A. (2003). Conceptualizing chronic poverty. *World Development*, 31(3), 403–423. https://doi.org/10.1016/S0305-750X(02)00222-X

Hurwitz, H. M., & Taylor, V. (2012). Women's cultures and social movements in global contexts. *Sociology Compass*, 6(10), 808–822. https://doi.org/10.1111/j.1751-9020.2012.00502.x

Hussain, T. M., & Smith, J. F. (1999). Women's physical mobility in rural Bangladesh: The role of socio-economic and community factors. *Contemporary South Asia*, 8(2), 177–186. https://doi.org/10.1080/09584939908719863

Hutchison, E. D. (2010). A life course perspective. In *Dimensions of human behavior: The changing life course* (Vol. 4, pp. 1–38).

Ibarra, H. (1992). Homophily and differential returns: Sex differences in network structure and access in an advertising firm. *Administrative Science Quarterly*, 37(3), 422–447. https://psycnet.apa.org/doi/10.2307/2393451

___. (1993). Personal networks of women and minorities in management: A conceptual framework. *Academy of Management Review*, 18(1), 56–87. https://psycnet.apa.org/doi/10.2307/258823

Idris, I. B., Hamis, A. A., Bukhori, A. B. M., Hoong, D. C. C., Yusop, H., Shaharuddin, M. A., Fauzi, N. A. F. A., & Kandayah, T. (2023). Women's autonomy in healthcare decision making: A systematic review. *BMC Women's Health*, 23(1), Article 643. https://doi.org/10.1186/s12905-023-02792-4

Ikenwilo, D., Olajide, D., Obembe, O., Ibeji, N., & Akindola, R. (2016). *The impact of a rural microcredit scheme on women's household vulnerability and empowerment: Evidence from southwest Nigeria* (PEP Working Paper No. 2016–01). Partnership for Economic Policy. https://papers.ssrn.com/sol3/papers.cfm?abstract_id=3167363

Institute of Medicine. (2001). *Health and behavior: The interplay of biological, behavioral, and societal influences.* The National Academies Press. https://doi.org/10.17226/9838

___. (2002). *Speaking of health: Assessing health communication strategies for diverse populations.* The National Academies Press. https://doi.org/10.17226/10018

International Committee of the Red Cross. (2015). *What is economic security?* https://www.icrc.org/en/document/introduction-economic-security

International Labour Office. (1999). *Decent work: Report of the director-general at the 87th session of International Labour Conference* (ILO Report). International Labour Office. https://webapps.ilo.org/public/english/standards/relm/ilc/ilc87/rep-i.htm

Jackman, R. W., & Miller, R. A. (1998). Social capital and politics. *Annual Review of Political Science*, 1(1), 47–73. https://doi.org/10.1146/annurev.polisci.1.1.47

Jackson, P. (2007). A prehistory of the Millennium Development Goals. *UN Chronicle*, 44(4), 6–7. https://doi.org/10.18356/86089317-en

Jain, A. K. (2011). Measuring the effect of fertility decline on the maternal mortality ratio. *Studies in Family Planning*, 42, 247–260. https://doi.org/10.1111/j.1728-4465.2011.00288.x

James, S. L., Abate, D., Abate, K. H., Abay, S. M., Abbafati, C., Abbasi, N., Abbastabar, H., Abd-Allah, F., Abdela, J., Abdelalim, A., Abdollahpour, I., Abdulkader, R. S., Abebe, Z., Abera, S. F., Abil, O. Z., Abraha, H. N., Abu-Raddad, L. J., Abu-Rmeileh, N. M. E., Accrombessi, M. M. K., ... Murray, C. J. L. (2018). Global, regional, and national incidence, prevalence, and years lived with disability for 354 diseases and injuries for 195 countries and territories, 1990–2017: A systematic analysis for the Global Burden of Disease Study 2017. *The Lancet*, 392(10159), 1789–1858. https://doi.org/10.1016/ s0140-6736(18)32279-7

Jayachandran, S. (2017). Fertility decline and missing women. *American Economic Journal: Applied Economics*, 9(1), 118–139. https://doi.org/10.1257/app.20150576

Jayachandran, S., & Kuziemko, I. (2011). Why do mothers breastfeed girls less than boys? Evidence and implications for child health in India. *Quarterly Journal of Economics*, 126(3), 1485–1538. https://doi.org/10.1093/qje/qjr029

Jejeebhoy, S. J., Santhya, K., Acharya, R., Zavier, A. J. F., Pandey, N., Singh, S.K., Saxena, K., Basu, S., & Gogoi, A. (2017). *Empowering women and addressing violence against them through self-help groups (SHGs)* (Population Council Report). Population Council, Centre for Catalyzing Change, & The London School of Hygiene. http://dx.doi.org/10.13140/ RG.2.2.12580.27524

Jennings, L., Na, M., Cherewick, M., Hindin, M., Mullany, B., & Ahmed, S. (2014). Women's empowerment and male involvement in antenatal care: Analyses of Demographic and Health Surveys (DHS) in selected African countries. *BMC Pregnancy and Childbirth*, 14, 1–11. https://doi.org/10.1186/1471-2393-14-297

Jensen, R. (2012). Do labor market opportunities affect young women's work and family decisions? Experimental evidence from India. *The Quarterly Journal of Economics*, 127(2), 753–792. https://doi.org/10.1093/qje/qjs002

Johansson, S. R. (1984). Deferred infanticide: Excess female mortality during childhood. In G. Hausfater & S. B. Hausfater (Eds.), *Infanticide: Comparative and evolutionary perspectives* (pp. 463–486). Aldine.

Jones, N., Presler-Marshall, E., Kassahun, G., & Kebedi, M. (2020a). Constrained choices: Exploring the complexities of adolescent girls' voice and agency in child marriage decisions in Ethiopia. *Progress in Development Studies*, 20(4), 296–311. https://doi. org/10.1177/1464993420958215

Jones, R. E., Haardörfer, R., Ramakrishnan, U., Yount, K. M., Miedema, S. S., Roach, T. D., & Girard, A. W. (2020b). Intrinsic and instrumental agency associated with nutritional status of East African women. *Social Science & Medicine*, 247, Article 112803. https:// doi.org/10.1016/j.socscimed.2020.112803

J-PAL Policy Bulletin. (2018). *Reducing pregnancy among adolescents* [Issue Brief]. https:// www.povertyactionlab.org/sites/default/files/publication/reducing-pregnancy-among- adolescents.pdf

Kabeer, N. (1997). Women, wages and intra-household power relations in urban Bangladesh. *Development and Change*, 28(2), 261–302. http://dx.doi.org/10.1111/1467-7660.00043

___. (1999a). *The conditions and consequences of choice: Reflections on the measurement of women's empowerment* (UNRISD Report No. 108). United Nations Research Institute for Social Development. https://www.files.ethz.ch/isn/28994/dp108.pdf

___. (1999b). Resources, agency, achievements: Reflections on the measurement of women's empowerment. *Development and Change*, 30(3), 435–464. http://dx.doi.org/10. 1111/1467-7660.00125

___. (2001). Conflicts over credit: Re-evaluating the empowerment potential of loans to women in rural Bangladesh. *World Development*, 29(1), 63–84. https://doi.org/10.1016/ S0305-750X(00)00081-4

___. (2005). *The Beijing platform for action and the millennium development goals: Different processes, different outcomes* (DAW Report Ep. 11). United Nations Division for the Advancement of Women. https://www.un.org/womenwatch/daw/egm/bpfamd2005/experts-papers/EGM-BPFA-MD-MDG-2005-EP.11.pdf

___. (2011). Between affiliation and autonomy: Navigating pathways of women's empowerment and gender justice in rural Bangladesh. *Development and Change, 42*(2), 499–528. https://doi.org/10.1111/j.1467-7660.2011.01703.x

___. (2016). Gender equality, economic growth, and women's agency: The "endless variety" and "monotonous similarity" of patriarchal constraints. *Feminist Economics, 22*(1), 295–321. https://doi.org/10.1080/13545701.2015.1090009

Kabeer, N., Mahmud, S., & Tasneem, S. (2018). The contested relationship between paid work and women's empowerment: Empirical analysis from Bangladesh. *The European Journal of Development Research, 30*(2), 235–251. https://doi.org/10.1057/s41287-017-0119-y

Kabir, A., Rashid, M. M., Hossain, K., Khan, A., Sikder, S. S., & Gidding, H. F. (2020). Women's empowerment is associated with maternal nutrition and low birth weight: Evidence from Bangladesh Demographic Health Survey. *BMC Women's Health, 20*(1), Article 93. https://doi.org/10.1186/s12905-020-00952-4

Kaestle, C. E., Morisky, D. E., & Wiley, D. J. (2002). Sexual intercourse and the age difference between adolescent females and their romantic partners. *Perspectives on Sexual and Reproductive Health, 34*(6), 304–309. https://doi.org/10.2307/3097749

Kalamar, A. M., Lee-Rife, S., & Hindin, M. J. (2016). Interventions to prevent child marriage among young people in low-and middle-income countries: A systematic review of the published and gray literature. *Journal of Adolescent Health, 59*(Suppl 3), S16–S21. https://doi.org/10.1016/j.jadohealth.2016.06.015

Kandiyoti, D. (1988). Bargaining with patriarchy. *Gender & Society, 2*(3), 274–290. http://dx.doi.org/10.1177/089124388002003004

Karimli, L., Lecoutere, E., Wells, C. R., & Ismayilova, L. (2021). More assets, more decision-making power? Mediation model in a cluster-randomized controlled trial evaluating the effect of the graduation program on women's empowerment in Burkina Faso. *World Development, 137*, Article 105159. https://doi.org/10.1016/j.worlddev.2020.105159

Karlan, D., Thuysbaert, B., & Gray, B. (2017). Credit with health education in Benin: A cluster randomized trial examining impacts on knowledge and behavior. *The American Journal of Tropical Medicine and Hygiene, 96*(2), 501–510. https://doi.org/10.4269/ajtmh.16-0126

Karp, C., Wood, S. N., Galadanci, H., Sebina Kibira, S. P., Makumbi, F., Omoluabi, E., Shiferaw, S., Seme, A., Tsui, A., & Moreau, C. (2020). "I am the master key that opens and locks": Presentation and application of a conceptual framework for women's and girls' empowerment in reproductive health. *Social Science & Medicine, 258*. https://doi.org/10.1016/j.socscimed.2020.113086

Karra, M., Canning, D., & Wilde, J. (2017). The effect of fertility decline on economic growth in Africa: A macrosimulation model. *Population and Development Review, 43*(S1), 237–263. https://doi.org/10.1111/padr.12009

Karra, M., Maggio, D., Guo, M., Ngwira, B., & Canning, D. (2022). The causal effect of a family planning intervention on women's contraceptive use and birth spacing. *Proceedings of the National Academy of Sciences of the United States of America, 119*(22), Article e2200279119. https://doi.org/10.1073/pnas.2200279119

Kaur, R. (2016). *Too many men, too few women: Social consequences of gender imbalance in India and China*. Orient Blackswan.

Kavanaugh, G., Sviatschi, M. M., & Trako, I. (2019). *Female officers, gender violence and human capital: Evidence from all-women's justice centers in Peru* (Working Paper). https://doi.org/10.2139/ssrn.3022670

Kawachi, I., Subramanian, S. V., & Kim, D. (2008). *Social capital and health: A decade of progress and beyond*. Springer. https://link.springer.com/book/10.1007/978-0-387-71311-3

Kawaguchi, D., & Lee, S. (2017). Brides for sale: Cross-border marriages and female immigration. *Economic Inquirer*, *55*(2), 633–654. https://doi.org/10.1111/ecin.12411

Keats, A. (2018). Women's schooling, fertility, and child health outcomes: Evidence from Uganda's free primary education program. *Journal of Development Economics*, *135*, 142–159. https://doi.org/10.1016/j.jdeveco.2018.07.002

Keyes, C. L. M., & Shapiro, A. D. (2004). Social well-being in the United States: A descriptive epidemiology. In O. G. Brim, C. D. Ryff, & R. C. Kessler (Eds.), *How healthy are we? A national study of well-being at midlife* (pp. 350–372). The University of Chicago Press.

Khader, S. (2016). Beyond autonomy fetishism: Affiliation with autonomy in women's empowerment. *Journal of Human Development and Capabilities*, *17*(1), 125–139. https://doi.org/10.1080/19452829.2015.1025043

Khatiwada, J., Muzembo, B. A., Wada, K., & Ikeda, S. (2020). Dimensions of women's empowerment on access to skilled delivery services in Nepal. *BMC Pregnancy and Childbirth*, *20*(622). https://doi.org/10.1186/s12884-020-03309-9

Kiani, Z., Simbar, M., Hajian, S., & Zayeri, F. (2020). Quality of life among infertile women living in a paradox of concerns and dealing strategies: A qualitative study. *Nursing Open*, *8*(1), 251–261. https://doi.org/10.1002/nop2.624

___. (2021). The prevalence of depression symptoms among infertile women: A systematic review and meta-analysis. *Fertility Research and Practice*, *7*(1), Article 6. https://doi.org/10.1186/s40738-021-00098-3

Kilburn, K. N., Pettifor, A., Edwards, J. K., Selin, A., Twine, R., MacPhail, C., Wagner, R., Hughes, J. P., Wang, J., & Kahn, K. (2018). Conditional cash transfers and the reduction in partner violence for young women: An investigation of causal pathways using evidence from a randomized experiment in South Africa (HPTN 068). *Journal of the International AIDS Society*, *21*(Suppl 1), 47–54. https://doi.org/10.1002/jia2.25043

King, G., & Murray, C. J. L. (2001). Rethinking human security. *Political Science Quarterly*, *116*(4), 585–610. https://doi.org/10.2307/798222

King, M. T. (2014). *Between birth and death: Female infanticide in nineteenth-century China*. Stanford University Press. https://doi.org/10.11126/stanford/9780804785983.001.0001

Klasen, S. (2002). Low schooling for girls, slower growth for all? Cross-country evidence on the effect of gender inequality in education on economic development. *The World Bank Economic Review*, *16*(3), 345–373. https://doi.org/10.1093/wber/lhf004

Klasen, S., & Lamanna, F. (2009). The impact of gender inequality in education and employment on economic growth: New evidence for a panel of countries. *Feminist Economics*, *15*(3), 91–132. http://dx.doi.org/10.1080/13545700902893106

Kleven, H., Landais, C., & Leite-Mariante, G. (2023). *The child penalty atlas* (NBER Working Paper No. 31649). National Bureau of Economic Research. https://doi.org/10.3386/w31649

Klugman, J. (2022). *The gender dimensions of forced displacement: A synthesis of new research* (The World Bank Report No. 168165). The World Bank Group. https://documents1.worldbank.org/curated/en/895601643214591612/pdf/The-Gender-Dimensions-of-Forced-Displacement-A-Synthesis-of-New-Research.pdf

Klugman, J., Hanmer, L., Twigg, S., Hasan, T., McCleary-Sills, J., & Santamaria, J. (2014). *Voice and agency: Empowering women and girls for shared prosperity*. The World Bank Group. https://hdl.handle.net/10986/19036

Kneip, T., Bauer, G., & Reinhold, S. (2014). Direct and indirect effects of unilateral divorce law on marital stability. *Demography*, *51*(6), 2103–2126. https://doi.org/10.1007/s13524-014-0337-2

Kohno, A., Techasrivichien, T., Suguimoto, S. P., Dahlui, M., Daliana, N., Farid, N., & Nakayama, T. (2020). Investigation of the key factors that influence the girls to enter into child marriage: A meta-synthesis of qualitative evidence. *PLOS One*, *15*(7), 1–20. https://doi.org/10.1371/journal.pone.0235959

Komter, A. (1989). Hidden power in marriage. *Gender & Society*, *3*(2), 187–216. https://doi.org/10.1177/089124389003002003

Kotschy, R., & Bloom, D. E. (2023). *Population aging and economic growth: From demographic dividend to demographic drag?* (NBER Working Paper No. 31585). National Bureau of Economic Research. https://www.nber.org/papers/w31585

Krishnan, S., Subbiah, K., Chandra, P., & Srinivasan, K. (2012). Minimizing risks and monitoring safety of an antenatal care intervention to mitigate domestic violence among young Indian women: The Dil Mil trial. *BMC Public Health*, *12*(943). https://doi.org/10.1186/1471-2458-12-943

Krook, M. L., & Zetterberg, P. (2014). Introduction: Gender quotas and women's representation—New directions in research. *Representation*, *50*(3), 287–294. https://doi.org/10.1080/00344893.2014.951168

Kudamatsu, M. (2012). Has democratization reduced infant mortality in sub-Saharan Africa? Evidence from micro data. *Journal of the European Economic Association*, *10*(6), 1294–1317. https://doi.org/10.1111/j.1542-4774.2012.01092.x

Kudeva, R., Halaas, B., Kagotho, N., Lee, G., & Biswas, B. (2020). Optimal birth interval and empowerment: A closer look at women's agency in Kenya. *African Journal of Midwifery and Women's Health*, *14*(4), 1–10. https://doi.org/10.12968/ajmw.2019.0028

Kumar, N., & Quisumbing, A. R. (2012). Beyond "death do us part": The long-term implications of divorce perceptions on women's well-being and child schooling in rural Ethiopia. *World Development*, *40*(12), 2478–2489. https://doi.org/10.1016/j.worlddev.2012.08.001

Kumar, N., Raghunathan, K., Arrieta, A., Jilani, A., & Pandey, S. (2021). The power of the collective empowers women: Evidence from self-help groups in India. *World Development*, *146*, Article 105579. https://doi.org/10.1016/J.WORLDDEV.2021.105579

Kumari, T. (2020). Women's economic empowerment: An integrative review of its antecedents and consequences. *Journal of Poverty, Investment and Development*, *56*. https://doi.org/10.7176/JPID/56-05

Lancaster, G., Maitra, P., & Ray, R. (2006). Endogenous intra-household balance of power and its impact on expenditure patterns: Evidence from India. *Economica*, *73*(291), 435–460. https://doi.org/10.1111/j.1468-0335.2006.00502.x

Lane, S. D., Jok, J. M., & El-Mouelhy, M. T. (1998). Buying safety: The economics of reproductive risk and abortion in Egypt. *Social Science & Medicine*, *47*(8), 1089–1099. https://doi.org/10.1016/S0277-9536(98)00129-4

Langer, A., Meleis, A., Knaul, F. M., Atun, R., Aran, M., Arreola-Ornelas, H., Bhutta, Z. A., Binagwaho, A., Bonita, R., Caglia, J. M., Claeson, M., Davies, J., Donnay, F. A., Gausman, J. M., Glickman, C., Kearns, A. D., Kendall, T., Lozano, R., Seboni, N., … Frenk, J. (2015). Women and health: The key for sustainable development. *The Lancet*, *386*(9999), 1165–1210. https://doi.org/10.1016/S0140-6736(15)60497-4

Larsen, U., Chung, W., & Gupta, M. D. (1998). Fertility and son preference in Korea. *Population Studies*, *52*(3), 317–325. https://doi.org/10.1080/0032472031000150496

Larson, J. S. (1993). The measurement of social well-being. *Social Indicators Research*, *28*(3), 285–296. https://doi.org/10.1007/BF01079022

Lecoutere, E., d'Exelle, B., & Van Campenhout, B. (2015). Sharing common resources in patriarchal and status-based societies: Evidence from Tanzania. *Feminist Economics*, *21*(3), 142–167. http://dx.doi.org/10.1080/13545701.2015.1024274

Lecoutere, E., Spielman, D. J., & Van Campenhout, B. (2023). Empowering women through targeting information or role models: Evidence from an experiment in agricultural extension in Uganda. *World Development, 167*, Article 106240. https://doi.org/10.1016/j.worlddev.2023.106240

Lecoutere, E., & Wuyts, E. (2021). Confronting the wall of patriarchy: Does participatory intrahousehold decision making empower women in agricultural households? *The Journal of Development Studies, 57*(6), 882–905. https://doi.org/10.1080/00220388.2020.1849620

Leder, S. (2016). *Linking women's empowerment and resilience: Literature review.* https://doi.org/10.13140/RG.2.1.3395.0809

Lee, H. (2010). *Family migration issues in North-east Asia* (IOM Research Paper). International Organization for Migration. https://publications.iom.int/system/files/pdf/wmr2010_family_migration_neasia.pdf

Lee, J. T., & Yen, H. W. (2007). Randomized controlled evaluation of a theory-based postpartum sexual health education programme. *Journal of Advanced Nursing, 60*(4), 389–401. https://doi.org/10.1111/j.1365-2648.2007.04395.x

Lee, M. (2024). Allocation of female talent and cross-country productivity differences. *The Economic Journal, 134*(664), 3333–3359. https://doi.org/10.1093/ej/ueae056

Lee, M., & Murdie, A. (2021). The global diffusion of the #MeToo movement. *Politics & Gender, 17*(4), 827–855. http://dx.doi.org/10.1017/S1743923X20000148

Lee-Rife, S. M. (2010). Women's empowerment and reproductive experiences over the lifecourse. *Social Science & Medicine, 71*(3), 634–642. https://doi.org/10.1016/j.socscimed.2010.04.019

Leight, J., Pedehombga, A., Ganaba, R., & Gelli, A. (2022). Women's empowerment, maternal depression, and stress: Evidence from rural Burkina Faso. *SSM Mental Health, 2*, Article 100160. https://doi.org/10.1016/j.ssmmh.2022.100160

Leventhal, K. S., Gillham, J., DeMaria, L., Andrew, G., Peabody, J., & Leventhal, S. (2015). Building psychosocial assets and wellbeing among adolescent girls: A randomized controlled trial. *Journal of Adolescence, 45*, 284–295. https://doi.org/10.1016/j.adolescence.2015.09.011

Levitt, P. (1998). Social remittances: Migration driven local-level forms of cultural diffusion. *The International Migration Review, 32*(4), 926–948. https://www.jstor.org/stable/pdf/2547666.pdf

Li, C., & Sun, D. (2023). Women's bargaining power and spending on children's education: Evidence from a natural experiment in China. *International Journal of Educational Development, 100*, Article 102787. https://doi.org/10.1016/j.ijedudev.2023.102787

Li, Z. (2023). Does intrahousehold bargaining power enhance women's marital satisfaction? A perspective from two competing forces in China. *Review of Development Economics, 27*(1), 476–498. https://doi.org/10.1111/rode.12947

Lindsay, S., Khudejha, A., Ilana, S., Gary, Y., Teame Tesfay, G., Leora, W., Asham Assazenew, B., Amy, N., & Kathryn, L. F. (2018). Preventing violence against refugee adolescent girls: Findings from a cluster randomised controlled trial in Ethiopia. *BMJ Global Health, 3*(5). https://doi.org/10.1136/bmjgh-2018-000825

Lokot, M., Shakya, H. B., & Cislaghi, B. (2022). The limits of child agency? Dissonances and contradictions in conceptualisations of agency within child-led marriages in Somalia and Cameroon. *International Journal of Children's Rights, 30*(1), 173–203. http://dx.doi.org/10.1163/15718182-30010007

Longwe, H. S. (1995a). *Framework for Gender Analysis.*

___. (1995b). *Women's Empowerment Framework.*

Lopes, S. C., Constant, D., Fraga, S., & Harries, J. (2022). How women's empowerment influences fertility-related outcomes and contraceptive practices: A cross-sectional study in Mozambique. *PLOS Global Public Health, 2*(9). http://dx.doi.org/10.1371/journal.pgph.0000670

Luke, N. (2003). Age and economic asymmetries in the sexual relationships of adolescent girls in Sub-Saharan Africa. *Studies in Family Planning*, *34*, 67–86. https://doi.org/10.1111/j.1728-4465.2003.00067.x

Lutter, M. (2015). Do women suffer from network closure? The moderating effect of social capital on gender inequality in a project-based labor market, 1929 to 2010. *American Sociological Review*, *80*(2), 329–358. http://dx.doi.org/10.1177/0003122414568788

Lutz, W., & Pachauri, S. (2023). *Systems analysis for sustainable wellbeing: 50 years of IIASA research, 40 years after the Brundtland Commission, contributing to the post-2030 Global Agenda*. International Institute for Applied Systems Analysis (IIASA). https://doi.org/10.5281/zenodo.8214208

Maara, J., Cirillo, C., Angeles, G., Prencipe, L., deMilliano, M., Lima, S. M., Palermo, T., Ghana LEAP 1000 Evaluation Team, Tanzania Adolescent Cash Plus Evaluation Team, & Malawi SCT Evaluation Team. (2023). Impacts of cash transfer and "cash plus" programs on self-perceived stress in Africa: Evidence from Ghana, Malawi, and Tanzania. *SSM Population Health*, *22*, Article 101403. https://doi.org/10.1016/j.ssmph.2023.101403

Madajewicz, M., Tsegay, A. H., & Norton, M. (2013). *Managing risks to agricultural livelihoods: Impact evaluation of the HARITA program in Tigray, Ethiopia, 2009-2012* (Oxfam America Report). Oxfam America. http://www.oxfamamerica.org/static/media/files/Oxfam_America_Impact_Evaluation_of_HARITA_2009-2012_English.pdf

Mainuddin, A., Begum, H. A., Rawal, L. B., Islam, A., & Islam, S. S. (2015). Women empowerment and its relation with health seeking behavior in Bangladesh. *Journal of Family & Reproductive Health*, *9*(2), 65–73.

Makino, M., Ngo, T. D, Psaki, S., Amin, S., & Austrian, K. (2021). Heterogeneous impacts of interventions aiming to delay girls' marriage and pregnancy across girls' backgrounds and social contexts. *Journal of Adolescent Health*, *69*(6), S39–S45. https://doi.org/10.1016/j.jadohealth.2021.09.016

Malhotra, A., & Mather, M. (1997). Do schooling and work empower women in developing countries? Gender and domestic decisions in Sri Lanka. *Sociological Forum*, *12*(4), 599–630. https://doi.org/10.1023/A:1022126824127

Malhotra, A., Schuler, S. R., & Boender, C. (2002). *Measuring women's empowerment as a variable in international development*. The World Bank Workshop on Poverty and Gender: New Perspectives. http://ereserve.library.utah.edu/Annual/ECON/Knowledge/Memis/meas.pdf

Marcus, R. (2021). Gender, social norms, and women's economic empowerment. In K. Grantham, G. Dowie, & A. de Haan (Eds.), *Women's economic empowerment* (1st ed., pp. 126–153). Routledge. https://doi.org/10.4324/9781003141938

Martimort, D., & Stole, L. (2009). Market participation in delegated and intrinsic common-agency games. *The RAND Journal of Economics*, *40*(1), 78–102. https://doi.org/10.1111/j.1756-2171.2008.00056.x

Martínez, C. A., & Perticará, M. (2017). Childcare effects on maternal employment: Evidence from Chile. *Journal of Development Economics*, *126*, 127–137. https://doi.org/10.1016/j.jdeveco.2017.01.001

Masis, L., Gichaga, A., Zerayacob, T., Lu, C., & Perry, H. B. (2021). Community health workers at the dawn of a new era: 4. Programme financing. *Health Research Policy and Systems*, *19*(Suppl 3), Article 107. https://doi.org/10.1186/s12961-021-00751-9

Mason, K. (2002). Measuring women's empowerment: Learning from cross-national research. In D. Narayanan (Ed.), *Measuring empowerment*. The World Bank.

Mason, K. O., & Smith, H. L. (2000). Husbands' versus wives' fertility goals and use of contraception: The influence of gender context in five Asian countries. *Demography*, *37*(3), 299–311. https://doi.org/10.2307/2648043

Mason, K. O., & Taj, A. M. (1987). Differences between women's and men's reproductive goals in developing countries. *Population and Development Review*, *13*(4), 611–638. http://www.jstor.org/stable/1973025

Matouschek, N., & Rasul, I. (2008). The economics of the marriage contract: Theories and evidence. *Journal of Law and Economics, 51*(1), 59–110. http://dx.doi.org/10.1086/588596

Mavisakalyan, A., & Tarverdi, Y. (2019). Gender and climate change: Do female parliamentarians make difference? *European Journal of Political Economy, 56,* 151–164. https://doi.org/10.1016/j.ejpoleco.2018.08.001

McChesney, K. Y. (2015). Successful approaches to ending female genital cutting. *Journal of Sociology and Social Welfare, 42,* Article 2.

McDougal, L., Jackson, E. C., McClendon, K. A., Belayneh, Y., Sinha, A., & Raj, A. (2018). Beyond the statistic: Exploring the process of early marriage decision-making using qualitative findings from Ethiopia and India. *BMC Women's Health, 18*(1), 1–16. https://doi.org/10.1186/s12905-018-0631-z

McDougal, L., Klugman, J., Dehingia, N., Trivedi, A., & Raj, A. (2019). Financial inclusion and intimate partner violence: What does the evidence suggest? *PLoS One, 14,* Article e0223721.

McElroy, M. B., & Horney, M. J. (1981). Nash-bargained household decisions: Toward a generalization of the theory of demand. *International Economic Review,* 333–349. https://doi.org/10.2307/2526280

McFarland, J. (1988). Review essay: The construction of women and development theory. *Canadian Review of Sociology, 25*(2), 299–308. http://dx.doi.org/10.1111/j.1755-618X.1988.tb00107.x

McKelway, M. (2018). *Women's self-efficacy and women's employment: Experimental evidence from India* (Working Paper). https://barrett.dyson.cornell.edu/NEUDC/paper_571.pdf

___. (2021). *Women's agency and women's employment: How women's sense of agency affects their labor supply* (King Center on Global Development Working Paper No. 1083). Stanford University. https://kingcenter.stanford.edu/sites/g/files/sbiybj16611/files/media/file/wp1083_0.pdf

McKinney, L. A., & Fulkerson, G. M. (2015). Gender equality and climate justice: A cross-national analysis. *Social Justice Research, 28,* 293–317. https://doi.org/10.1007/s11211-015-0241-y

McPherson, M., Smith-Lovin, L., & Cook, J. M. (2001). Birds of a feather: Homophily in social networks. *Annual Review of Sociology, 27,* 415–444. https://doi.org/10.1146/annurev.soc.27.1.415

Meinzen-Dick, R., Quisumbing, A., Doss, C., & Theis, S. (2019). Women's land rights as a pathway to poverty reduction: Framework and review of available evidence. *Agricultural Systems, 172,* 72–82. https://doi.org/10.1016/j.agsy.2017.10.009

Mersha, A. A., & Van Laerhoven, F. (2016). A gender approach to understanding the differentiated impact of barriers to adaptation: Responses to climate change in rural Ethiopia. *Regional Environmental Change, 16*(6), 1701–1713. https://doi.org/10.1007/s10113-015-0921-z

Miedema, E., Koster, W., & Pouw, N. (2020). Taking choice seriously: Emic understandings of decision-making about child marriage. *Progress in Development Studies, 20*(4), 261–269. http://dx.doi.org/10.1177/1464993420965315

Miedema, S. S., Haardörfer, R., Girard, A. W., & Yount, K. M. (2018). Women's empowerment in East Africa: Development of a cross-country comparable measure. *World Development, 110,* 453–464. https://doi.org/10.1016/j.worlddev.2018.05.031

Milazzo, A. (2018). Why are adult women missing? Son preference and maternal survival in India. *Journal of Development Economics, 134,* 467–484. https://doi.org/10.1016/j.jdeveco.2018.06.009

Miller, G. (2008). Women's suffrage, political responsiveness, and child survival in American history. *Quarterly Journal of Economics, 123*(3), 1287–1327. https://doi.org/10.1162/qjec.2008.123.3.1287

Minasyan, A., Zenker, J., Klasen, S., & Vollmer, S. (2019). Educational gender gaps and economic growth: A systematic review and meta-regression analysis. *World Development, 122*, 199–217. https://doi.org/10.1016/j.worlddev.2019.05.006

Minckas, N., Shannon, G., & Mannell, J. (2020). The role of participation and community mobilisation in preventing violence against women and girls: A programme review and critique. *Global Health Action, 13*(1). https://doi.org/10.1080/16549716.2020.1775061

Mittal, S. (2016). Role of mobile phone-enabled climate information services in gender-inclusive agriculture. *Gender, Technology and Development, 20*(2), 200–217. https://doi.org/10.1177/0971852416639772

Mokam, B., & Zamo Akono, C. (2022). The association between women's empowerment and reproductive health care utilization in Cameroon. *International Journal for Quality in Health Care, 34*(2). https://doi.org/10.1093/intqhc/mzac032

Molitoris, J., Barclay, K., & Kolk, M. (2019). When and where birth spacing matters for child survival: An international comparison using the DHS. *Demography, 56*(4), 1349–1370. https://doi.org/10.1007/s13524-019-00798-y

Molyneux, M., & Thomson, M. (2011). Cash transfers, gender equity and women's empowerment in Peru, Ecuador and Bolivia. *Gender & Development, 19*(2), 195–212. https://doi.org/10.1080/13552074.2011.592631

Moore, L., Chersich, M. F., Steen, R., Reza-Paul, S., Dhana, A., Vuylsteke, B., Lafort, Y., & Scorgie, F. (2014). Community empowerment and involvement of female sex workers in targeted sexual and reproductive health interventions in Africa: A systematic review. *Globalization and Health, 10*(47). https://doi.org/10.1186/1744-8603-10-47

Mootz, J. J., Spencer, C. M., Ettelbrick, J., Kann, B., Fortunato dos Santos, P., Palmer, M., & Stith, S. M. (2022). Risk markers for victimization and perpetration of male-to-female physical intimate partner violence in sub-Saharan Africa: A meta-analysis. *Trauma, Violence, & Abuse, 5*. https://doi.org/10.1177/15248380221129589

Moreau, C., Karp, C., Wood, S. N., Galadanci, H., Kibira, S. P. S., Makumbi, F., Omoluabi, E., Shiferaw, S., Seme, A., & Tsui, A. (2020). Reconceptualizing women's and girls' empowerment: A cross-cultural index for measuring progress toward improved sexual and reproductive health. *International Perspectives on Sexual and Reproductive Health, 46*, 187–198. https://doi.org/10.1363/46e9920

Mosedale, S. (2005). Assessing women's empowerment: Towards a conceptual framework. *Journal of International Development, 17*(2), 243–257. https://doi.org/10.1002/jid.1212

___. (2006). *Global research framework for CARE's strategic impact inquiry on women's empowerment* (CARE Paper). Cooperative for Assistance and Relief Everywhere. https://www.care.org/wp-content/uploads/2020/06/SII-Womens-Empowerment-Global-Research-Framework-with-annexes-2006.pdf

Moser, C. O. (1989). Gender planning in the Third World: Meeting practical and strategic gender needs. *World Development, 17*(11), 1799–1825. https://doi.org/10.1016/0305-750X(89)90201-5

Mpiima, D. M., Manyire, H., Kabonesa, C., & Espiling, M. (2019). Gender analysis of agricultural extension policies in Uganda: Informing practice? *Gender, Technology and Development, 23*, 187–205. https://doi.org/10.1080/09718524.2019.1657610

Mukherjee, S. (2013). Skewed sex ratio and migrant brides in Haryana: Reflections from the field. *Social Change, 43*(1), 37–52. https://doi.org/10.1177/0049085713475725

Mukoya, F. (2020). ICTs as enablers of resilient social capital for ethnic peace. In *Proceedings of the 3rd ACM SIGCAS Conference on Computing and Sustainable Societies* (pp. 116–126). http://dx.doi.org/10.1145/3378393.3402266

Muluneh, M. D., Francis, L., Agho, K., & Stulz, V. (2021). A systematic review and meta-analysis of associated factors of gender-based violence against women in sub-Saharan Africa. *International Journal of Environmental Research and Public Health, 18*(9), Article 4407. https://doi.org/10.3390/ijerph18094407

Muralidharan, K., & Prakash, N. (2017). Cycling to school: Increasing secondary school enrollment for girls in India. *American Economic Journal: Applied Economics, 9*(3), 321–350. http://www.jstor.org/stable/26598064

Muthumbi, J., Svanemyr, J., Scolaro, E., Temmerman, M., & Say, L. (2015). Female genital mutilation: A literature review of the current status of legislation and policies in 27 African countries and Yemen. *African Journal of Reproductive Health, 19*(3), 32–40.

Mwaikambo, L., Speizer, I. S., Schurmann, A., Morgan, G., & Fikree, F. (2011). What works in family planning interventions: A systematic review. *Studies in Family Planning, 42*(2), 67–82. https://doi.org/10.1111/j.1728-4465.2011.00267.x

Nahar, S., & Mengo, C. W. (2022). Measuring women's empowerment in developing countries: A systematic review. *Journal of International Development, 34*(2), 322–333. https://doi.org/10.1002/jid.3594

Nanda, P., Datta, N., Lamba, S., & Pradhan, E. (2016). *Impact of a conditional cash transfer program on girls' education and age of marriage in India: Synthesis of findings* (ICRW Report). International Center for Research on Women. https://www.icrw.org/publications/making-change-with-cash-impact-of-a-conditional-cash-transfer-program-on-age-of-marriage-in-india-4/

Nanda, V., Nayak, M., & Goldstein, J. (2020). Global efforts to realize the essential but elusive goal of gender equality and women's empowerment (SDG 5). *Denver Journal of International Law & Policy, 48*(1).

Nandi, A. (2015). The unintended effects of a ban on sex-selective abortion on infant mortality: Evidence from India. *Oxford Development Studies, 43*(4), 466–482. https://doi.org/10.1080/13600818.2014.973390

Nanvubya, A., Wanyenze, R. K., Abaasa, A., Nakaweesa, T., Mpendo, J., Kawoozo, B., Matovu, F., Nabukalu, S., Omoding, G., Kaweesi, J., Ndugga, J., Bagaya, B., Chinyenze, K., Price, M. A., & Van Geertruyden, J. P. (2022). Evaluating the effectiveness of enhanced family planning education on knowledge and use of family planning in fishing communities of Lake Victoria in Uganda: A randomized controlled trial. *BMC Health Services Research, 22*, Article 506. https://doi.org/10.1186/s12913-022-07898-3

Narayan-Parker, D. (2002). *Empowerment and poverty reduction: A sourcebook.* The World Bank. http://documents.worldbank.org/curated/en/827431468765280211/Empowerment-and-poverty-reduction-a-sourcebook

Natarajan, M., & Babu, D. (2020). Women police stations: Have they fulfilled their promise? *Police Practice and Research, 21*(5), 442–458. http://dx.doi.org/10.1080/15614263.2020.1809827

National Academies of Sciences, Engineering, and Medicine. (2021). *Family planning, women's empowerment, and population and societal impacts: Proceedings of a workshop.* The National Academies Press. https://doi.org/10.17226/26023

National Research Council. (1986). *Population growth and economic development: Policy questions.* The National Academies Press. https://doi.org/10.17226/620

___. (1994). *Science priorities for the human dimensions of global change.* The National Academies Press. https://doi.org/10.17226/9175

Navarro-Mantas, L., de Lemus, S., García-Sánchez, E., McGill, L., Hansen, N., & Megías, J. L. (2022). Defining power and agency in gender relations in El Salvador: Consequences for intimate partner violence and women's mental health. *Frontiers in Psychology, 13.* https://doi.org/10.3389/fpsyg.2022.867945

Naved, R. T., Mahmud, S., Al Mamun, M., Parvin, K., Kalra, S., Laterra, A., & Sprinkel, A. (2024). Effectiveness of combined interventions to empower girls and address social norms in reducing child marriage in a rural sub-district of Bangladesh: A cluster randomised controlled trial of the tipping point initiative. *Journal of Global Health, 14*, 04020. https://doi.org/10.7189/jogh.14.04020

Naz, S., & Acharya, Y. (2021). The effect of reframing the goals of family planning programs from limiting fertility to birth spacing: Evidence from Pakistan. *Studies in Family Planning, 52*(2), 125–142. https://doi.org/10.1111/sifp.12155

Newton, K. (2001). Trust, social capital, civil society, and democracy. *International Political Science Review, 22*(2), 201–214. https://doi.org/10.1177/019251210122200

Nieuwenhuijze, M., & Leahy-Warren, P. (2019). Women's empowerment in pregnancy and childbirth: A concept analysis. *Midwifery, 78*, 1–7. https://doi.org/10.1016/j.midw.2019.07.015

Njue, C., Karumbi, J., Esho, T., Varol, N., & Dawson, A. (2019) Preventing female genital mutilation in high income countries: A systematic review of the evidence. *Reproductive Health, 16*, 1–20. https://doi.org/10.1186/s12978-019-0774-x

Ntoimo, L. F. C., Okonofua, F. E., Aikpitanyi, J., Yaya, S., Johnson, E., Sombie, I., Aina, O., & Imongan, W. (2022). Influence of women's empowerment indices on the utilization of skilled maternity care: Evidence from rural Nigeria. *Journal of Biosocial Science, 54*(1), 77–93. https://doi.org/10.1017/s0021932020000681

Nussbaum, M. (2011). *Creating capabilities: The human development approach*. Harvard University Press. https://archive.org/details/creatingcapabili0000nuss/page/n2/mode/1up

Olney, D. K., Bliznashka, L., Pedehombga, A., Dillon, A., Ruel, M. T., & Heckert, J. (2016). A 2-year integrated agriculture and nutrition program targeted to mothers of young children in Burkina Faso reduces underweight among mothers and increases their empowerment: A cluster-randomized controlled trial. *The Journal of Nutrition, 146*(5), 1109–1117. https://doi.org/10.3945/jn.115.224261

Orkin, K., Garlick, R., Mahmud, M., Sedlmayr, R., Haushofer, J., & Dercon, S. (2023). *Aspiring to a better future: Can a simple psychological intervention reduce poverty?* (NBER Working Paper No. 31735). National Bureau of Economic Research. https://www.nber.org/system/files/working_papers/w31735/w31735.pdf

Orsini, M. M., Ewald, D. R., & Strack, R. W. (2022). Development and validation of the 4-Factor Critical Consciousness Scale. *SSM - Population Health, 19*, Article 101202. https://doi.org/10.1016/j.ssmph.2022.101202

Orton, L., Pennington, A., Nayak, S., Sowden, A., White, M., & Whitehead, M. (2016). Group-based microfinance for collective empowerment: A systematic review of health impacts. *Bull World Health Organization, 94*(9), 694–704a. https://doi.org/10.2471/blt.15.168252

Osamor, P. E., & Grady, C. (2016). Women's autonomy in health care decision-making in developing countries: A synthesis of the literature. *International Journal of Women's Health, 8*, 191–202. https://doi.org/10.2147/IJWH.S105483

Osili, U. O., & Long, B. T. (2008). Does female schooling reduce fertility? Evidence from Nigeria. *Journal of Development Economics, 87*(1), 57–75. https://doi.org/10.1016/j.jdeveco.2007.10.003

Ostrom, E. (2000). Collective action and the evolution of social norms. *Journal of Economic Perspectives, 14*(3), 137–158. https://pubs.aeaweb.org/doi/pdfplus/10.1257/jep.14.3.137

Our World in Data Team. (2023). *Achieve gender equality and empower all women and girls*. https://ourworldindata.org/sdgs/gender-equality

Ozier, O. (2018). The impact of secondary schooling in Kenya: A regression discontinuity analysis. *Journal of Human Resources, 53*(1), 157–188. https://doi.org/10.3368/jhr.53.1.0915-7407R

Özler, B., Hallman, K., Guimond, M. F., Kelvin, E. A., Rogers, M., & Karnley, E. (2020). Girl Empower – A gender transformative mentoring and cash transfer intervention to promote adolescent wellbeing: Impact findings from a cluster-randomized controlled trial in Liberia. *SSM Population Health, 10*, Article 100527. https://doi.org/10.1016/j.ssmph.2019.100527

Palriwala, R. (1993). Economics and patriliny: Consumption and authority within the household. *Social Scientist, 21*(9/11), 47–73. https://doi.org/10.2307/3520426

Parvez Butt, A. (2020). *Communities changing social norms to end female genital cutting in West Africa.* Oxfam. https://oxfamilibrary.openrepository.com/handle/10546/621088

Perera, C., Bakrania, S., Ipince, A., Nesbitt-Ahmed, Z., Obasola, O., Richardson, D., Van de Scheur, J., & Yu, R. (2022). Impact of social protection on gender equality in low- and middle-income countries: A systematic review of reviews. *Campbell Systematic Reviews, 18*(2). https://doi.org/10.1002/cl2.1240

Pesando, L. M. (2022). Safer if connected? Mobile technology and intimate partner violence. *Demography, 59*(2), 653–684. https://doi.org/10.1215/00703370-9774978

Pesando, L. M., & Qiyomiddin, K. (2023). Mobile phones and infant health at birth. *PLOS One, 18*(9), Article e0288089. https://doi.org/10.1371/journal.pone.0288089

Pesando, L. M., & Rotondi, V. (2020). Mobile technology and gender equality. In W. Leal Filho, A. Azul, L. Brandli, A. Lange Salvia, & T. Wall (Eds.), *Gender equality. Encyclopedia of the UN Sustainable Development Goals.* Springer, Cham. https://doi.org/10.1007/978-3-319-70060-1_140-1

Peterman, A., Pereira, A., Bleck, J., Palermo, T. M., & Yount, K. M. (2017). Women's individual asset ownership and experience of intimate partner violence: Evidence from 28 international surveys. *American Journal of Public Health, 107*(5), 747–755. https://doi.org/10.2105/AJPH.2017.303694

Picard, M. (2021). *Empowering women in climate, environment and disaster risk governance: From national policy to local action* [Virtual conference session]. UN Women Expert Group Meeting. http://dx.doi.org/10.13140/RG.2.2.19131.69925

Pike, K., & English, B. (2022). And roses too: How "better work" facilitates gender empowerment in global supply chains. *Gender, Work & Organization, 29*(1), 188–204. https://doi.org/10.1111/gwao.12740

Pizzamiglio, R., & Kovacs, P. (2021). Accelerating women's empowerment through legal empowerment and social accountability strategies. *Journal of Human Development and Capabilities, 22*(3), 517–526. https://doi.org/10.1080/19452829.2021.1890005

Polis, C. B., Cox, C. M., Tunçalp, Ö., McLain, A. C., & Thoma, M. E. (2017). Estimating infertility prevalence in low-to-middle-income countries: An application of a current duration approach to Demographic and Health Survey data. *Human Reproduction, 32*(5), 1064–1074. https://doi.org/10.1093%2Fhumrep%2Fdex025

Poteat, V. P., Calzo, J. P., & Yoshikawa, H. (2018). Gay-Straight Alliance involvement and youths' participation in civic engagement, advocacy, and awareness-raising. *Journal of Applied Developmental Psychology, 56*, 13–20. https://doi.org/10.1016/j.appdev.2018.01.001

Poudel, S., Adhikari, C., Yadav, R. K., Yadav, D. K., Thapa, D. K., & Jakovljevic, M. (2022). Disempowered mothers have undernourished children: How strong is the intrinsic agency? *Frontiers in Public Health, 10*, Article 817717. https://doi.org/10.3389/fpubh.2022.817717

Pouw, N., & Gupta, J. (2017). Inclusive development: A multi-disciplinary approach. *Current Opinion in Environmental Sustainability, 24*, 104–108. https://doi.org/10.1016/j.cosust.2016.11.013

Pradhan, M. R., Unisa, S., Rawat, R., Surabhi, S., Saraswat, A., Reshmi, R. S., & Sethi, V. (2023). Women empowerment through involvement in community-based health and nutrition interventions: Evidence from a qualitative study in India. *PLOS One, 18*(4). https://doi.org/10.1371/journal.pone.0284521

Prakash, N., & Vadlamannati, K. C. (2019). Girls for sale? Child sex ratio and girl trafficking in India. *Feminist Economics, 25*(4), 267–308. https://doi.org/10.1080/13545701.2019.1666212

Pratley, P. (2016). Associations between quantitative measures of women's empowerment and access to care and health status for mothers and their children: A systematic review of evidence from the developing world. *Social Science & Medicine, 169*, 119–131. https://doi.org/10.1016/j.socscimed.2016.08.001

Prillaman, S. A. (2023). *Strength in numbers: How women's groups close India's political gender gap. American Journal of Political Science,* 67(2), 390–410. https://doi.org/10.1111/ajps.12651

Priya, P., Venkatesh, A., & Shukla, A. (2021). *Two decades of theorising and measuring women's empowerment: Literature review and future research agenda.* Women's Studies International Forum. https://doi.org/10.1016/j.wsif.2021.102495

Pronyk, P. M., Harpham, T., Busza, J., Phetla, G., Morison, L. A., Hargreaves, J. R., Kim, J. C., Watts, C. H., & Porter, J. D. (2008). Can social capital be intentionally generated? A randomized trial from rural South Africa. *Social Science & Medicine,* 67(10), 1559–1570. https://doi.org/10.1016/j.socscimed.2008.07.022

Prost, A., Colbourn, T., Seward, N., Azad, K., Coomarasamy, A., Copas, A., Houweling, T. A., Fottrell, E., Kuddus, A., Lewycka, S., MacArthur, C., Manandhar, D., Morrison, J., Mwansambo, C., Nirmala, N., Nambiar, B., Osrin, D., Pagel, C., Phiri, T., ... Costello., A. (2013). Women's groups practising participatory learning and action to improve maternal and newborn health in low-resource settings: A systematic review and meta-analysis. *The Lancet,* 381(9879), 1736–1746. https://doi.org/10.1016/S0140-6736(13)60685-6

Pulgaron, E. R., Marchante, A. N., Agosto, Y., Lebron, C. N., & Delamater, A. M. (2016). Grandparent involvement and children's health outcomes: The current state of the literature. *Families, Systems, & Health,* 34(3), 260–269. https://doi.org/10.1037/fsh000021

Purvis, B., Mao, Y., & Robinson, D. (2019). Three pillars of sustainability: In search of conceptual origins. *Sustainability Science,* 14(3), 681–695. https://dx.doi.org/10.1007/s11625-018-0627-5

Putnam, R. D. (1995). Bowling alone: America's declining social capital. *Journal of Democracy,* 6(1), 65–78. https://doi.org/10.1353/jod.1995.0002

Qian, N. (2008). Missing women and the price of tea in China: The effect of sex-specific earnings on sex imbalance. *The Quarterly Journal of Economics,* 123(3), 1251–1285. https://doi.org/10.1162/qjec.2008.123.3.1251

Questa, K., Das, M., King, R., Everitt, M., Rassi, C., Cartwright, C., Ferdous, T., Barua, D., Putnis, N., Snell, A. C., Huque, R., Newell, J., & Elsey, H. (2020). Community engagement interventions for communicable disease control in low- and lower- middle-income countries: Evidence from a review of systematic reviews. *International Journal for Equity in Health,* 19(51). https://doi.org/10.1186/s12939-020-01169-5

Quisumbing, A. R. (2003). *Household decisions, gender, and development* (IFPRI Report). International Food Policy Research Institute. https://www.efdinitiative.org/sites/default/files/publications/genderbook.pdf

Quisumbing, A. R., & Kumar, N. (2014). *Land rights knowledge and conservation in rural Ethiopia: Mind the gender gap* (IFPRI-Discussion Paper No. 01386). International Food Policy Research Institute. http://ebrary.ifpri.org/cdm/ref/collection/p15738coll2/id/128480

Quisumbing, A. R., & Maluccio, J. A. (2003). Resources at marriage and intrahousehold allocation: Evidence from Bangladesh, Ethiopia, Indonesia, and South Africa. *Oxford Bulletin of Economics and Statistics,* 65(3), 283–327. http://dx.doi.org/10.1111/1468-0084.t01-1-00052

Quisumbing, A. R., Meinzen-Dick, R., Malapit, H. J., Seymour, G., Heckert, J., Doss, C., Johnson, N., Rubin, D., Thai, G., Ramani, G., Myers, E., & the GAAP2 for pro-WEAI Study Team. (2024). Enhancing agency and empowerment in agricultural development projects: A synthesis of mixed methods impact evaluations from the Gender, Agriculture, and Assets Project, Phase 2 (GAAP). *Journal of Rural Studies, 108*, Article 103295, https://doi.org/10.1016/j.jrurstud.2024.103295

Rahman, M. (2012). Women's autonomy and unintended pregnancy among currently pregnant women in Bangladesh. *Maternal and Child Health Journal, 16*(6), 1206–1214. https://doi.org/10.1007/s10995-011-0897-3

Rahman, R., Rahman, M., & Haque, S. E. (2021). Empowerment dimensions and their relationship with continuum care for maternal health in Bangladesh. *Scientific Reports, 11*(1), Article 18760. https://doi.org/10.1038/s41598-021-98181-8

Raj, A., Dey, A., Lundgren, R., & EMERGE Team. (2021). *A conceptual framework for measuring women's empowerment* (EMERGE Paper). University of California, San Diego's Center on Gender Health and Equity. https://emerge.ucsd.edu/wp-content/uploads/2021/04/emerge-conceptual-framework-to-measure-empowerment.pdf

Raj, A., Dey, A., Rao, N., Yore, J., McDougal, L., Bhan, N., Silverman, J. G., Hay, K., Thomas, E. E., Fotso, J. C., & Lundgren, R. (2024). The EMERGE framework to measure empowerment for health and development. *Social Science & Medicine, 351*(Suppl. 1). https://doi.org/10.1016/j.socscimed.2024.116879

Raj, A., Ghule, M., Johns, N. E., Battala, M., Begum, S., Dixit, A., Vaida, F., Saggurti, N., Silverman, J. G., & Averbach, S. (2022). Evaluation of a gender synchronized family planning intervention for married couples in rural India: The CHARM2 cluster randomized control trial. *EClinicalMedicine, 45*, Article 101334. https://doi.org/10.1016/j.eclinm.2022.101334

Raj, A., Ghule, M., Ritter, J., Battala, M., Gajanan, V., Nair, S., Dasgupta, A., Silverman, J. G., Balaiah, D., & Saggurti, N. (2016). Cluster randomized controlled trial evaluation of a gender equity and family planning intervention for married men and couples in rural India. *PLOS One, 11*(5). https://doi.org/10.1371/journal.pone.0153190

Rajkhowa, P., & Qaim, M. (2022). Mobile phones, women's physical mobility, and contraceptive use in India. *Social Science and Medicine, 305*, Article 115074. https://doi.org/10.1016/j.socscimed.2022.115074

Rangel, M. A. (2006). Alimony rights and intrahousehold allocation of resources: Evidence from Brazil. *The Economic Journal, 116*(513), 627–658. https://doi.org/10.1111/j.1468-0297.2006.01104.x

Rangel, M., & Thomas, D. (2019). *Decision-making in complex households* (NBER Working Paper No. 26511). National Bureau of Economic Research. https://www.nber.org/papers/w26511

Rao, N. (2015). Marriage, violence, and choice: Understanding Dalit women's agency in rural Tamil Nadu. *Gender and Society, 29*(3), 410–433. http://dx.doi.org/10.1177/0891243214554798

Rao, N., Lawson, E. T., Raditloaneng, W. N., Solomon, D., & Angula, M. N. (2019). Gendered vulnerabilities to climate change: Insights from the semi-arid regions of Africa and Asia. *Climate and Development, 11*(1), 14–26. https://doi.org/10.1080/17565529.2017.1372266

Rappaport, J. (1995). Empowerment meets narrative: Listening to stories and creating settings. *American Journal of Community Psychology, 23*(5), 795–807. https://doi.org/10.1007/BF02506992

Rastogi, G., & Sharma, A. (2022). Unwanted daughters: The unintended consequences of a ban on sex-selective abortions on the educational attainment of women. *Journal of Population Economics, 35*, 1473–1516. https://doi.org/10.1007/s00148-022-00896-z

Ray, R., & Korteweg, A. C. (1999). Women's movements in the Third World: Identity, mobilization, and autonomy. *Annual Review of Sociology*, *25*(1), 47–71. http://dx.doi. org/10.1146/annurev.soc.25.1.47

Reggio, I. (2011). The influence of the mother's power on her child's labor in Mexico. *Journal of Development Economics*, *96*(1), 95–105. https://doi.org/10.1016/j.jdeveco.2010.07.002

Reifsnider, E., Gallagher, M., & Forgione, B. (2005). Using ecological models in research on health disparities. *Journal of Professional Nursing*, *21*(4), 216–222. https://doi.org/ 10.1016/j.profnurs.2005.05.006

Reniers, G. (2003). Divorce and remarriage in rural Malawi. *Demographic Research*, *1*(6), 175–206. http://dx.doi.org/10.4054/DemRes.2003.S1.6

Resurrección, B. P. (2013). Persistent women and environment linkages in climate change and sustainable development agendas. *Women's Studies International Forum*, *40*, 33–43. https://doi.org/10.1016/j.wsif.2013.03.011

Richardson, R. A. (2018a). Measuring women's empowerment: A need for context and caution. *The Lancet Global Health*, *6*(1), Article e30. https://doi.org/10.1016/s2214-109x(17)30460-6

___. (2018b). Measuring women's empowerment: A critical review of current practices and recommendations for researchers. *Social Indicators Research*, *137*(2), 539–557. https:// doi.org/10.1007/s11205-017-1622-4

Richardson, R. A., Harper, S., Bates, L. M., & Nandi, A. (2019). The effect of agency on women's mental distress: A prospective cohort study from rural Rajasthan, India. *Social Science & Medicine*, *233*, 47–56. https://doi.org/10.1016/j.socscimed.2019.05.052

Riley, E. (2024). Resisting social pressure in the household using mobile money: Experimental evidence on microenterprise investment in Uganda. *American Economic Review*, *114*(5), 1415–1447. https://doi.org/10.1257/aer.20220717

Rivera, A. I. V., Mondragón-Sánchez, E. J., Vasconcelos, F. K. A., Pinheiro, P. N. D. C., Ferreira, A. G. N., & Galvão, M. T. G. (2021). Actions to prevent sexual violence against adolescents: An integrative literature review. *Revista Brasileira de Enfermagem*, *74*(Suppl. 4), Article e20190876. https://doi.org/10.1590/0034-7167-2019-0876

Robinson, J. L., Narasimhan, M., Amin, A., Morse, S., Beres, L. K., Yeh, P. T., & Kennedy, C. E. (2017). Interventions to address unequal gender, power relations, and improve self-efficacy and empowerment for sexual and reproductive health decision-making for women living with HIV: A systematic review. *PLOS One*, *12*(8). https://doi.org/10.1371/ journal.pone.0180699

Rocca, C. H., Rathod, S., Falle, T., Pande, R. P., & Krishnan, S. (2009). Challenging assumptions about women's empowerment: Social and economic resources and domestic violence among young married women in urban south India. *International Journal of Epidemiology*, *38*(2), 577–585. https://doi.org/10.1093/ije/dyn226

Rodella, A., Cuevas, F., & Atuesta, B. (2015). *Haiti Adolescent Girl Initiative (AGI)* (The World Bank Project Report No. 98201). The World Bank Group. https://documents1.worldbank. org/curated/en/106851468186565029/pdf/98201-WP-P123483-Box391506B-PUBLIC-Haiti-Adolescent-Girls-Initiative.pdf

Roff, J. (2017). Cleaning in the shadow of the law? Bargaining, marital investment, and the impact of divorce law on husbands' intrahousehold work. *Journal of Law & Economics*, *60*(1), 115–134. http://dx.doi.org/10.1086/692806

Rogers, B. L., & Schlossman, N. P. (Eds.). (1990). *Intra-household resource allocation: Issues and methods for development policy and planning: Papers prepared for the Workshop on Methods of Measuring Intra-household Resource Allocation, Gloucester, Massachusetts, USA, October 1983* (Vol. 15). United Nations University Press.

Rogers, E. S., Chamberlin, J., Ellison, M. L., & Crean, T. (1997). A consumer-constructed scale to measure empowerment among users of mental health services. *Psychiatric Services*, *48*(8), 1042–1047. https://doi.org/10.1176/ps.48.8.1042

Rose, E. (1999). Consumption smoothing and excess female mortality in rural India. *Review of Economics and Statistics*, *81*(1), 41–49. https://doi.org/10.1162/003465399767923809

Rossi, P., & Godard, M. (2022). The old-age security motive for fertility: Evidence from the extension of social pensions in Namibia. *American Economic Journal: Economic Policy*, *14*(4), 488–518. http://dx.doi.org/10.2139/ssrn.3457324

Rotondi, V., Kashyap, R., Pesando, L. M., Spinelli, S., & Billari, F. C. (2020). Leveraging mobile phones to attain sustainable development. *Proceedings of the National Academy of Sciences of the United States of America*, *117*(24), 13413–13420. https://doi.org/10.1073/pnas.1909326117

Rowlands, J. (1995). Empowerment examined. *Development in Practice*, *5*(2), 101–107. https://doi.org/10.1080/0961452951000157074

___. (1997). *Questioning empowerment: Working with women in Honduras*. Oxfam.

Rowther, A. A., Kazi, A. K., Nazir, H., Atiq, M., Atif, N., Rauf, N., Malik, A., & Surkan, P. J. (2020). "A woman is a puppet." Women's disempowerment and prenatal anxiety in Pakistan: A qualitative study of sources, mitigators, and coping strategies for anxiety in pregnancy. *International Journal of Environmental Research and Public Health*, *17*(14), Article 4926. https://doi.org/10.3390/ijerph17144926

Roy, S., Ara, J., Das, N., & Quisumbing, A. R. (2015). "Flypaper effects" in transfers targeted to women: Evidence from BRAC's Targeting the Ultra-poor Program in Bangladesh. *Journal of Development Economics*, *117*, 1–17. https://doi.org/10.1016/j.jdeveco.2015.06.004

Ruck, D. J., Bentley, R. A., & Lawson, D. J. (2020). Cultural prerequisites of socioeconomic development. *Royal Society Open Science*, *7*(2), Article 190725. https://doi.org/doi:10.1098/rsos.190725

Ruel, M. T., & Alderman, H. (2013). Nutrition-sensitive interventions and programmes: How can they help to accelerate progress in improving maternal and child nutrition? *Lancet*, *382*, 536–551. http://dx.doi.org/10.1016/S0140-6736(13)60843-0

Ryan, R. M., & Deci, E. L. (2000). Intrinsic and extrinsic motivations: Classic definitions and new directions. *Contemporary Educational Psychology*, *25*(1), 54–67. https://doi.org/10.1006/ceps.1999.1020

Saggurti, N., Atmavilas, Y., Porwal, A., Schooley, J., Das, R., Kande, N., Irani, L., & Hay, K. (2018). Effect of health intervention integration within women's self-help groups on collectivization and healthy practices around reproductive, maternal, neonatal and child health in rural India. *PLOS One*, *13*(8), Article e0202562. https://doi.org/10.1371/journal.pone.0202562

Salem, R., Cheong, Y. F., & Yount, K. M. (2018). Is women's work a pathway to their agency in rural Minya, Egypt? *Social Indicators Research*, *136*(2). https://doi.org/10.1007/s11205-017-1573-9

Saluja, O. B., Singh, P., & Kumar, H. (2023). Barriers and interventions on the way to empower women through financial inclusion: A 2 decades systematic review (2000–2020). *Humanities and Social Sciences Communications*, *10*(148). https://doi.org/10.1057/s41599-023-01640-y

Samari, G. (2017). Women's agency and fertility: Recent evidence from Egypt. *Population Research and Policy Review*, *36*(4), 561–582. https://doi.org/10.1007/s11113-017-9427-3

___. (2019). Women's empowerment in Egypt: The reliability of a complex construct. *Sexual and Reproductive Health Matters*, *27*(1), 146–159. https://doi.org/10.1080/26410397.2019.1586816

Santos Silva, M., & Klasen, S. (2021). Gender inequality as a barrier to economic growth: A review of the theoretical literature. *Review of Economics of the Household*, *19*, 581–614. https://doi.org/10.1007/s11150-020-09535-6

Santoso, M. V., Kerr, R. B., Hoddinott, J., Garigipati, P., Olmos, S., & Young, S. L. (2019). Role of women's empowerment in child nutrition outcomes: A systematic review. *Advances in Nutrition*, *10*(6), 1138–1151. https://doi.org/10.1093/advances/nmz056

Sapkal, R. S. (2017). From mother to daughter: Does equal inheritance property laws reform improve female labor supply and educational attainments in India? *Asian Journal of Law and Economics*, *8*(1). https://doi.org/10.1515/ajle-2015-0028

Sardinha, L., Maheu-Giroux, M., Stöckl, H., Meyer, S. R., & García-Moreno, C. (2022). Global, regional, and national prevalence estimates of physical or sexual, or both, intimate partner violence against women in 2018. *The Lancet*, *399*(10327), 803–813. https://doi.org/10.1016/S0140-6736(21)02664-7

Scales, P. C., Benson, P. L., Dershem, L., Fraher, K., Makonnen, R., Nazneen, S., Syvertsen, A. K., & Titus, S. (2013). Building developmental assets to empower adolescent girls in rural Bangladesh: Evaluation of project Kishoree Kontha. *Journal of Research on Adolescence*, *23*(1), 171–184. http://dx.doi.org/10.1111/j.1532-7795.2012.00805.x

Schaffnit, S. B., Wamoyi, J., Urassa, M., Dardoumpa, M., & Lawson, D. W. (2021). When marriage is the best available option: Perceptions of opportunity and risk in female adolescence in Tanzania. *Global Public Health*, *16*(12), 1820–1833. https://doi.org/10.1080/17441692.2020.1837911

Schierl, T., Tanaka, L. F., Klug, S. J., Winkler, A. S., & Stelzle, D. (2023). The association of women's empowerment with HIV-related indicators: A pooled analysis of demographic and health surveys in sub-Saharan Africa. *Journal of Epidemiology and Global Health*, *13*, 816–824. https://doi.org/10.1007/s44197-023-00153-w

Scrimshaw, S. C. (1978). Part two: Stages in women's lives and reproductive decision-making in Latin America. *Medical Anthropology*, *2*(3), 41–58. https://doi.org/10.1080/01459740.1978.9986954

Scrimshaw, S. C., Lane, S. D., Rubinstein, R. A., & Fisher, J. (2022). Introduction. In S. C. Scrimshaw, S. D. Lane, R. A. Rubenstein, & J. Fisher (Eds.), *The SAGE handbook of social studies of health and medicine* (2nd ed.). SAGE Publications.

Scrimshaw, S. C. M. (1984). Infanticide in human populations: Societal and individual concerns. In G. Hausfater & S. B. Hardy (Eds.), *Infanticide: Comparative and evolutionary perspectives* (pp. 439–462). Aldine.

____. (1985). Bringing the period down: Government and squatter settlement confront induced abortion in Ecuador. In P. J. Pelto & W. deWalt (Eds.), *Macro and micro levels of analysis in anthropology* (pp. 121–146). Westview Press. http://dx.doi.org/10.4324/9780429036071-6

Sear, R., & Coall, D. (2011). How much does family matter? Cooperative breeding and the demographic transition. *Population and Development Review*, *37*, 81–112. https://doi.org/10.1111/j.1728-4457.2011.00379.x

Sear, R., & Mace, R. (2008). Who keeps children alive? A review of the effects of kin on child survival. *Evolution and Human Behavior*, *29*(1), 1–18. https://doi.org/10.1016/j.evolhumbehav.2007.10.001

Sedlmayr, R., Shah, A., & Sulaiman, M. (2018). Cash-plus: Poverty impacts of transfer-based intervention alternatives. *Journal of Development Economics*, *144*, Article 102418. https://doi.org/10.1016/j.jdeveco.2019.102418

Segal, S. P., Silverman, C., & Temkin, T. (1995). Measuring empowerment in client-run self-help agencies. *Community Mental Health Journal*, *31*(3), 215–227. https://doi.org/10.1007/bf02188748

Seider, S., Clark, S., & Graves, D. (2020). The development of critical consciousness and its relation to academic achievement in adolescents of color. *Child Development, 91*(2), e451–e474. https://doi.org/10.1111/cdev.13262

Sekabira, H., & Qaim, M. (2017). Can mobile phones improve gender equality and nutrition? Panel data evidence from farm households in Uganda. *Food Policy, 73*, 95–103. https://doi.org/10.1016/j.foodpol.2017.10.004

Sen, A. (1987). *Gender and cooperative conflicts.* World Institute for Development Economics Research.

___. (1990). More than 100 million women are missing. *The New York Review of Books, 37*(20), 219–222.

___. (1992). Missing women. *British Medical Journal, 304*, 587–588. https://doi.org/10.1136/bmj.304.6827.587

___. (1999). *Development as freedom.* Alfred Knopf.

___. (2006). Development as freedom: An India perspective. *Indian Journal of Industrial Relations, 42*(2), 157–169.

Sen, G., & Grown, C. (1987). *Development crises and alternative visions: Third World women's perspectives.* Routledge.

Sen, G., & Ostlin, P. (2011). *Gender inequality in health.* In J. H. Lee & R. Saldana (Eds.), *Improving equality in health by addressing social determinants* (pp. 59–87). World Health Organization.

Seymour, G., Heckert, J., Quisumbing, A., Meinzen-Dick, R., Malapit, H., Paz, F., Faas, S., Myers, E., Doss, C., Sinharoy, S. S., Cheong, Y. F., Yount, K. M., Hassan, M. Z., Hassan, M. I., Sharma, S., Pokhrel, P., Sagastume, M. D., Kanyanda, S. S. E., Vundru, W. D., & Moylan, H. (2024). *Measuring women's empowerment in national surveys: Development of the Women's Empowerment Metric for National Statistical Systems (WEMNS)* (IFPRI Discussion Paper No. 2254). International Food Policy Research Institute.

Shah, M., Seager, J., Montalvao, J., & Goldstein, M. (2023). *Sex, power, and adolescence: Intimate partner violence and sexual behaviors* (NBER Working Paper No. 31624). National Bureau of Economic Research. https://www.nber.org/system/files/working_papers/w31624/w31624.pdf

Shah, M., Seager, J., & Rubio, G. (2022). *Supplying contraceptives to adolescents: When pure access does not breed use* (Working Paper).

Shakya, H. B., Cislaghi, B., Fleming, P., Levtov, R. G., Boyce, S. C., Raj, A., & Silverman, J. G. (2022). Associations of attitudes and social norms with experiences of intimate partner violence among married adolescents and their husbands in rural Niger: A dyadic cross-sectional study. *BMC Women's Health, 22*(1), Article 180. https://doi.org/10.1186/s12905-022-01724-y

Sharaunga, S., Mudhara, M., & Bogale, A. (2016). Effects of 'women empowerment' on household food security in rural KwaZulu-Natal province. *Development Policy Review, 34*(2), 223–252. https://doi.org/10.1111/dpr.12151

___. (2019). Conceptualisation and measurement of women's empowerment revisited. *Journal of Human Development and Capabilities, 20*(1), 1–25. https://doi.org/10.1080/19452829.2018.1546280

Sharma, S., Mehra, D., Akhtar, F., & Mehra, S. (2020). Evaluation of a community-based intervention for health and economic empowerment of marginalized women in India. *BMC Public Health, 20*(1), Article 1766. https://doi.org/10.1186/s12889-020-09884-y

Shibre, G., Mekonnen, W., & Haile, M. D. (2023). Decomposition analysis of women's empowerment-based inequalities in the use of maternal health care services in Ethiopia: Evidence from demographic and health surveys. *PLOS One, 18*(4). https://doi.org/10.1371/journal.pone.0285024

Shiell, A., Hawe, P., & Kavanagh, S. (2020). Evidence suggests a need to rethink social capital and social capital interventions. *Social Science & Medicine, 257*, Article 111930. https://doi.org/10.1016/j.socscimed.2018.09.006

Shimamoto, K., & Gipson, J. D. (2019). Investigating pathways linking women's status and empowerment to skilled attendance at birth in Tanzania: A structural equation modeling approach. *PLOS One, 14*(2). https://doi.org/10.1371/journal.pone.0212038

Singh, S., Mohan, A., Saran, A., Puskur, R., Mishra, A., Etale, L., Cole, S. M., Masset, E., Waddington, H. S., MacDonald, H., & White, H. (2022a). Protocol: Gender transformative approaches in agriculture for women's empowerment: A systematic review. *Campbell Systematic Reviews, 18*(3). http://dx.doi.org/10.1002/cl2.1265

Singh, S., Prowse, M., White, H., Warsame, A., Waddington, H. S., Vijayamma, R., Umezawa, H., Tolin, L., Reumann, A., & Puri, J. (2022b). *Effectiveness of life skills training interventions for the empowerment of women in developing countries: A systematic review* (IFAD Report). International Fund of Agricultural Development. https://www.ifad.org/documents/38714170/47117768/egm-gender-systematic-review-top_1.pdf/f46cdf8d-fa73-f581-e756-093ae34ebb87?t=1674807443489

Sinharoy, S. S., McManus, S., Conrad, A., Patrick, M., & Caruso, B. A. (2023). The Agency, Resources, and Institutional Structures for Sanitation-related Empowerment (ARISE) Scales: Development and validation of measures of women's empowerment in urban sanitation for low- and middle-income countries. *World Development, 164*, Article 106183. https://doi.org/10.1016/j.worlddev.2023.106183

Snoxell, S., Harpham, T.,Grant, E., & Rodriguez, C. (2006). Social capital interventions: A case study from Cali, Colombia. *Canadian Journal of Development Studies, 27*, 65–81. https://doi.org/10.1080/02255189.2006.9669121

Solar, O., & Irwin, A. (2010). *A conceptual framework for action on the social determinants of health* (WHO Discussion Conceptual Paper No. 2). World Health Organization. https://iris.who.int/bitstream/handle/10665/44489/9789241500852_eng.pdf?sequence=1

Sripad, P., Warren, C. E., Hindin, M. J., & Karra, M. (2019). Assessing the role of women's autonomy and acceptability of intimate-partner violence in maternal health-care utilization in 63 low- and middle-income countries. *International Journal of Epidemiology, 48*(5), 1580–1592. https://doi.org/10.1093/ije/dyy299

Stark, L., Asghar, K., Seff, I., Yu, G., Tesfay Gessesse, T., Ward, L., Assazenew Baysa, A., Neiman, A., & Falb, K. L. (2018). Preventing violence against refugee adolescent girls: Findings from a cluster randomised controlled trial in Ethiopia. *BMJ Global Health, 3*(5), e000825. https://doi.org/10.1136/bmjgh-2018-000825

Steckermeier, L. C. (2019). Better safe than sorry. Does agency moderate the relevance of safety perceptions for the subjective well-being of young children? *Child Indicators Research, 12*, 29–48. https://doi.org/10.1007/s12187-017-9519-y

Stevenson, B. (2007). The impact of divorce laws on marriage-specific capital. *Journal of Labor Economics, 25*(1), 75–94. http://dx.doi.org/10.2139/ssrn.911880

Stevenson, B., & Wolfers, J. (2006). Bargaining in the shadow of the law: Divorce laws and family distress. *Quarterly Journal of Economics, 121*(1), 267–288. https://doi.org/10.1093/qje/121.1.267

Stoebenau, K., Pande, R., & Malhotra, A. (2013). *Has fertility decline contributed to improvements in women's lives?* (ICRW Working Paper No. 012-2013-ICRW-FE). International Center for Research on Women. https://www.icrw.org/wp-content/uploads/2016/10/ICRW_FEN_WPS_2013_FINAL.pdf

Suri, T., & Jack, W. (2016). The long-run poverty and gender impacts of mobile money. *Science, 354*(6317), 1288–1292. https://doi.org/10.1126/science.aah5309

Sviatschi, M. M., & Trako, I. (2024). Gender violence, enforcement, and human capital: Evidence from women's justice centers in Peru. *Journal of Development Economics, 9*, Article 103262. https://doi.org/10.1016/j.jdeveco.2024.103262

Swamy, A., Knack, S., Lee, Y., & Azfar, O. (2001). Gender and corruption. *Journal of Development Economics, 64*(1), 25–55. https://doi.org/10.1016/S0304-3878(00)00123-1

Tarozzi, A., Desai, J., & Johnson, K. (2015). The impacts of microcredit: Evidence from Ethiopia. *American Economic Journal: Applied Economics*, 7(1), 54–89. https://doi.org/10.1257/app.20130475

Tavenner, K., van Wijk, M., Fraval, S., Hammond, J., Baltenweck, I., Teufel, N., Kihoro, E., de Haan, N., van Etten, J., Steinke, J., Baines, D., Carpena, P., Skirrow, T., Rosenstock, T., Lamanna, C., Ng'endo, M., Chesterman, S., Namoi, N., & Manda, L. (2019). Intensifying inequality? Gendered trends in commercializing and diversifying smallholder farming systems in East Africa. *Frontiers in Sustainable Food Systems*, 3(10). https://doi.org/10.3389/fsufs.2019.00010

Tertilt, M. (2005). Polygyny, fertility, and savings. *Journal of Political Economy*, 113(6), 1341–1371. http://dx.doi.org/10.1086/498049

___. (2006). Polygyny, women's rights, and development. *Journal of the European Economic Association*, 4(2-3), 523–530. http://dx.doi.org/10.1162/jeea.2006.4.2-3.523

Thorpe, S., VanderEnde, K., Peters, C., Bardin, L., & Yount, K. M. (2016). The influence of women's empowerment on child immunization coverage in low, lower-middle, and upper-middle income countries: A systematic review of the literature. *Maternal and Child Health Journal*, 20(1), 172–186. https://doi.org/10.1007/s10995-015-1817-8

Tyner, J. A. (1999). The global context of gendered labor migration from the Philippines to the United States. *American Behavioral Scientist*, 42(4), 671–689. https://doi.org/10.1177/00027649921954417

Uberoi, P. (Ed.). (1993). *Family, kinship and marriage in India*. Oxford University Press.

Uduji, J. I., & Okolo-Obasi, E. N. (2018). Young rural women's participation in the e-wallet programme and usage intensity of modern agricultural inputs in Nigeria. *Gender, Technology and Development*, 22, 59–81. https://doi.org/10.1080/09718524.2018.1445894

United Nations. (1948). *The universal declaration of human rights*. https://www.un.org/en/about-us/universal-declaration-of-human-rights

___. (1995, September 4–15). *Report of the Fourth World Conference on Women*. Beijing, China. https://documents.un.org/doc/undoc/gen/n96/273/01/pdf/n9627301.pdf

___. (2015). *Transforming our world: the 2030 Agenda for Sustainable Development* https://docs.un.org/en/A/RES/70/1

___. (2023). *Sustainable development goals: Extended report*. https://unstats.un.org/sdgs/report/2023/extended-report/

United Nations Development Programme. (2006). *Resouce guide: Mainstraming gender in water management*. https://www.undp.org/sites/g/files/zskgke326/files/publications/IWRM GenderResourceGuide-English-200610.pdf

United Nations for Human Rights Office of the High Commissioner. (n.d.). *About good governance*. https://www.ohchr.org/en/good-governance/about-good-governance

___. (2021). *Human rights and elections: A handbook on international human rights standards on elections* (OHCHR Report). https://www.ohchr.org/sites/default/files/2022-02/Human-Rights-and-Elections.pdf

United Nations Population Fund & International Organization for Migration. (2006). *Female migrants: Bridging the gaps throughout the life cycle*. https://www.unfpa.org/sites/default/files/resource-pdf/bridging_gap.pdf

Upadhyay, U. D., Gipson, J. D., Withers, M., Lewis, S., Ciaraldi, E. J., Fraser, A., Huchko, M. J., & Prata, N. (2014). Women's empowerment and fertility: A review of the literature. *Social Science & Medicine*, 115, 111–120. https://doi.org/10.1016/j.socscimed.2014.06.014

Upadhyay, U. D., & Karasek, D. (2012). Women's empowerment and ideal family size: An examination of DHS empowerment measures in sub-Saharan Africa. *International Perspectives on Sexual and Reproductive Health*, 38(2), 78–89. https://doi.org/10.1363/3807812

van Eerdewijk, A., Wong, F., Vaast, C., Newton, J., Tyszler, M., & Pennington, A. (2017). *White paper: A conceptual model of women and girls' empowerment* (KIT Gender White Paper). Koninklijk Instituut voor de Tropen. https://www.kit.nl/wp-content/uploads/2018/10/BMGF_KIT_WhitePaper_web-1.pdf

VanderWeele, T. J., McNeely, E., & Koh, H. K. (2019). Reimagining health—flourishing. *JAMA, 321*(17), 1667–1668. https://doi.org/10.1001/jama.2019.3035

Vanhuyse, F., Stirrup, O., Odhiambo, A., Palmer, T., Dickin, S., Skordis, J., Batura, N., Haghparast-Bidgoli, H., Mwaki, A., & Copas, A. (2022). Effectiveness of conditional cash transfers (Afya credits incentive) to retain women in the continuum of care during pregnancy, birth and the postnatal period in Kenya: A cluster-randomised trial. *BMJ Open, 12*(1). https://doi.org/10.1136/bmjopen-2021-055921

Varkey, P., Kureshi, S., & Lesnick, T. (2010). Empowerment of women and its association with the health of the community. *Journal of Women's Health, 19*(1), 71–76. https://doi.org/10.1089/jwh.2009.1444

Varriale, C., Pesando, L. M., Kashyap, R., & Rotondi, V. (2022). Mobile phones and attitudes towards women's participation in politics: Evidence from Africa. *Sociology of Development, 8*(1), 1–37. https://doi.org/10.1525/sod.2020.0039

Vasquez, I., McMahon, F., Murphy, M., & Schneider, G. S. (2021). *The Human Freedom Index: A global measurement of personal, civil, and economic freedom.* CATO Institute. https://www.cato.org/human-freedom-index/2021

Villalonga-Olives, E., Wind, T. R., & Kawachi, I. (2018). Social capital interventions in public health: A systematic review. *Social Science & Medicine, 212*, 203–218. https://doi.org/10.1016/j.socscimed.2018.07.022

Vladutiu, C. J., Martin, S. L., & Macy, R. J. (2011). College- or university-based sexual assault prevention programs: A review of program outcomes, characteristics, and recommendations. *Trauma, Violence, & Abuse, 12*(2), 67–86. https://doi.org/10.1177/1524838010390708

Voena, A. (2015). Yours, mine, and ours: Do divorce laws affect the intertemporal behavior of married couples? *American Economic Review, 105*(8), 2295–2332. http://dx.doi.org/10.1257/aer.20120234

Vogelstein, R. B., & Stone, M. (2021). *Awakening #MeToo and the global fight for women's rights.* Public Affairs.

Waid, J. L., Wendt, A. S., Sinharoy, S. S., Kader, A., & Gabrysch, S. (2022). Impact of a homestead food production program on women's empowerment: Pro-WEAI results from the FAARM trial in Bangladesh. *World Development, 158*, Article 106001. https://doi.org/10.1016/j.worlddev.2022.106001

Waidler, J., Gilbert, U., Mulokozi, A., & Palermo, T. (2022). A "Plus" model for safe transitions to adulthood: Impacts of an integrated intervention layered onto a national social protection program on sexual behavior and health seeking among Tanzania's youth. *Studies in Family Planning, 53*(2), 233–258. https://doi.org/10.1111/sifp.12190

Weber, A. M., Cislaghi, B., Meausoone, V., Abdalla, S., Mejía-Guevara, I., Loftus, P., Hallgren, E., Seff, I., Stark, L., Victora, C. G., & Buffarini, R. (2019). Gender norms and health: Insights from global survey data. *The Lancet, 393*(10189), 2455–2468. https://doi.org/10.1016/S0140-6736(19)30765-2

Weitzman, A. (2014). Women's and men's relative status and intimate partner violence in India. *Population and Development Review, 40*(1), 55–75. https://doi.org/10.1111/j.1728-4457.2014.00650.x

Wekesah, F. M., Mutua, E. N., & Izugbara, C. O. (2019). Gender and conservation agriculture in sub-Saharan Africa: A systematic review. *International Journal of Agricultural Sustainability, 17*(1), 78–91. https://doi.org/10.1080/14735903.2019.1567245

Wekwete, N. N. (2014). Gender and economic empowerment in Africa: Evidence and policy. *Journal of African Economies, 23*(Suppl. 1), i87–i127. https://doi.org/10.1093/jae/ejt022

Williams, A. L., & Merten, M. J. (2014). Linking community, parenting, and depressive symptom trajectories: Testing resilience models of adolescent agency based on race/ethnicity and gender. *Journal of Youth and Adolescence*, 43(9), 1563–1575. https://doi.org/10.1007/s10964-014-0141-8

Woldemicael, G. (2007). *Do women with higher autonomy seek more maternal and child health-care? Evidence from Ethiopia and Eritrea*. Stockholm University. https://urn.kb.se/resolve?urn=urn:nbn:se:su:diva-7296

Wolfers, D., & Scrimshaw, S. (1975). Child survival and intervals between pregnancies in Guayaquil, Ecuador. *Population Studies*, 29(3), 479–496. https://doi.org/10.1080/0032 4728.1975.10412712

Wolfers, J. (2006). Did unilateral divorce laws raise divorce rates? A reconciliation and new results. *American Economic Review*, 96(5), 1802–1820. https://doi.org/10.1257/aer.96.5.1802

Wood, S. N., Karp, C., Tsui, A., Kibira, S. P. S., Desta, S., Galadanci, H., Makumbi, F., Omoluabi, E., Shiferaw, S., Seme, A., & Moreau, C. (2021). A sexual and reproductive empowerment framework to explore volitional sex in sub-Saharan Africa. *Culture, Health & Sexuality*, 23(6), 804–821. https://doi.org/10.1080/13691058.2020.1733667

World Health Organization. (n.d.). *Promoting wellbeing*. https://www.who.int/activities/promoting-well-being

___. (1948). *Summary report on proceedings minutes and final acts of the International Health Conference held in New York from 19 June to 22 July 1946*. https://iris.who.int/handle/10665/85573

___. (2022). *Abortion care guideline*. https://www.who.int/publications/i/item/9789240039483

___. (2023). *Infertility prevalence estimates, 1990–2021*. https://iris.who.int/bitstream/handle/10665/366700/9789240068315-eng.pdf

Wu, X., Ye, H., & He, G. G. (2012). *Fertility decline and women's empowerment in China* (ICRW Working Paper Series 006-2012-ICRW-FE). International Center for Research on Women. https://www.icrw.org/wp-content/uploads/2016/10/ICRW-WPS_Wu_sept-2012.pdf

Yang, W., Roig, M., Jimenez, M., Perry, J., & Shepherd, A. (2016). *Leaving no one behind: The imperative of inclusive development* (UN Report). United Nations Department of Economic and Social Affairs. https://www.un.org/esa/socdev/rwss/2016/full-report.pdf

Yaya, S., Uthman, O. A., Ekholuenetale, M., & Bishwajit, G. (2018). Women empowerment as an enabling factor of contraceptive use in sub-Saharan Africa: A multilevel analysis of cross-sectional surveys of 32 countries. *Reproductive Health*, 15(1), Article 214. https://doi.org/10.1186/s12978-018-0658-5

Yeo, S., Bell, M., Kim, Y. R., & Alaofè, H. (2022). Afghan women's empowerment and antenatal care utilization: A population-based cross-sectional study. *BMC Pregnancy and Childbirth*, 22(1), Article 970. https://doi.org/10.1186/s12884-022-05328-0

Yi, Z., Ping, T., Baochang, G., Yi, X., Bohua, L., & Yongpiing, L. (1993). Causes and implications of the recent increase in the reported sex ratio at birth in China. *Population and Development Review*, 19(2), 283–302. https://doi.org/10.2307/2938438

Yount, K. M. (2001). Excess mortality of girls in the Middle East in the 1970s and 1980s: Patterns, correlates and gaps in research. *Population Studies*, 55(3), 291–308. https://doi.org/10.1080/00324720127703

___. (2004). Maternal resources, proximity of services, and curative care of boys and girls in Minya, Egypt 1995–97. *Population Studies*, 58(3), 345–355. https://doi.org/10.1080/0032472042000272384

___. (2005). Resources, family organization, and domestic violence against married women in Minya, Egypt. *Journal of Marriage and Family*, 67(3), 579–596. http://dx.doi.org/10.1111/j.1741-3737.2005.00155.x

___. (2011). Women's conformity as resistance to intimate partner violence in Assiut, Egypt. *Sex Roles, 64*, 43–58. https://doi.org/10.1007/s11199-010-9884-1

Yount, K. M., & Carrera, J. S. (2006). Domestic violence against married women in Cambodia. *Social Forces, 85*(1), 355–387. http://dx.doi.org/10.1353/sof.2006.0151

Yount, K. M., Cheong, Y. F., Khan, Z., Miedema, S. S., & Naved, R. T. (2021). Women's participation in microfinance: Effects on women's agency, exposure to partner violence, and mental health. *Social Science & Medicine, 270*, Article 113686. https://doi.org/10.1016/j.socscimed.2021.113686

Yount, K. M., Crandall, A. A., & Cheong, Y. F. (2018a). Women's age at first marriage and long-term economic empowerment in Egypt. *World Development, 102*, 124–134. https://doi.org/10.1016/j.worlddev.2017.09.013

Yount, K. M., Durr, R. L., Bergenfeld, I., Sharma, S., Clark, C. J., Laterra, A., Kalra, S., Sprinkel, A., & Cheong, Y. F. (2023). Impact of the CARE Tipping Point Program in Nepal on adolescent girls' agency and risk of child, early, or forced marriage: Results from a cluster-randomized controlled trial. *SSM-Population Health, 22*, Article 101407. https://doi.org/10.1016/j.ssmph.2023.101407

Yount, K. M., Johnson, E., Sharma, K., Meinzen-Dick, R. S., & Sinharoy, S. (2022). *Conceptualizing and measuring women's empowerment: Insights from country stakeholders in Asia.* SSRN. https://dx.doi.org/10.2139/ssrn.4088823

Yount, K. M., Khan, Z., Miedema, S., Cheong, Y. F., & Naved, R. T. (2020). *The Women's Agency Scale 61 (WAS-61): A comprehensive measure of women's intrinsic, instrumental, and collective agency.* SSRN. https://dx.doi.org/10.2139/ssrn.3670180

Yount, K. M., Krause, K. H., & Miedema, S. S. (2017). Preventing gender-based violence victimization in adolescent girls in lower-income countries: Systematic review of reviews. *Social Science & Medicine, 192*, 1–13. https://doi.org/10.1016/j.socscimed.2017.08.038

Yount, K. M., Peterman, A., & Cheong, Y. F. (2018b). Measuring women's empowerment: A need for context and caution. *The Lancet Global Health, 6*(1). https://doi.org/10.1016/S2214-109X(17)30459-X

Yount, K. M., VanderEnde, K. E., Dodell, S., & Cheong, Y. F. (2016). Measurement of women's agency in Egypt: A national validation study. *Social Indicators Research, 128*(3), 1171–1192. https://doi.org/10.1007/s11205-015-1074-7

Yount, K. M., Zureick-Brown, S., Halim, N., & LaVilla, K. (2014). Fertility decline, girls' well-being, and gender gaps in children's well-being in poor countries. *Demography, 51*(2), 535–561. https://doi.org/10.1007/s13524-014-0282-0

Zakiyah, N., van Asselt, A. D., Roijmans, F., & Postma M. J. (2016). Economic evaluation of family planning interventions in low and middle income countries: A systematic review. *PLOS One, 11*(12). https://doi.org/10.1371/journal.pone.0168447

Zhang, H., & Assaad, R. (2024). Women's access to school, educational attainment, and fertility: Evidence from Jordan. *Journal of Development Economics, 170*. https://doi.org/10.1016/j.jdeveco.2024.103291

Zimmerman, C., Mak, J., Popock, N., & Kiss, L. (2021). Human trafficking: Results of a 5-year theory-based evaluation of interventions to prevent trafficking of women from south Asia. *Frontiers in Public Health, 9*, Article 645059. https://doi.org/10.3389/fpubh.2021.645059

Zimmerman, M. A. (2000). Empowerment theory: Psychological, organizational and community levels of analysis. In J. Rappaport & E. Seidman (Eds.), *Handbook of community psychology* (pp. 43–63). Springer.

Zinsser, J. P. (1990). The United Nations decade for women: A quiet revolution. *The History Teacher, 24*(1), 19–29. https://doi.org/10.2307/494202

Appendix A

Biographical Sketches of Committee Members

ANITA RAJ (*Co-Chair*, she/her/hers) is Nancy Reeves Dreux Endowed Chair in the School of Public Health and Tropical Medicine and the executive director of the Newcomb Institute at Tulane University. Previously, she was Tata Chancellor Professor of Society and Health and the director of the Center on Gender Equity and Health at the University of California, San Diego. Raj is a research scientist trained in developmental psychology and public health with a multidisciplinary research focus on gender equity in global health and development. She has led federal grant and foundation-funded studies on gender theory and measurement science, sexual and reproductive health, maternal and adolescent health, women's empowerment, and gender inequalities, including gender-based violence and child marriage. She created and leads the EMERGE platform, which provides open access evidence-based measures on gender empowerment, built indicators on gender empowerment in national surveys, and offers technical assistance to survey researchers and implementers working on gender empowerment. Raj also created and leads the Violence EXperiences study to assess state-wide data on experiences of violence, discrimination, and mental health, to support data-driven policy decision making on these issues. She has a Ph.D. in psychology from the University of Georgia.

SUSAN CROSBY SCRIMSHAW (*Co-Chair*, she/her/hers) was president of Russell Sage College, president of Simmons College, dean of the School of Public Health at the University of Illinois at Chicago, and associate dean of public health and associate director of the Latin American Center at the University of California, Los Angeles. Her research includes community

187

participatory research, research methods, reproductive health, health communication, and social determinants of health internationally and with Latino and African American populations in the United States. Scrimshaw is an American Association for the Advancement of Science fellow and American Anthropological Association fellow. She serves on the board of directors of Speare Memorial Hospital in Plymouth, New Hampshire. Scrimshaw also served on the Chicago and Illinois State Boards of Health, on the New York State Minority Health Council, as chair of the Association of Schools of Public Health, and on the board and as board president of the US-Mexico Foundation for Science. She lived in Guatemala until age 16. Honors include the Yarmolinsky Medal (National Academy of Medicine), the Margaret Mead Award (Society for Applied Anthropology/ American Anthropological Association), and Hero of Public Health gold medal (Mexico). She has a Ph.D. in medical anthropology from Columbia University. Scrimshaw is a member of the National Academy of Medicine.

RAGUI ASSAAD (he/him/his) is a professor in the Humphrey School of Public Affairs at the University of Minnesota. He is also a research fellow at the Economic Research Forum (ERF) in Cairo, Egypt, and a nonresident research fellow of the Institute of Labor Economics in Bonn, Germany. Assaad previously served as regional director for West Asia and North Africa at the Population Council. His current research focuses on labor markets and human development in the Arab World, with a focus on youth and gender issues as they relate to education, transition from school to work, labor force participation, employment and unemployment, informality, migration, and family formation. Under the auspices of ERF, Assaad led the design and implementation of several nationally representative longitudinal surveys of labor market conditions in Arab countries. He earned the Outstanding Research Award of the Minnesota Population Center, University of Minnesota, and the Award for Global Engagement for exceptional contributions to global education, research, and engagement at the University of Minnesota. Assaad received a Ph.D. in city and regional planning from Cornell University.

SONALDE DESAI (she/her/hers) is a professor of sociology at University of Maryland and the center director of the National Council of Applied Economic Research–National Data Innovation Centre, New Delhi. Prior to joining the University of Maryland, she was an associate in the Policy Research Division at the Population Council. Desai is a demographer whose work deals primarily with social inequalities in developing countries, with a particular focus on gender and class inequalities. She studies inequalities in education, employment, and maternal and child health outcomes by locating them within the region's political economy. While much of Desai's research focuses on South Asia, she has also engaged in comparative studies across Asia, Latin America, and Sub-Saharan Africa. She currently leads the India Human Development Survey of over 40,000 households. Desai has been elected as the president of the Population Association of India and was the president of the Population Association of America. She has been named a fellow of the American Association for the Advancement of Science and is a member of the National Academies of Sciences, Engineering, and Medicine's Committee on Population. Desai received a Ph.D. in sociology from Stanford University and post-doctoral training at the University of Chicago and RAND Corporation.

ALETHEIA DONALD (she/her/hers) is a development economist and thematic leader within the World Bank's Gender Innovation Lab in the Office of the Chief Economist for Africa. At the World Bank, she leads research projects across Côte d'Ivoire, Senegal, the Democratic Republic of the Congo, Turkey, and the Philippines as well as the cross-institutional Measures for Advancing Gender Equality initiative. She is a nonresidential fellow at the Center for Global Development as well as an affiliate of the Institute of Labor Economics. Before joining the World Bank, she was a research fellow at Harvard University's Evidence for Policy Design and head of research for Empower Dalit Women of Nepal. Donald's research spans the study of poverty, social norms, labor, and methodological work on survey data collection. Her current work centers on issues of gender and economic activity, including the effects of marriage, redistributive norms, mechanization, childcare, women's land rights, and intrahousehold cooperation. Donald holds a Ph.D. in economics from Sapienza University.

PASCALINE DUPAS (she/her/hers) is professor of economics and public affairs at Princeton University. Previously, she was professor of economics and the Kleinheinz Family Professor of International Studies at Stanford University and the faculty director of the Stanford King Center on Global Development. Dupas is a development economist seeking to identify interventions and policies that can help reduce global poverty. Her ongoing research includes studies on the gendered impacts of education policy in Ghana, family planning policy in Burkina Faso, digital credit regulation in Malawi, and government subsidized health insurance in India, among others. Dupas is co-chair of the health sector at the Jameel Poverty Action Lab, on the board of directors of the Bureau for Research and Economic Analysis of Development, and a research associate at the National Bureau for Economic Research. She is a National Science Foundation CAREER award winner, a fellow of the Econometric Society, a former Sloan fellow, and a former Guggenheim fellow. Dupas obtained a Ph.D. in economics from the École des Hautes Études en Sciences Sociales in Paris, France.

KELLI STIDHAM HALL (she/her/hers) is the associate dean of research, Thomas Keller Professor of Diversity, and professor of epidemiology in the School of Public Health and Tropical Medicine at Tulane University. Previously, she was an associate professor in Columbia University's Mailman School of Public Health, Heilbrunn Department of Population & Family Health. A social epidemiologist and advanced practice nurse, her research program focuses on the social and structural determinants of maternal-child and reproductive health in the United States and globally. Hall studies the effects of poverty, policies, structural racism, health systems factors, and toxic social stress on disparities in maternal mental health, maternal morbidity, and mortality, and the role of community-driven solutions, multilevel interventions, and integrated models of care. She is currently the multiple principal investigator of Columbia University's National Institutes of Health U54 Maternal Health Research Center of Excellence and is the former principal investigator and founding director of the Center for Reproductive Health Research in the Southeast at Emory University. Hall serves on the editorial boards of the *Maternal Child Health Journal* and *Contraception*, on the board of directors of the Society for Family Planning, on the executive committee of the National Medical Committee of Planned Parenthood Federation of America, and as section counselor for American Public Health Association's Population, Sexual and Reproductive Health Section. She has a Ph.D. from Columbia University in maternal child health (nursing) and epidemiology. In 2020, Hall was elected as a National Academy of Medicine Emerging Leader in Health and Medicine.

POONAM MUTTREJA (she/her/hers) is executive director of the Population Foundation of India (PFI), a leading nongovernmental organization in the fields of population dynamics, gender equity, and sexual and reproductive health. Before joining PFI, she served as the India country director of the John D. and Catherine T. MacArthur Foundation for 15 years and has also co-founded and led the Ashoka Foundation, Dastkar, and the Society for Rural, Urban and Tribal Initiative. For over 40 years, Muttreja has been a strong advocate for women's health, reproductive and sexual rights, and rural livelihoods. She has co-conceived the popular transmedia initiative, Main Kuch Bhi Kar Sakti Hoon (I, A Woman, Can Achieve Anything). The program has introduced an artificial intelligence–powered chat bot, SnehAI, a first of its kind initiative for a behavior change communication initiative in India. She has an M.A. in public administration from Harvard University.

LUCA MARIA PESANDO (he/him/his) is an associate professor of social research and public policy at New York University Abu Dhabi (NYUAD) and was a visiting scholar at the Weatherhead Center for International Affairs at Harvard University. Before joining NYUAD, he was an assistant professor of sociology and demography in the Department of Sociology and Centre on Population Dynamics at McGill University. Pesando's research lies in the areas of social, economic, and digital demography. He is interested in issues of family poverty, inequality, gender, social stratification, intra- and intergenerational processes, technology adoption, and interactions between life-cycle events and human capital accumulation. Pesando's overarching research aim is to produce better knowledge on the link between family change, gender, and educational inequalities in areas where these dynamics are changing rapidly and scant research is available. Most of his work takes an international comparative perspective and focuses on low- and middle-income contexts undergoing economic, social, and demographic transformations, mainly across Sub-Saharan Africa. At McGill, he was nominated as William Dawson Scholar (outstanding early-career researcher), and he was recently awarded a fellowship from the Jacobs Foundation. Pesando has a Ph.D. in demography and sociology from the University of Pennsylvania.

GOLEEN SAMARI (she/her/hers) is associate professor of population and public health sciences at the University of Southern California. Previously, she was assistant professor in the Heilbrunn Department of Population and Family Health and the Mailman School of Public Health at Columbia University. Samari was also a faculty affiliate of the Columbia University Population Research Center, and faculty in the Columbia Program on Forced Migration and Health and Columbia Program on Global Health Justice and Governance. Her research focuses on several dimensions of social inequities and reproductive and population health. She considers how structural oppression based on race, gender, and migration shapes reproductive and population health both domestically and globally, with a particular focus on communities in or from the Middle East and North Africa. Cutting across all her research areas is an interest in the way structural constructs are measured and policy relevant research. She has received several honors for her early career contributions to health equity, and she is a term member with the Council on Foreign Relations. She has a Ph.D. in public health and demography from the University of California, Los Angeles.

TOM VOGL (he/him/his) is associate professor of economics at the University of California, San Diego. He was previously assistant professor of economics and international affairs at Princeton University and associate professor of economics at the University of Texas at Austin. As a development economist and economic demographer, Vogl studies health and population issues in low- and middle-income countries. His recent research has focused on the co-evolution of fertility and the education of adults and children, the intergenerational persistence of child mortality, and the aggregate consequences of differential fertility. Vogl is a fellow of the Bureau for

Research and Economic Analysis of Development and a research associate of the National Bureau of Economic Research, where he serves on the Advisory Board of the Study Group on Gender in the Economy. He received his Ph.D. in economics from Harvard University.

YOHANNES DIBABA WADO (he/him/his) is a research scientist in the Sexual, Reproductive Maternal, Newborn Child and Adolescent Health unit of the African Population and Health Research Center (APHRC) based in Nairobi, Kenya. Before joining APHRC, he worked as senior advisor for research and evaluation with Ipas in Ethiopia and was a lecturer in population studies at Jimma University in southwest Ethiopia. Wado is a population health researcher with experience in research, as well as monitoring and evaluation of programs in the areas of population and sexual and reproductive health and rights. He has experiences in leading and implementing large national surveys, longitudinal studies, randomized controlled trials, systematic and scoping reviews, and analysis of large surveys. Currently, Wado provides technical leadership to research and evaluation projects on population health and sexual and reproductive health and rights, including on family planning, unsafe abortion, and adolescent health. He has a Ph.D. in public health from Addis Ababa University.

KATHRYN YOUNT (she/her/hers) is Asa Griggs Candler Professor of Global Health and sociology at Emory University. Her research examines the intersections of women's health, empowerment, and exposure to gender-based violence, including mixed-methods randomized controlled trials of social-norms and empowerment-based programs to improve these outcomes in underserved populations. Yount has received funding from U.S. federal agencies, private foundations, and foreign agencies to conduct research in Asia, Latin America, the Middle East, Sub-Saharan Africa, and underserved communities in Atlanta. She was as an elected member of the board of directors for the Population Association of America and is a frequent advisor for women's empowerment and gender-based violence prevention initiatives funded by the UKAID and the Bill & Melinda Gates Foundation. Yount was elected as a fellow of the American Association for the Advancement of Science. At Emory University, she is a recipient of the Women of Excellence Award for Mentoring, Marion V. Creekmore Award for Internationalization, and Eleanor Main Graduate Mentor Award. She holds a Ph.D. in demography from Johns Hopkins University.

Appendix B

Frameworks of Women's Empowerment

TABLE B-1 Frameworks of Women's Empowerment

Framework	Empowerment	Agency	Choice	Critical Consciousness	Power	Resources	Achievements/ Outcomes	Institutional Structures
CARE (2006)	Uses the Narayan-Parker (2002) definition of empowerment: "the expansion of assets and capabilities of poor people to participate in, negotiate with, influence, control, and hold accountable the institutions that affect their lives" (p. xviii) and the Kabeer (1999a) definition.	Carrying out one's own analyses, making one's own decisions, and taking one's own actions.	Choice involves the critical components of agency, resources, and achievements.	Practical consciousness is not normally accessible to agents: it is unconscious. Discursive consciousness is precisely what people can articulate about their own actions and motivations. The discrepancy between practical and discursive consciousness is critical to structures of power within society.	Personal (power within, power to) self- and other-images, skills, capabilities, and resources. Interpersonal (power over, power with) visible (organizations, rules/ processes), hidden (agenda-setting), or invisible (meaning-making through socialization and control of information).	Allocative resources are those capabilities that command control over objects, goods, or material life. Authoritative resources refers to control over people. Resources include social relationships through which women negotiate their needs and rights with other social actors, including men. Both agency and structure are mediated through relationships between and	No definition given but references Kabeer (1999a).	Routines, conventions, relationships, and taken-for-granted behavior. Institutions that establish agreed-upon significations (meanings), accepted forms of domination (who has power over what or whom), and agreed criteria for legitimizing the social order. Structure includes culture, legal/ judicial, market/ economic,

Framework	Empowerment	Agency	Choice	Critical Consciousness	Power	Resources	Achievements/ Outcomes	Institutional Structures
						among social actors while, at the same time, forms and patterns of relationships are deeply influenced, frequently in hidden ways, by agency and structure.		political, bureaucratic, and organizational.
Caruso et al. (2022) and Sinharoy et al. (2023) [based on Gates and applied to WASH]	The expansion of choice and strengthening of voice through the transformation of power relations so women and girls have more control over their lives and futures; a process of ongoing change.	Women and girls pursuing goals, expressing voice, and influencing and making decisions free from violence and retribution. Agency includes decision making, leadership, and collective action.		Women and girls identifying and questioning how inequalities in power operate in their lives, and asserting and affirming their sense of self and their entitlement.		The tangible and intangible capital and sources of power that women and girls have, own, or use, individually or collectively, in the exercise of agency. Resources include bodily integrity, critical consciousness, and assets.	The possible outcomes of exercising agency. This framework is focused on water and sanitation outcomes (WASH).	The social arrangements of formal and informal rules and practices that enable and constrain the agency of women and girls, and govern the distribution of resources. Institutional structures include formal laws and policies, norms, and relations.

continued

TABLE B-1 Continued

Framework	Empowerment	Agency	Choice	Critical Consciousness	Power	Resources	Achievements/ Outcomes	Institutional Structures
Donald et al. (2017, 2020)	Empowerment includes components such as resources (preconditions) and achievement (outcomes); agency is the process that binds the two, although well-being outcomes and resources can themselves affect agency (based on Kabeer, 1999a).	Agency is the ability to define one's goals and act on them (based on Kabeer, 1999a). Agency includes goal setting, the ability to achieve goals, and acting on goals, and can be exercised at the individual, household, and community levels. To achieve agency, individuals have to define goals that are in line with their values, to perceive a sense of control and ability, and to act on goals.	Choice and goal setting are precursors to and part of agency. Observed choices may be based on expectations from others or one's own preferences.			Resources are preconditions to agency, and resources can be internal or external to the household and are affected by informal institutions, formal policies (including laws on inheritance and marriage), and the interaction between them.	Achievement by choice is equivalent to an outcome.	Norms and institutional barriers prevent achievement of goals. Institutions can act as resources in the empowerment process.

continued

Framework	Empowerment	Agency	Choice	Critical Consciousness	Power	Resources	Achievements/ Outcomes	Institutional Structures
Edmeades et al. (2018) [USAID funded]	The ability to assert one's opinions, desires, and interests in ways that shape discussions and decisions, and to make and influence decisions, and to challenge and change individual and community circumstances. The result of the interaction of individual and macro-level or structural factors, such as social norms or the legal environment.	The capacity for purposive action that draws on social and material resources at multiple levels to realize preferences and choices, enhance voice, and increase power and influence. The three components of agency are choice, voice, and power.	The ability of individuals to make and influence decisions that affect their lives.	Individuals can observe and critique cultural and social norms around reproduction and conceptualize alternatives to these.	Power and its exercise by individuals toward and from others plays a central role in constraining or enabling voice and choice. Various forms of power may be more or less relevant at different social levels, but power is decidedly present in all social interactions and plays a critical role in the ability to express voice and choice.	Enabling factors that serve as catalysts for empowerment within the context of specific relationships and societal levels. Resources are multilevel and include the individual, the immediate relational (family and peers), and the distant relational (social institutions and structures).	Outcomes include decision making, leadership, and collective action.\n\nThis framework is focused on sexual and reproductive health outcomes.	Social and cultural norms, available infrastructure, and social institutions.

TABLE B-1 Continued

Framework	Empowerment	Agency	Choice	Critical Consciousness	Power	Resources	Achievements/ Outcomes	Institutional Structures
Galie & Farnworth (2019)	Empowerment through: a person's ability to exercise agency (or not) rests to an important extent on processes beyond their personal control. Changes in the empowerment of individuals are mediated by the empowerment status of significant people associated with them (parents, siblings, spouses, children, and other relatives),	The ability to define goals, have meaningful choices, and act to achieve desired outcomes (Kabeer, 1999a definition).			Power through: individual power won and lost through changes in the empowerment status of others, or through relating to others.	No definition given but references Kabeer (1999a).	No definition given but references Kabeer (1999a).	No definition given but discusses the influence of social norms that lie outside the immediate control of individuals and can greatly influence individual choice; alongside political and economic constraints.

Framework	Empowerment	Agency	Choice	Critical Consciousness	Power	Resources	Achievements/ Outcomes	Institutional Structures
	the way personal characteristics are considered to affect how an individual relates to others, and the judgment by the immediate community within which they live.							

continued

TABLE B-1 Continued

Framework	Empowerment	Agency	Choice	Critical Consciousness	Power	Resources	Achievements/ Outcomes	Institutional Structures
Bill & Melinda Gates Foundation (2018); Van Eerdewijk et al. (2017)	The expansion of choice and strengthening of voice through the transformation of power relations so women and girls have more control over their lives and futures; a process of ongoing change. Transformation of power relations occurs through women and girls exercising agency and taking action, through the redistribution of resources towards women and	Capacity of women and girls to take purposeful action and pursue goals, free from the threat of violence or retribution. The model highlights three specific expressions of agency: decision making, leadership, and collective action.	The ability of women and girls to make and influence choices that affect their lives and futures.	Women and girls identifying and questioning how inequality in power operates in their lives and asserting and affirming their sense of self and their entitlements.	Power can enable and constrain action and agency. It operates in visible, invisible, and hidden terms. Expressions of power include power-over, but this includes positive and generative forces; power-to, or a woman's or girl's ability to act and shape her life; power-within, or a woman's or girl's sense of self-worth, self-knowledge,	Tangible and intangible capital and sources of power that women and girls have, own, or use individually or collectively in the exercise of agency. Resources include women's and girls' critical consciousness, bodily integrity (health, safety, and security), and assets (financial and productive assets, knowledge and skills, time, social capital).	Achievement of choice is whether the choice brings the desired outcome. Achievements and outcomes are the results of the empowerment process. This framework is focused on sexual and reproductive health outcomes.	Social arrangements, including both formal and informal rules and practices that shape and influence women's and girls' ability to express agency and assert control over resources. Institutional structures include formal laws and policies, norms, and relations.

Framework	Empowerment	Agency	Choice	Critical Consciousness	Power	Resources	Achievements/ Outcomes	Institutional Structures
	girls and through shifting the institutional structures that shape women's and girls' choice and voice, and ultimately, their lives and futures.				and self-confidence; and power-with or collaborative power.			

continued

TABLE B-1 Continued

Framework	Empowerment	Agency	Choice	Critical Consciousness	Power	Resources	Achievements/ Outcomes	Institutional Structures
Kabeer (1999a)	Empowerment is the process of agency that links the precondition of resources with the outcomes or achievements.	The ability to define one's goals and act upon them. Agency is about more than observable action; it also encompasses the meaning, motivation, and purpose that individuals bring to their activity or sense of agency, or what feminists have called the power within. Agency is often operationalized as decision making but it can also take the form of bargaining and negotiation,	Choice involves the critical components of agency, resources, and achievements.	Practical consciousness is not normally accessible to agents: it is unconscious. Discursive consciousness is precisely what people can articulate about their own actions and motivations. The discrepancy between practical and discursive consciousness is critical to structures of power within society.	Personal (power within, to) self- and other-images, skills, capabilities, and resources. Interpersonal (power over, with) visible (organizations, rules/ processes), hidden (agenda-setting), or invisible (meaning-making through socialization and control of information).	Allocative resources are those capabilities that command control over objects, goods, or material life. Authoritative resources refer to control over people. Resources include social relationships through which women negotiate their needs and rights with other social actors, including men. Both agency and structure are mediated through relationships	No definition given but references	Routines, conventions, relationships, and taken-for-granted behavior. Institutions that establish agreed-upon significations (meanings), accepted forms of domination (who has power over what or whom), and agreed criteria for legitimizing the social order. Structure includes culture, legal/ judicial, market/ economic,

continued

Framework	Empowerment	Agency	Choice	Critical Consciousness	Power	Resources	Achievements/ Outcomes	Institutional Structures
		deception and manipulation, subversion and resistance, as well as more intangible, cognitive processes of reflection and analysis. It can be exercised by an individual as an individual or by individuals organized as formal or informal groups. Agency refers to the cognitive capacity for critical analysis, reflection, and goal setting; to the practical capacity to achieve these goals; as well as to a subjective				between and among social actors while, at the same time, forms and patterns of relationships are deeply influenced, frequently in hidden ways, by agency and structure.		political, bureaucratic, and organizational.

TABLE B-1 Continued

Framework	Empowerment	Agency	Choice	Critical Consciousness	Power	Resources	Achievements/ Outcomes	Institutional Structures
		capability that reflects how women view themselves and their place in society, their "sense of agency," self-worth, and personhood.						
Karp et al. (2020) & Wood et al. (2021) [Gates funded; based on The World Bank/ Kabeer, 1999a]	Empowerment represents a process for achieving specific development outcomes, as well as a goal in and of itself. Empowerment is defined by a transition from one state to another; this transition involves the enhancement of one's ability to act on one's	Agency includes existence of choice and exercise of choice (based on Donald et al., 2017). Existence of choice is a woman's internal and external motivations for setting her sexual and reproductive goals (motivational	The existence of choice encompasses a variety of skills, particularly women's self-efficacy and decision making. Once existence of choice has been established, the next step is for a woman to recognize that she can act on her		No definition given but recognize that power relations operate at multiple levels including couple, family, community, and societal levels, and include common discussions of power to, power within, and power with.	Opportunity structures like education, economic conditions, and employment.	Achievement by choice of a self-determined set of sexual and reproductive health outcomes. This framework is focused on sexual and reproductive health outcomes.	Opportunity structures (financial, physical, or educational) are included as part of resources.

Framework	Empowerment	Agency	Choice	Critical Consciousness	Power	Resources	Achievements/ Outcomes	Institutional Structures
	preferences. Third, empowerment involves individual attributes of agency, or an individual's ability to set goals and act on them. External resources and opportunity structures play a fundamental role in one's pursuit of their goals. Power relations are key in achievement of goals. Define sexual and reproductive health empowerment as the progression from the existence of	autonomy). Exercise of choice is encompassing a variety of skills, particularly a woman's level of confidence in acting on her choices (self-efficacy), her negotiation abilities with her partner (negotiation), and her capacity to make decisions (decision making).	preferences, also described as having "power to" act. When both existence of choice and exercise of choice are met, an individual can achieve their goals.					

continued

TABLE B-1 Continued

Framework	Empowerment	Agency	Choice	Critical Consciousness	Power	Resources	Achievements/ Outcomes	Institutional Structures
	choice through the exercise of choice to the achievement of choice.							
Kumari (2020) [based on Kabeer, 1999a]	Uses Organisation for Economic Co-operation and Development definition: "women's economic empowerment is the capacity of women to participate in, contribute to and benefit from growth processes in a way that recognizes the value of the contributions, respect their dignity and make it possible to negotiate a fairer distribution of the benefits	Agency provides access to resources as a necessary precondition of empowerment (based on Kabeer, 1999a).			The ability to influence decisions that affect one's life, both private and public domains.	Resources are the preconditions for the process of agency. Resources enable but do not guarantee empowerment because of the broader structural and normative environment for women and girls.	The consequences of choices made. This framework is focused on economic outcomes.	

Framework	Empowerment	Agency	Choice	Critical Consciousness	Power	Resources	Achievements/ Outcomes	Institutional Structures
	of growth" (p. 34) and the Kabeer (1999a) definition. Women's economic empowerment increases propensity of savings, accumulating investment, and financial well-being, and paves the way for inclusive growth. Financial literacy and inclusion are central to women's economic empowerment.							

continued

TABLE B-1 Continued

Framework	Empowerment	Agency	Choice	Critical Consciousness	Power	Resources	Achievements/ Outcomes	Institutional Structures
Longwe (1995a,b)	Describes women's empowerment as the process by which women achieve increased control over public decision making. The five levels of empowerment in this model are welfare, access, conscientization, mobilization, and control.	Agency is not a term directly used in this framework, but the levels of empowerment described in the model align with agency measures from other frameworks, specifically, (1) *access* or use of welfare services or opportunities made available for advancement, and (2) *mobilization* or collective action to create social change to advance women's equality.		Uses the word *conscientization* to describe the awareness building among women that women's equality should be their right.		Welfare is defined as the foundation for empowerment, inclusive of the resources that are made available for women to advance their social position toward equality.	The highest level of empowerment in this framework is control, which would be the stage at which women have control over their lives and equal positioning in society.	Focus of this framework is on women's equality in government structures that hold decision-making authority over society.

continued

Framework	Empowerment	Agency	Choice	Critical Consciousness	Power	Resources	Achievements/ Outcomes	Institutional Structures
Mosedale (2005)	Describes women's empowerment as the process through which women redefine and extend their possibilities to be and do what they choose and prefer, individually and collectively, in spheres where they have experienced restriction relative to men; these efforts can be for the woman herself or for women collectively regardless of whether she personally benefits. Disempowerment is the process by which women's gendered identities restrict their ability to be and do in both public spheres and in their households.	Agency in this framework focuses on women's actions, individually or as a collective, to achieve their goals. Actions are based on women's decision making to act upon their goals toward achievement.	Choice is the extension of possibilities to be and do in the empowerment process.	This term is not used, but the framework references the participatory process in which women can reflect on their circumstances, identify constraints to their opportunities, and develop awareness of their own interests and options to secure those interests.	Power-over: who has control over women in ways that maintain constraints; power-with: who allies with women to support their empowerment; power-within: inner strength or self-efficacy to act.			

TABLE B-1 Continued

Framework	Empowerment	Agency	Choice	Critical Consciousness	Power	Resources	Achievements/Outcomes	Institutional Structures
Raj et al. (2024)	A process of transformation for oppressed individuals and groups or collectives to move from critical consciousness to agency to self-determined goal achievement for self-actualization.	To act on choice and achieve self-determined goals. Agency can result in backlash or retaliation from those with power over a person, and resistance from that person in the face of backlash. Agency includes the elements of can-act-resist.	Critical consciousness and choice: gain consciousness of choice, for a choice beyond what a person is allowed or expected based on social characteristics such as gender. Aspire and goal set one's choice, creating a plan for how to achieve it. Feel conviction in that choice, as there may be many barriers or costs to working toward the choice; it is reasonable to vacillate in the decision. Acting on the choice is easier when a person has confidence in the choice they are making.		Power is defined as authority, with emphasis being on "power structures" that have control over vulnerable or marginalized groups.	Comprised of the social and capital assets and opportunities that can meet people's needs. These exist in the context in which empowerment can occur. Resources are an input into the empowerment process.	People self-determine goals and gain self-determination and self-actualization.	Discussed as part of resources that may be used for empowerment or may be held back from use by power structures that seek to impede empowerment.
Sharaunga et al. (2019) [based on Kabeer, 1999a]	The multi-dimensional process of increasing the capacities/	No definition given but references Kabeer (1999a).	Making choices and transforming choices into desired			No definition given but references Kabeer (1999a).	No definition given but references Kabeer (1999a).	Structures include levels of government and the

Framework	Empowerment	Agency	Choice	Critical Consciousness	Power	Resources	Achievements/ Outcomes	Institutional Structures
	capabilities (e.g., resources and agency) of individuals or groups to make choices and to transform those choices into desired actions and outcomes. Empowerment includes economic empowerment, social empowerment, empowerment in agriculture, and civic forms of empowerment.	Agency is depicted as the process that links the resources (preconditions) to achievements (empowerment outcomes) (Kabeer, 1999a).	outcomes are distinct pieces of empowerment. No further definition of choice provided.				Outcomes include more income, increased well-being, reduced vulnerability, improved food security, self-reliance. This framework is focused on sustainable livelihood outcomes.	private sector as well as processes like laws, policies, culture, and institutions.

continued

TABLE B-1 Continued

Framework	Empowerment	Agency	Choice	Critical Consciousness	Power	Resources	Achievements/ Outcomes	Institutional Structures
Yount et al. (2017) & Singh et al. (2022a) [based on Kabeer, 1999a]	Follows Kabeer (1999a) definition: resources, agency, achievements. Both an individual process and a collective process of facilitating transformation of gender norms and relations through building collective agency, shared ownership of resources (collective resources), and developmental outcomes (collective achievements).	Agency is the capacity to articulate preferences and to make decisions.				Resources include human resources such as schooling attainment, skill development, and self-efficacy; social resources such as participation in organizations, access to peer networks, and access to role models outside the family; and economic resources or material assets such as earnings, property, and land.	Includes both individual- and community-level or collective achievements. Some examples include perception and awareness about gender norms and roles, community ownership of assets, political representation, women's nutrition, and children's nutrition.	

Framework	Empowerment	Agency	Choice	Critical Consciousness	Power	Resources	Achievements/ Outcomes	Institutional Structures
Yount et al. (2020)	Inspired by Freire's conscientization approach, or the process by which oppressed people move from dominated consciousness to understanding and action; and Kabeer's (1999a) resources, agency, achievements framework. Multidimensional process by which women claim enabling resources to enhance their agency.	Ability to make strategic choices under constraints; multidimensional construct involving internal states of being, ways of acting, and ways of being and acting with others. Intrinsic agency (power within): critical awareness of one's rights and aspirations, confidence in one's capabilities, and motivation to pursue self-defined goals. Instrumental agency: creative power to exercise one's capabilities; make one's own strategic choices; pursue	Defines "choice" as strategic and exercised under constraints.	Defined as critical awareness of one's rights (part of intrinsic agency).	Rejects notions of power as exerting control over others in favor of experiencing power within to overcome internalized oppression, creative power to achieve one's aspirations, the collective power with others to advance change.	Human resources may entail schooling or skills-based training; economic resources may entail work, income, property, or other assets; social resources may entail nonfamilial networks of solidarity and support.	Emphasizes women's broader well-being.	Includes prevailing gender norms and institutional constraints; process of empowerment differs for diverse women.

continued

TABLE B-1 Continued

Framework	Empowerment	Agency	Choice	Critical Consciousness	Power	Resources	Achievements/ Outcomes	Institutional Structures
		one's rights, goals, and aspirations; and affect desired change in one's life (e.g., express views opposing prevailing norms/power relations, influence household decisions, move freely in public spaces historically reserved for men). Collective agency: engagement in or leadership of groups/ networks with shared goals, confidence						

Framework	Empowerment	Agency	Choice	Critical Consciousness	Power	Resources	Achievements/ Outcomes	Institutional Structures
		in group's/ network's ability to act on shared goals, and influential joint actions in pursuit of shared goals; agency can arise in all spheres of life and across the life course.						

SOURCE: Created by the committee based on existing frameworks.